Crime and Empire

Crime and Empire

The Colony in Nineteenth-Century Fictions of Crime

UPAMANYU PABLO MUKHERJEE

OXFORD
UNIVERSITY PRESS

OXFORD

UNIVERSITY PRESS

Great Clarendon Street, Oxford OX2 6DP

Oxford University Press is a department of the University of Oxford.
It furthers the University's objective of excellence in research, scholarship,
and education by publishing worldwide in

Oxford New York

Auckland Bangkok Buenos Aires Cape Town Chennai
Dar es Salaam Delhi Hong Kong Istanbul Karachi Kolkata
Kuala Lumpur Madrid Melbourne Mexico City Mumbai Nairobi
São Paulo Shanghai Taipei Tokyo Toronto

Oxford is a registered trade mark of Oxford University Press
in the UK and in certain other countries

Published in the United States
by Oxford University Press Inc., New York

British Library Cataloguing in Publication Data

Data available

Library of Congress Cataloging in Publication Data

Data applied for

ISBN 0-19-926105-9

1 3 5 7 9 10 8 6 4 2

Typeset by Cambrian Typesetters,
Frimley, Surrey
Printed in Great Britain
on acid-free paper by
Biddles Ltd,
Guildford and King's Lynn

Preface

THE LANGUAGE OF crime surrounds us everywhere. It may be no exaggeration to say that the 'new world order' ushered in by the US president George Bush (sen.) in his state of the union address in 1991 has seen 'justice' and 'criminality' (and related terms like 'crimes against humanity') replace 'security', 'containment', and 'negotiation' as the key terms in the Anglo-American ideological landscape. Playing a vital role in the representation and formulation of social relationships within these societies, this language is perhaps most spectacularly evident in global relationships now, where new imperial configurations are being forged in a seemingly unipolar world. Yet this is not unique to the 'new world order'. Narratives of crime have always enjoyed a special relationship with power, whether in the domestic or imperial contexts. This book excavates moments in the life of the 'old' European world order, and of Britain, the power in paramount position in the concert of nations from the late eighteenth century onwards. It looks at the role played by the narratives of crime in the formation of British attitudes towards the linchpin of their imperial fortunes—India. But it also shows how these narratives and attitudes were formed in conjunction with those working inside Britain, within the boundaries of its domestic social relations. This study of the narratives of crime and 'old' empire may provide us with a context for understanding the prevalence of the language of power today.

Two major concerns that registered in a large number of nineteenth-century British fictional as well as non-fictional narratives were the issues of crime, and Britain's status of being the paramount imperial power in the world. In what follows, I will examine the interplay between these two issues by focusing on the interplay between Britain and India. One of the aims of this exercise will be to re-evaluate the role played by fiction in the construction of British authority, both domestic and colonial. Recent works on the nineteenth-century novel have tended to read the genre as a kind of cultural police that covertly inserted the interest of the ruling classes in its unsuspecting readers. But by looking at the genre's peculiar use of the rhetoric of crime, and comparing it to a variety of other non-fictional narratives, I will suggest that its relationship with the dominant ideology was much more problematic.

Chronologically, the main focus of the discussion will be on the period between Robert Peel's police reform Bill in 1829 and the publication of the so-called 'first' English detective novel by Wilkie Collins in 1868. But I have looked at the lines of continuity between the representation of the criminal and the colony both before and after this period. With the emergence and entrenchment of industrial capitalism in Britain, there came a growing demand for legal and police reforms that designated an unprecedented range of activities as criminal and implemented suitable degrees of punishment for it. Crime thus became a political and cultural preoccupation (as seen in the novel), and the rule of law became central to the construction of authority in British society.

At the same time, however, there was never any consensus about crime throughout this period, as my examination of conflicting ideas and practices about criminality shows. All the narratives of crime, and especially the novel, registered this historical situation to varying degrees. The effects of this were seen in a colony like India, where the East India Company tried to invest its colonialist regime with the moral justification of bringing law to what was shown to be an essentially anarchic and criminal country. But since it employed the contested rhetoric of crime, it was never able to construct an unproblematic ideology of its authority.

As the most influential cultural product of the period, the novel best embodied this complex relationship between authority and the rhetoric of crime. The genre used the representations of 'criminal' India as well as of British criminality simultaneously to empower and question British rulership. This revision in the model of the nineteenth-century British novel's role within the dominant ideology also hopes to insert a historical strain into the framework of post-colonial theory. While theorists have pointed out that colonialist/imperialist discourse is plagued with 'fractures, fissures and inconsistencies' that constantly subvert its overt ideological aim, they have frequently attributed this to the semantic instabilities inherent in the texts themselves. By isolating one of the dominant rhetorics of colonialism, that of crime, and by showing how it worked as an accurate register of the conflicts within its historical and material conditions, I will submit that theories of the text must look beyond and around it to understand its fundamental features.

What does this study of crime narratives in the life of 'old' empire have to tell us today? First, that we should be aware of the particular history and the global significance of the language of crime and justice. Second, that even as 'crime' has served as an important ideological tool, it is also the site from where challenges to authority have been, and continue to be mounted. At least at the level of ideology and consensus, narratives of crime, punishment, and justice are double-edged tools that both empower and question authority. This strategy at once defines a strong and weak point in the façade of imperial ideologies, both new and old. The challenges to our 'New World Order' must necessarily focus on this fact.

The ideas behind this book took shape between 1998 and 2001 while I was doing an M.Phil. and then a Ph.D. in the universities of Oxford and Cambridge. There, I was fortunate enough to enjoy the supervision of two outstanding teachers, Kate Flint and Ian Donaldson. Several other exceptional scholars and teachers, in both India and Britain, have shaped my beliefs about life and work. Stephen Gill, Gillian Beer, Nicholas Shrimpton, and Dinah Birch in Britain, and Swapan Chakraborty, Supriya Chowdhury, Sukanta Chowdhury, Jasodhara Bagchi, Malini Bhattacharya, Mihir Bhattacharya, Malabika Sarkar, and Arup Rudra in India, taught me to think with passion. Of course, I could never have had the chance to work in the two leading universities of the world without the support, at various times, of the Rhodes Trust, the Cambridge Commonwealth Trust, and St John's College, Cambridge. The first three years of my life in Britain were made smooth and comfortable by everyone working in Rhodes House. I have yet to see any other office that combines such efficiency with so much genuine smile and caring. And since it all started with an interview on a cold Delhi morning, I would like to let Prof. Vir Chauhan know how grateful I am for his donation of canny advice and a pair of smart shoes. Dr Anil Seal of the Cambridge Commonwealth Trust also excelled in the role of a contemporary Magwitch. When all further avenues seemed blocked, he waved his magic wand and made the continuation of the Ph.D. in Cambridge possible. St John's College and, in particular, my college tutor, Mr Ray Jobling, have my gratitude not only for taking care of all existing and prospective financial needs, but also for the latter's rather effective pep talks that sent me once more unto the breach.

The translating of mere ideas into a book was done 2001–3 while I was teaching in the university of Newcastle upon Tyne. Again, I have been fortunate in having the most supportive of colleagues on the face of the planet. All of them, without exception, made me feel welcomed and helped me settle into a new job and a new city. Linda Anderson, Kate Chedzgoy, Jenny Richards, Gemma Robinson, Anne Whitehead, Terry Wright, Mike Rossington, Mike Pincombe, John Stonham, Ricardo Bermudez-Otero, Bruce Babington, and Hermann Moisl have all offered invaluable advice and support. The frighteningly able administrative outfit run by Rowena Bryson, Rob Walton, and Melanie Birch has soothed nerves frayed by bruising encounters with the photocopying machines and computers. I also have to thank the staff of the various libraries I have haunted over the past few years—the Bodleian Library and the English Faculty library in Oxford; Cambridge University Library; the British Library, London; and the Robinson Library in Newcastle—for putting up with me. Sophie Goldsworthy at the Oxford University Press has been always at hand to nudge me in the right direction. Frances Whistler and Jackie Pritchard's immaculate editing intuition imposed some shape on the primeval chaos of the manuscript.

I do not have the space to mention all the friends who have touched my life with hope and love while I was mired in research. They have been thanked with hours of passionate argument, midnight coffees, and the collective dreaming of the possible and impossible. Some, however, must be named. The Hiltons, by some strange alchemy, have adopted me as one of the clan. Mary redefined the word shelter by sharing her space, time, and intellect with me in the basement of 1 Carlyle Road. Zoe was the best of housemates and a patient sufferer of the tyranny of my opinions. Boyd forgave me for placing him alongside Foucault in my book. Tom coped well with the surprise of finding yet another 'lodger' in the house. But I would not have the chance to know these wonderful people without Eliza. For this, and countless other unasked for precious gifts, she has all I can give for what it is worth. Tim and Gilly Greenwood, Yug, Marcus, Tim, James, Hannah, Maria, Fan, Clea, Katherine, Chiki, Ami, Pete, Jason, Anne-Marie, Jerry, Johnny, Matt, along with many others, have always been there when I needed them. Tithi, despite her penchant for long absences, has never let me walk alone since we were one.

I am struck by the absurdity of trying to express my thanks for my family. Their love for me makes nonsense of the attempts at such civility. Very few people can understand what we have been through over the years. My brother and my sister are with me wherever I am. My father, through all the reverses, has held on to his blind belief in me. But this one is for my mother, who, in many ways, has had the longest and the loneliest of waits. This is my way of letting her know that the waiting is over.

U.P.M.

Contents

I

Introduction

'The problematic of empire', write Hardt and Negri in their recent influential work *Empire*, 'is determined in the first place by one simple fact that there is world order. This order is expressed as a juridical formation.'[1] Of course, for these authors, empire is distinctly different from 'old' European imperialism. It is a form of sovereignty that has emerged in the context of a unipolar world, the collapse of the old colonies and the Soviet bloc, and the dominance of a new order that was made spectacularly visible with the Gulf Crisis of 1990–1. The empire is not a nation: 'The United States does indeed occupy a privileged position in Empire, but this privilege derives not from its similarities to the old European imperialist powers, but from its difference.'[2] This latest theory of 'new' imperialism is obviously not without its critics. But the authors' insistence on the central importance of the juridical—that is, the entire spectrum of the issues relating to order, deviance, and above all policing—to the formation of empire is surely borne out daily by a range of global events from Iraq, to Palestine, the Balkans, Bali, and the twin towers of New York. The common rhetorical and representative strategies employed, at least in the West, to document the birth pangs of this new form of globalized power have been precisely those of order, deviance, and punishment. Over the last decade US sanctions and war on Iraq, its future plans for Iran and North Korea, the US-led UN war against Serbia and the subsequent trial of Milošović, and the so-called 'war on terror' have all been performed through a language where the ethics for such actions is manufactured through concepts of crime and policing. Unrestricted global

[1] Michael Hardt and Antonio Negri, *Empire* (Cambridge, Mass.: Harvard University Press, 2000), 3.   [2] Ibid. p. xiv.

intervention, the cornerstone of this empire, is predicated on a right to police:

The formation of a new right is inscribed in the deployment of prevention, repression, and rhetorical force aimed at the reconstruction of social equilibrium: all this is proper to the activity of the police. We can thus recognize the initial and implicit source of imperial right in terms of police action and the capacity of the police to create and maintain order. The legitimacy of the imperial ordering supports the exercise of police power, while at the same time the activity of the global police force demonstrates the real effectiveness of the imperial ordering.[3]

The cultural importance of the narratives of crime may have received a new boost in these days of empire. But it is precisely this rhetoric and these practices of producing and managing criminality, the ideas of order and disorder, of the ethical duties of policing, that intimately connect Hardt and Negri's 'empire' to older forms of imperialism.

What we shall see in the following pages is the centrality of the language of policing, of law, of crime and punishment to the formation of authority and 'rights' of one of the most powerful of the 'old' European empires—the British empire—in its relationship with its most prized possession, India. One of the implicit aims, certainly, will be to remind ourselves that the language that we are hearing today, especially from Anglo-American political leaders— of intervening, ordering, punishing, bringing to account—has a venerable lineage in the West's imperial relationship with the world. But I hope in thus reminding ourselves, we will also do much more. At least two other claims will be made and hopefully substantiated. First, that this language of crime or the juridical grew out of an intimate and symbiotic relationship between the colonizing/metropolitan and the colonized societies. We cannot understand why crime and policing assumed a particular importance in a particular way within imperial rhetoric unless we link it to the evolution of this strategy of power within the domestic boundaries of empire. Second, this strategy was necessarily ambiguous, releasing possibilities of dissent in the very moment of its articulation of authority. However, the critical and ideological pitfalls of automatically assigning ambiguity to imperialist

---

[3] Michael Hardt and Antonio Negri, *Empire*, 17.

discourses have been dealt with ably and eloquently by critics like Benita Parry.[4] I do not want to suggest that the juridical was (and still is) an ambiguous tool of empire because of the instabilities of writing and techniques of representation. But I do not want to allocate to it, in my view, a false aura of the perfect imperial weapon either. Rather, we will trace the social and historical contexts of this culture of the juridical and see how these stories of order and disorder could interrogate empire even as they played a central role in its entrenchment. In many ways, the Anglo-Indian relationship formed the paradigm of this relationship between crime, narratives, and empire.

EMPIRE, FICTION

In her review of *The Moonstone* in 1868 Geraldine Jewsbury pointed out the extraordinary amount of sympathy that Wilkie Collins elicited from his readers for the three Indian priests who commit murder in order to take a precious gem back to their temple in India.[5] In a decade when the racist discourse of colonialism saturated large sections of British society with stereotypical representation of 'criminal' Indians, Africans, and Caribbeans, Collins's use of the Hindu priests to avenge the despoliation of their country seems remarkable.[6] In the pages that follow, I will suggest a genesis of the problematic figures of these 'criminal Indians', not so much in Collins's own work, as in the variety of narratives about the British colonial contact with India that provided the context of his novel. We shall see that by the 1860s, there was already a long tradition of British writing that used

[4] See Benita Parry, *Delusions and Discoveries* (London: Verso, 1998).

[5] 'Few will read of the final destiny of *The Moonstone* without feeling the tears rise in their eyes as they catch the last glimpse of the three men, who have sacrificed their cast in the service of their God . . . as they embrace each other and separate to begin their lonely and never-ending pilgrimage of expiation. The deepest emotion is certainly reserved to the last.' In Norman Page (ed.), *Wilkie Collins: The Critical Heritage* (London: Routledge, 1974), 170–1.

[6] Robert Young has shown how the Mutiny of 1857, the debates about slavery in the American Civil War, and Governor Eyre's massacres during the Jamaican insurrection all formed the widespread British claims of racial superiority and, consequently, the perceptions about rights to rule and punish 'inferior and criminal' races in the 1860s. See Robert Young, *Colonial Desire* (London: Routledge, 1995), 92.

'criminal India' to interrogate, rather than empower, colonialist/ imperialist ventures. We will also see that it was the novel, more than the legal, historical, political, and geographical narratives, that used the rhetoric of crime to air the possibilities of dissent. This novelistic dissent, as much as the British propaganda of the 'civilizing mission', was the context in which Collins's Hindu priests took shape.

Could the fictions of crime effect any meaningful interrogation of the ideology of British colonial authority? Or is this claim no more than a misplaced wish to force some radical, dissenting qualities on a narrative that has frequently been diagnosed to be essentially a conservative one? Certainly, the nexus between fiction and crime has been well documented. Jon Thompson has observed that this went right back to the originary moments of the English novel, and Christine Marlin has testified that there was scarcely a major nineteenth-century work that did not in some way concern itself with legality and deviance.[7] D. A. Miller and John Bender have gone as far as to claim that not only was crime a thematic concern of nineteenth-century novels, but the genre itself was a covert tool of the 'new' policing techniques developed by the British state to enforce norms of law and order on society.[8] In fact, I will argue that the novels engaging with criminality had a much more problematic relationship with authority and dominant ideologies than this label of a 'cultural police' suggests. At any rate, what is clear is that ideas, discussions, debates, practices of crime and punishment were important to English fiction in the nineteenth century. And it

[7] See Jon Thompson, *Fiction, Crime and Empire* (Urbana: University of Illinois Press, 1993) and Christine Marlin, 'The Depiction of the Criminal in Victorian Fiction' (M.Phil. thesis, Oxford, 1994).

[8] See D. A. Miller, *The Novel and the Police* (Berkeley and Los Angeles: University of California Press, 1988) and John Bender, *Imagining the Penitentiary* (Chicago: University of Chicago Press, 1987). These valuable works, to my mind, are still open to modifications. While the novel could certainly be a cultural tool to manufacture consensus, its relationship with the dominant ideology was almost always problematic and ambiguous. Even Foucauldian analysis of literature must bear Foucault's own observation in mind—'there are no relations of power without resistances; the latter are all the more real and effective because they are formed right at the point where relations of power are exercised ... nor is it inexorably frustrated through being the compatriot of power. It exists all the more by being in the same place as power.' Michel Foucault, *Power/Knowledge: Selected Interviews and Other Writings 1972–1977*, ed. Colin Gordon (Brighton: Harvester Press, 1980), 142. Novels certainly did register this interfacing of power and resistance.

is this rhetoric of crime that we shall examine to show how, even as it came to play a central role in the construction of authority at home and abroad, it could also provide an opportunity to interrogate the very premiss of that authority.

A look at a wide variety of English narratives from the late eighteenth to the nineteenth century reveals that at no time were the representations of the criminal, or for that matter policing and punishment, ever free of contests, disagreements, and debates. If legality and deviance became the crucial sites of empowerment of the British state, they also defined points of resistance where the power of that state was challenged. Divergent and conflicting opinions about crime, policing, and punishment could be seen even in official documents like parliamentary Select Committee reports and debates. As the dominant literary genre in an era of increasing mass literacy and publishing, the novel was compelled to engage with the discourse of criminality.[9]

This becomes clear as we examine a range of popular authors ranging from W. H. Ainsworth to Mary Braddon and genres like the 'Newgate' and 'sensation' fictions. We shall also see that the very historical conditions that shaped the rhetoric of crime ensured that the narratives employing it could never unproblematically present one particular viewpoint about rulership, justice, legality, morality, or deviance. Tony Bennett has pointed out that 'popular culture . . . is neither the site of a people's deformation, nor of their own self-making, but a field shaped by those conflicting presences'.[10] The nineteenth-century popular novelists used the rhetoric of crime to sustain this conflictual, rather than consensual, nature of culture.

If the rhetoric of crime was (as we will see) conditioned by its historical roots to contain within it seeds of both dissent and consensus, why should it find in fiction a more congenial host than any other kind of writing? There have, of course, been a number of important critical formulations of the special relationship between literature and ideology. Pierre Macherey has suggested that although ideology is formed independently of the literary author, they exist to make ideologies 'visible'.[11] Dennis Porter has glossed

[9] For an account of mass publishing, rising literacy, and popularity of the novel, see Ken Worpole, *Reading by Numbers* (London: Comedia, 1984).
[10] Quoted in Thompson, *Fiction, Crime and Empire*, 71.
[11] Quoted by Dennis Porter in *The Pursuit of Crime* (New Haven: Yale University Press, 1981), 128–9.

Macherey's work by pointing out how literature brings out the
contradictions inherent in ideologies: 'the point is, finally, that
ideologies are not embedded in literary works passively but they
come to appear there objectified in all their fullness and contradictions.'[12] Here we may also take note of the work of Lennard
Davies, for whom novels share an intricate relationship with ideology, when the latter is described as

move from Gothic

The vast signifying system that, in its interpenetration with the individual
psyche, makes things 'mean' something to a culture and individuals in that
culture. Ideology constitutes *the sum of that which a culture needs to
believe about itself and its aspirations as opposed to what really is.* (my
emphasis)[13]

The novel, according to Davies, is a crucial tool of the gigantic
process of storytelling that 'makes sense' by offering a complete
and evident explanation of the state of affairs of a society.[14] At the
vanguard of the cultural forms that rose to prominence under
modern capitalism, novels are 'regularising and normalising' agents
that helped form a collective political consensus, a willingness to
accept the status quo rather than to change it.[15] Yet, if the novel is
complicit in the operation of dominant ideology, it is by no means
an unambiguous or unproblematic tool. Davies sees ambiguity
embedded in the material history of the genre: 'It is Janus-faced in
that sense, since it holds onto an earlier form related to craft and
cottage industry for its creation, but it is reliant on technology and
merchandising for its distribution and effect.'[16] And this Janus-like
quality of the novel is hardly limited to its own genesis as a
commodity. It also flavours its contents. Davies concedes:

Like any complex social formation, novels are highly ambivalent in their
message . . . Novels can offer in their heroes and stories various kinds of
opposition to stasis and power, but at the same time it would seem that the
formal elements of the novel add up to a social formation that resists
change.[17]

This is a far more flexible conclusion than Miller's and one that registers the novel as a genre in permanent tension between its radical and

---

[12] Quoted by Dennis Porter in *The Pursuit of Crime*, 128–9.
[13] Lennard Davies, *Resisting Novels: Ideology and Fiction* (New York: Methuen,
1987), 24.   [14] Ibid. 25–6.
[15] Ibid. 3–18.   [16] Ibid. 4.   [17] Ibid. 17–18.

authoritarian impulses. And once we see the novel in this light, we may consider how its increasing popularity throughout the nineteenth century could also be a testament to its ability to absorb and generate the impulses towards dissent. Fredric Jameson has noted that popular cultural forms situate themselves at a troubled distance from dominant ideologies:

if the ideological function of mass culture is understood as a process whereby otherwise dangerous and protopolitical impulses are 'managed' and defused, rechanneled and offered spurious objects, then some preliminary step must also be theorised in which these same impulses—the raw material upon which the process works—are initially awakened within the very text that seeks to still them.[18]

Novels, as the dominant popular nineteenth-century cultural form, can thus be seen to be responsible both for the entrenchment of 'Britishness' as well as the interrogation of the central features of this ideological construct.[19]

It may be that critical focus on the popular novel's complicity in the managing of the 'proto-political' impulses of the nineteenth-century has had the unfortunate (side?) effect of wrinkling out its ambiguous and 'mixed' nature. The genre proved to be adept at housing the ideas and representations of crime precisely because they were registers of the larger conflicts raging throughout nineteenth-century imperial Britain. We will attempt to recover the historical context of the contradictions registered by the novel's use of the rhetoric of crime, and then underline its problematic relationship with the dominant domestic and colonialist/imperialist ideologies of the period.

The purpose of our exercise will emphatically not be to slip into the delusional comfort zone where we can assume that imperial narrative's unease unproblematically reflected the historical reality of British imperialism. As Benita Parry reminds us:

Because fiction by working on ideology can reinvent, defamiliarize or undermine authorized versions, the uncertainty which is discernible in colonial writings should be read as a troubled response to a condition but

---

[18] Fredric Jameson, *The Political Unconscious: Narrative as a Socially Symbolic Act* (Ithaca, NY: Cornell University Press, 1981), 287.

[19] Jameson identifies the genre as both a product of ideology and 'a revolt against that reification and a symbolic act which involves a whole Utopian compensation for increasing dehumanization on the level of daily life'. Ibid. 42.

not as testimony to the events of a historical moment with which it can be discontinuous. When Conrad wrote his anguished books, Western regimes were pursuing aggressively expansionist ambitions and engaged in violent territorial acquisitions in Africa; when Kipling cryptically contemplated the insecurity of the Raj, British rule was intensifying its bureaucracy in India and flexing its military muscle to deal with growing opposition.[20]

But on the other hand, we shall see that the pursuit of metropolitan advantage was not always silenced by the fiction of the Raj. Indeed, we shall see that one of the central components of that fiction, the rhetoric of crime, frequently served to bring forth the brutal nature of the pursuit of metropolitan power in all its nakedness.

EMPIRE, POST-COLONIAL PERSPECTIVES

The period 1829–70 spans both the introduction and establishment of Robert Peel's reformed 'new police' in England and the political dominance of the British East India Company in India that eventually led to the passing of the colony under the direct rule of the crown. As the example of Wilkie Collins shows, it is far from accidental that two of the major concerns of British politics and culture—crime and empire—came together in the novels being written around this time. As in the context of 'domestic' Britain, criminality and law came to occupy a crucial position in Britain's relationship with its most important colony. Domestic compliance with colonial expansionism in the subcontinent was secured at the material level with the lure of enormous profits and on the ideological level with the moral appeal of the 'rule of law'. In this narrative of the triumph of free trade and progress, the degenerate Indians would wake up to the blessings of civilization with the introduction of British law and education. On the other hand, built around the same notions of criminality and justice, there grew up a competing and powerful criticism of colonialism that proposed to interrogate the crimes committed by the so-called lawgivers in the colony. This rhetoric of crime became widely prevalent in English narratives from the 1770s onwards. There are important differences between late eighteenth-century British attitudes towards

---

[20] Parry, *Delusions*, 11.

crime and the colony, and those being formed by the liberal-evan-
gelical currents of the early nineteenth century, and to my mind no
one has charted these as convincingly and eloquently as Eric
Stokes.[21] But the lines of continuity between pre- and post-'new
policing', and between pre- and post-colonial paramountcy, are too
vivid to be ignored.

Accordingly, the chapters that follow will run a parallel enquiry
into the debate about the 'criminal' in both the domestic and the
colonial contexts and explore the symbiotic relationship between
the two. Thus, as one chapter tells the story of police reform in
England and its impact on British culture, another moves on to
consider the colony. The aim throughout will be to read the
cultural and ideological histories of the colony and the 'centre' not
as separate, but as enmeshed entities. The discussions of the fiction
of British 'domestic' crime will always invite a comparison to the
fiction of Indian crime to show how the latter was able to question
the premises of colonial ideology by drawing on the debates found
in the former. I will conclude by suggesting that by the late 1860s,
during the germination of the English detective novel, the figure of
the criminal Indian was already being used not only to interrogate
colonial ideology, but also to outline a critique of British domestic
society. At the level of what Althusser called 'Ideological State
Apparatus', fiction, we shall see, often played a disruptive rather
than a monolithically constitutive role.[22] This reading will also
hope to modify some of the more extreme textual practices of post-
colonial theory by foregrounding the links between the material
practices of statecraft and the cultural representations of it.

One of the greatest achievements of discourse theorists who
have drawn on the work of Michel Foucault has been precisely to
highlight the coercive ideological strategies embedded in texts. Yet,

[21] See Eric Stokes, *The English Utilitarians and India* (New Delhi: Oxford
University Press, 1982).
[22] See Louis Althusser, *Essays on Ideology* (London: Verso, 1984), 7. This reading of literature's relationship with ideology may be seen as an extension of
Althusser's point that 'the Ideological State Apparatuses may be not only the stake,
but also the site of class struggle . . . because the resistance of the exploited masses
is able to find means and occasions to express itself there, either by the utilisation
of their contradictions, or by conquering combat positions in them in struggle', ibid.
21. Allowing for the fact that the colonial situation gave a peculiar slant to capitalism, my point is precisely that as a part of the ideological apparatus of the state,
literature defined a unique *utilization* of the contradictions inherent there.

paradoxically, this important insight has sometimes been achieved at the cost of isolating the texts from their socio-political context. Once the literary narrative is seen in isolation from the materiality of history of which it is a part, the contradictions embodied in it cease to relate properly to the conditions of the societies in which they are produced. Ideology comes to be seen as a product of discourses, and its contradictions as a result of semiotic instabilities or *textual* conflicts. For all its insistence on establishing a political engagement with culture, post-colonial criticism has often accepted this textual exclusiveness with little protest. For instance, an influential study of narratives of colonialism begins on the premiss that they are shot through with the 'idiom of dubiety' and the 'instability of its own facts'.[23] As David Spurr points out in his discussion on what he calls the rhetoric of empire, these instabilities cannot be contained within a bounded *textual* field.[24] However, and quite often, no sooner does one look to these discussions for linkages made between historical reality and these textual instabilities, than one is brought up short against 'culture', 'discourse', and 'semiotics'. To borrow from Said, here are the text and the critics indeed, but what of the world?

Even the important work of Homi Bhabha may be profitably modified by historical contextualization. Each of Bhabha's key concepts of the colonialist discourse revolves around ambiguity and other allied terms—'slippages', 'irony', 'repetition':

The discourse of post-enlightenment English colonialism often speaks in a tongue that is forked . . . the epic intention of the civilising mission . . . often produces a text rich in traditions of *trompe l'œil*, irony, mimicry and repetition . . . the discourse of mimicry is constructed around an ambivalence; in order to be effective, mimicry must continually produce its slippage, its excess, its difference. The authority of that mode of colonial discourse that I have called mimicry is therefore stricken by an indeterminacy.[25]

As students of literature, culture, and history, we are indebted to Bhabha for the important analysis of the condition of the colonial

[23] Sara Suleri, *The Rhetoric of English India* (Chicago: University of Chicago Press, 1992), 3.
[24] David Spurr, *The Rhetoric of Empire* (Durham, NC: Duke University Press, 1993), 2.
[25] Homi K. Bhabha, 'Of Mimicry and Man', in *The Location of Culture* (London: Routledge, 1994), 85–6. On theories of ambivalence and slippages also see his 'The Other Question', ibid. 66–83.

texts. But if we stop short of exploring the relationship between these textual/discursive slippages and the specific historical reality that conditioned them, we will fail to cultivate one of the most fundamental potentials of this analysis. In a seminar at the Jawaharlal Nehru University in Delhi, questions were raised about the ideological aims of such an analytical practice

Bhabha is sanguine in his faith that the ambivalence, the splitting of 'the subject of culture' originates in phenomena explained by the general law of semiotics. . . . What authorises [this subject], it seems to me, is not only its methodological and narrative paradigms . . . but its genealogy, in which the congruent discourses of imperialism and humanism (to name only the big guns!) feature prominently. Their historical logic, in all its continuing institutional authority and transformative power, is at stake too, and that suggests to me that the play of self and other, or self as other, is not reducible, even as a heuristic, to the splitting of the subject at the moment of [its] enunciation.[26]

As Ania Loomba points out, 'Even theories of reading should make it possible to attribute the inefficiency of the master-text to more than the internal instabilities of the text itself, otherwise it follows that the doubting recipient subject is reduced to the effect of the text itself.'[27] What we shall find in the chapters below is precisely an attempt to locate the relationship between instabilities of the master texts of colonialism/imperialism and the material practices of rulership that were formed in conjunction with it. As I have indicated before, I will not claim that there is an unproblematic relationship between these texts and their historical context. But perhaps our critical efforts can be profitably directed towards understanding the problematics of this relationship between texts and history.

CONTRADICTIONS, NARRATIVES

Contradictions, slippages, paradoxes were of course far from being the exclusive property of British attitudes towards crime and

---

[26] Suvir Kaul, 'The Indian Academic and Resistance to Theory', paper presented at JNU, New Delhi, March 1990, quoted by Ania Loomba, 'Overworlding the Third World', in Patrick Williams and Laura Chrisman (eds.), *Colonial Discourse and Post-colonial Theory* (New York: Harvester/Wheatsheaf, 1993), 309.

[27] Ibid. 310.

punishment in the nineteenth century. These were the very stuff of the contemporary British social fabric. They were embedded in the material, economic base of a society caught in the throes of industrial revolution, as Marx understood clearly. Theorizing about the self-expanding nature of capital, he observed:

> But from the fact that capital posits every such limit as a barrier and hence gets ideally beyond it, does not by any means follow that it has really overcome it, and since every such barrier contradicts its character, its production *moves in contradictions which are constantly overcome but just as constantly posited.* (my emphasis)[28]

All crucial ideological concepts were marked by them. For example, that great entity the 'individual', which received such enhancement through the contemporary forms of social control—the 'new' police, 'new' prisons, and 'new' education—was also accompanied by the contradictory and concerted efforts towards limiting the potentials of the individual. Indeed, this, for Lucien Goldman, was the elemental essence of the novel:

> In the liberal market societies, there was a set of values, which, though not trans-individual, nevertheless had a universal aim and . . . a general validity. These were the values of liberal individualism that were bound up with the very existence of the competitive market . . . On the basis of these values, there developed the category of individual biography that became the constitutive element of the novel. Here it assumed the form of the problematic individual on the basis of . . . internal contradictions between individualism as a universal value produced by the bourgeois society and the important and painful limitations that the society itself brought to the possibilities of the development of the individual.[29]

So entrenched was this play of contradiction throughout every stratum of nineteenth-century British society, that, speaking of the 'mind' of its most influential section, Boyd Hilton has noted: 'it is not an easy mind to characterise, for there was no consensus, but

---

[28] Karl Marx, *Grundrisse* (Harmondsworth: Penguin, 1973), 410. Discussing this section of the work, Ranajit Guha glosses: 'the discrepancy between the universalising tendency of capital as an ideal and the frustration of that tendency in reality was, for him, a measure of the contradictions of western bourgeois societies of his time . . . he used this measure to define and explain the uneven character of development in the contemporary bourgeois world.' In Ranajit Guha, *Dominance without Hegemony* (Cambridge, Mass.: Harvard University Press, 1997), 16.

[29] Lucien Goldman, 'Towards a Sociology of the Novel', in Terry Eagleton and Drew Milne (eds.), *Marxist Literary Theory* (Oxford: Blackwell, 1996), 215.

rather a "war of ideas" which left most thinking men ambivalent, or torn between "incompatible opposites" '.[30]

Inevitably, these contradictions were echoed in the British governing strategies of the period. In his history of power in modern society, Michel Foucault placed the emergence of the 'age of sobriety in punishment' at the beginning of the nineteenth century.[31] There is no need to go over his well-known thesis, but it must be noted that, unlike many of his followers, Foucault was well aware of the historical logic behind the rise of the carceral regime:

> The moment where it became understood that it was more efficient and profitable in terms of the economy of power to place people under surveillance than to subject them to exemplary penalty. This moment in time corresponds to the formation, gradual in some respects and rapid in others, of a new mode of exercise of power in the eighteenth and early nineteenth centuries.[32]

Efficient and profitable are the key terms here. What Foucault hints at is that the new regime of punishment (conducted through the reform of the police, 'new prisons', etc.) could only arise once the diffusion of the modern capitalist ethos of profit and economy had gained sufficient intensity. The importance of this to the dominance of the British middle classes cannot be overestimated. New policing and the production of criminality, part of what Foucault called the 'synaptic regime of power', were crucial to the rise of new groups and social classes towards the centre of political power at the expense of the older agrarian aristocracy.[33]

Working from a very different angle, Hilton reaches almost the same conclusions as Foucault about the centrality of the ideas of crime and punishment in such a society. If, as Hilton (and Stokes, in the context of India) has shown, evangelicalism became a crucial element in British society from the 1790s, then ideas of crime, guilt, and punishment grew in proportion as crucial ideological props: 'the telos was not, however, happiness but justice,

---

[30] Boyd Hilton, *The Age of Atonement* (Oxford: Clarendon Press, 1988), 3.

[31] Michel Foucault, *Discipline and Punish* (Harmondsworth: Penguin, 1979), 14.

[32] Quoted in Foucault, *Power/Knowledge*, 38.

[33] 'It was the instituting of this new local, capillary form of power which impelled society to eliminate certain elements such as the court and the king. The mythology of the sovereign was no longer possible once a certain kind of power was being exercised within the social body'. Foucault, *Discipline and Punish*, 39.

that is punishment—justice being regarded in an individualistic
rather than a distributive light—and this priority in turn led to an
emphasis on sin which may strike the modern mind as irrational.'[34]
What emerges from Hilton's analysis of the 'age of atonement' is
the connection between ideas of guilt and punishment and the
formation of what Foucault has called the 'soul' of the individual
in a modern capitalist society:

thus, by analysis of penal leniency as a technique of power, one might
understand both how man, the soul, the normal or abnormal have come
to duplicate crime as objects of penal intervention; and in what way a
specific mode of subjection was able to give birth to man as an object of
knowledge for a discourse with a 'scientific' status.[35]

If we connect Foucault's 'soul' to Hilton's account of the
'conscience' and Goldman's reading of the 'individual', we will
begin to grasp the importance of the idea of crime to the British
sense of the 'self' in this period.

The centrality of the rhetoric of crime in such a society as nineteenth-century England then cannot be doubted. But equally, as we
have seen, the pervasive nature of the contradictions and conflicts
within the ideas and practices of crime cannot be ignored either.
We will examine journals, parliamentary reports, and newspapers
to show just how contested and controversial these categories were.
A range of conflicting interests, from local neighbourhood allegiances to broader class alignments, meant that production and
containment of crime in Britain was never free from debates, oppositions, resistances, and contradictions. As Ruth Paley has argued,
'the Metropolitan Police Act did not come about as a simple knee-
jerk response to public demand; rather, it is highly likely that it was
an example of the way in which a reform . . . imposed from above
. . . can yet bring about permanent and decisive changes in public
attitudes and expectations.'[36] David Taylor has accused the
'Whiggish view of police history' of failing to take account of the
diversity and strength of opinions that existed among both the
proponents and opponents of police reform, and has called for a
closer examination of local studies to account for 'the persistence

[34] Hilton, *The Age of Atonement*, 21.
[35] Foucault, *Discipline and Punish*, 24.
[36] Ruth Paley, 'An Imperfect, Inadequate and Wretched System? Policing in
London before Peel', *Criminal Justice History*, 10 (1989), 97.

of varied and often violent responses to the new police'.[37] Taylor
demonstrates that it is misleading to see police reform as an
unproblematic diffusion of a metropolitan model 1829–56, and
how the phenomena of crime and punishment were made complex
by the simultaneous existence of various alternative policing practices and models.[38]

As we shall see, a lot of the resistance to 'new' policing was rural
in origin. However, this is not to imply that the only opposition to
the reformed policing came from the aristocracy and the agricultural poor. As the century advanced and the industrial urban society fostered a sense of identity among urban workers, the new
police came under increasingly radical opposition from papers like
the *Northern Star* and events like the 'battle' of Coine in 1840. We
shall review the cultural impact of such resistances, but what
matters to us is the realization that, shaped by these social practices, the rhetoric of crime in nineteenth-century Britain could not
be used in the construction of a homogeneous ideology. It embodied all the contradictions and fractures of the social reality that
provided its context. In turn, when used as the mortar to hold
together the ideological façade of British aggression in India, this
rhetoric of crime would ensure that colonialist discourse would be
marked by ambiguities and a constant failure of its ambition to
achieve coherence.

Here, I wish to emphasize that in no way do I wish to imply that
the contradictions of colonialist discourse *only* originated from the
social and material tensions inherent within the colonizing, metropolitan society. That would scandalously ignore the whole history
of the colony's resistance to domination as well as the contradictions in social and material reality there. I am not particularly keen
to be a part of that 'radical criticism coming out of the West . . .
[that] is the result of an interested desire to conserve the subject of
the West, or the West as subject . . . This much-publicised critique
of the sovereign subject thus actually inaugurates the Subject.'[39]
Much admirable and incisive critical labour has been spent on
recovering the history of colonial and other subaltern struggles

[37] See David Taylor, *The New Police in Nineteenth-Century England*
(Manchester: Manchester University Press, 1997), 2–5.
[38] Ibid. 5–10.
[39] Gayatri Chakravorty Spivak, 'Can the Subaltern Speak?', in Williams and
Chrisman (eds.), *Colonial Discourse*, 66.

against British rulership and their decisive cultural impact. My aim
here is a more modest one. It is to show that even as it came into
contact with Indian society and its ideologies, the British discourse
and practice of crime that played a central role in the establishment
of colonial dominance had already inherited all the contradictions
of the its domestic realities. Transported to the singularly different
colonial society, with its own well-entrenched codes of 'normalcy'
and power, the contradictions within this strategy of rulership
widened into fissures that destabilized the ideology of colonial
rulership. Bhabha's 'slippages' and 'ambivalences' were determined
not so much by semiotic or textual differences, but by the historically specific conditions that marked the violent moment of the
incursion of colonial capital in India. As students of English litera-
ture(s), our critical attentions are perhaps disproportionately
focused on the master texts and master voices. Nevertheless, by
showing how the fractures within these texts expose the basic
contradictions of colonial and metropolitan societies, we could see
how cultural criticism, if not recovering the voice of the subaltern,
may at least alert us to the consequences of these narratives.[40]

PARADOXES, THE COLONY

The route of the arrival of the 'new policing' (masquerading as civilizing mission) in India is well documented. As I have indicated
before, I think Eric Stokes's work remains unsurpassed in this
respect. There is no need or indeed space to discuss the entire scope
of his discussion of utilitarian and evangelical ideologies in the
context of empire here. For us, two of his arguments are of importance. First, that from the Regulating Act of 1773 onwards, a
central tone of the British empire in India was a juridical one. The
questions of law, order, justice, and crime came to reside at the
heart of British relationship with India. Again and again viceroys
like Hastings, Cornwallis, and Wellesley, administrators like

[40] Here I have hoped with David Spurr that 'the first step towards an alternative
to colonial discourse . . . has to be a critical understanding of its structures . . . given
the degree to which a colonising discourse penetrates Western writing . . . I have
suggested that this writing also contains at least the seeds of resistance . . . to the
temptations of a totalizing authority over the object of representation.' Spurr, *The
Rhetoric of Empire*, 187.

Charles Grant, Munro, and Metcalfe, and philosopher-historians like James Mill and Jeremy Bentham linked issues of crime and order to the very essence of British existence in India. The difference between the British regime and the entire Indian civilization was represented as the former's commitment to the rule of law. And this, in turn, provided ethical and moral justification of the colonization of the country.[41] Second, the British struggle to determine the precise course of the empire was frequently conducted through the language and practices of crime, justice, and policing. So, on the reformer's side (liberal, radical, utilitarian, or evangelical) Cornwallis insisted that the new order of things 'Should have for its foundation, the security of individual property, and the administration of justice, criminal and civil, by rules which were to disregard all conditions of persons . . . free of influence or control from the government itself'.[42]

Mill and the utilitarians would allow an 'immense and infinite influence to law and government' and later John Crawford would argue for law to be used 'in a revolutionary way, consciously employing it as a weapon to transform Indian society by breaking up the customary, communal tenures'.[43] Against them were ranged the 'paternalists', men like Munro and Malcolm, who argued to preserve aspects of Indian social and legal infrastructure in the colonial state. Followers of the Burkean notions of tradition and organic communities, they denied that British legal and social mores could be applied unmodified to India. Such a disruptive move would replace what they saw as negotiating, 'paternal' British rule by an impersonal and mechanical, ultimately repressive governing machine.[44] Law and order were not only central, but a contested terrain on which the British relationship with its most important colony was built. This would also have profound repercussions in the realm of contemporary culture.

There is little doubt that in the argument about the strategy of British power in the colony, the reformist voices would be the louder. The case of the evangelicals, for example, is an instructive one. The 'age of atonement' coincides exactly with the establishment of the political dominance of the East India Company in India. Serving precisely the social groups who were driven by, as

---

[41] See Stokes, *The English Utilitarians*, 1–80. [42] Ibid.
[43] Ibid. [44] Ibid. 14–15.

Stokes shows, the ethos of free trade, evangelicalism, and philosophical radicalism, it is not surprising that British dominance in
India should be fuelled by the same myths about criminality and
order that had become the centrepiece of domestic reform. Hilton
calculates that between 1784 and 1832, about 112 Members of the
English Parliament were formally classified as 'evangelical, and by
1850 about a third of Anglican clergymen could also be designated
as such'.[45] The evangelical ideology, it can be safely assumed, influenced many more and played an important role in political and
economic policies.[46]

But the arrival of new policing and the evangelical ethos along
with its cultural dimensions in India hardly translated into an
unproblematic 'disciplining' of the country. As David Arnold has
observed, it would not be difficult to 'contrast Foucault's paradig-
matic view of prison discipline and institutional surveillance with a
different perspective drawn from colonial India'.[47] Prison, that
centrepiece in the 'new' strategies of surveillance, seems to have
been of a fundamentally different nature in the colony: 'Far from
being a captive domain in which discipline might reign supreme,
the prison often became . . . a focus or symbol of wider defiance
against the British.'[48] Supposedly an instrument of British imposition of 'new order' in the colony, so permeable was the colonial
prison that by the mid-nineteenth century 'the colonial authorities
felt obliged to recognise a continuum between the prison and the
wider community and so abandoned any pretence at individualis-
ing or reforming prisoners'.[49] Such deep 'slippage' in the practice
of colonial discipline cannot be attributed exclusively to either
domestic or colonial realities, but must be seen as a product of the
intimate and symbiotic nature of the contact between the societies.

Certain Marxist critics have tried to explain the paradoxes in

[45] Hilton, *The Age of Atonement*, 26, 205. The fervent proponent of police
reform, Patrick Colquhoun's admiration of Robert Peel was often expressed in
singularly evangelical terms like 'the prophet of God' and 'instrument of a kind
providence'. Note how easily these terms were applied to numerous British 'heroes'
of India from Dalhousie to Nicholson to legitimize their violence as a part of the
'divine plan'.
[46] In addition to Stokes, see Javed Majeed's analysis of James Mill in his
'Orientalism, Utilitarianism and British India' (D.Phil. thesis, Oxford: 1988).
[47] David Arnold, 'The Colonial Prison: Power, Knowledge and Penology in
Nineteenth Century India', in Ranajit Guha (ed.), *A Subaltern Studies Reader*
(Minneapolis: University of Minnesota Press, 1997), 141–2.
[48] Ibid. 143.   [49] Ibid. 172.

colonialist discourse by highlighting the resistance offered by the native 'pre-capitalist' social organization to the assault of colonial capitalism.[50] In this reading, if the resistance to new strategies of surveillance in England itself testified to the durability of an agrarian/feudal social organization, in the India of maharajas and peasants this resistance was amplified many times. But to essentialize India as 'pre-capital' is in a sense to replicate the central assertions of a colonialist historiography that saw the country as primitive, lagging behind in the inexorable march towards progress and modernity. Historians like Raj Chandravarkar have stressed the fact that a dogmatic application of Marxism distorts the reality of both pre-colonial India and the process of industrialization itself. But the same historians are also the first to point out the material complexity of the colonial society. Chandravarkar himself hints at this:

The history of industrialisation in the West is taken primarily to mean the evolution of factory from craft industry, generally presupposing the prior development of a market economy, the social differentiation of the peasantry and the changing legal and social structure. *In India, all these forces were working together at the same time.* (my emphasis)[51]

This complex process of an industrial capitalism that aimed not to develop the country, but to secure profits for a foreign power, has been well documented by 'Dependency' theorists like Frank and Wallerstein.[52] What is relevant to us is that it was in this unique context of industrial capital in the colony that the roots of the 'paradoxes, slippages, and contradictions' of the colonialist discourse took hold. At the material base of colonialism lay the

[50] In a passage in *Capital* (vol. ii), Marx wrote: 'The obstacles presented by the internal solidity and organisation of pre-capitalistic, national modes of production to the corrosive influence of commerce are strikingly illustrated in the intercourse of the English with India and China.' Quoted in Anthony Brewer, *Marxist Theories of Imperialism* (London: Routledge & Kegan Paul, 1980), 38.

[51] Rajnarayan Chandravarkar, *Imperial Power and Popular Politics: Class, Resistance and the State in India 1850–1950* (Cambridge: Cambridge University Press, 1998), 31. He goes on to say, 'the crude distinction made between pre-industrial and industrial societies frequently fails to advance our understanding of the former or even its transition to the latter. Pre-industrial societies are often taken to be predominantly agrarian societies in which large-scale industry has not been established. They are thus lumped together irrespective of their levels of technology, economic activity or social organization,' Ibid. 34.

[52] For the classic account of Marxist theories of imperialism and 'Dependency theories' see Brewer, *Marxist Theories*.

paradox of the manipulation of raw materials and (enforced) use of cheap labour, not for the relentless transformation and development of a 'modern' society, but to improvise and use the 'old' semi-feudal system for the maximum profit of a foreign regime. Thus, although industrial capitalism brought with it the whole gamut of ideological apparatuses like the rhetoric of crime (themselves marked by contradictions) that had been used in new techniques of rulership in Britain, they were hopelessly at odds with the material reality of the colony. The narratives of colonialism were geared towards the production of 'discipline', 'consent', and 'persuasion', when in fact, in the colony, there was little need of such techniques. All 'master-texts', fictions and non-fictions, were ultimately rooted in this contradiction of legitimizing colonial expansionism in the name of capitalist progress, when the state was, as Radhika Singha has put it, a 'despotism of law'.

Despite the criticism levelled at the 'Subaltern Studies' group by a number of historians, Ranajit Guha's basic reading of the paradox of colonial power relations, it seems to me, remains valid.[53] If the material conditions of the metropolis were crucially different from those of the colony, then so were the strategies of dominance and the construction of authority. Briefly, while in Britain social power was secured through a strategy where the 'moment of persuasion' outweighed that of coercion, in the colonial non-hegemonic (or at least, very partially hegemonic) society, the reverse was true.[54] Thus, policing practices in colonial India were much less concerned with producing consent and discipline than with confirming the arbitrary autocratic nature of the state. While the

---

[53] This is not the place to analyse the usefulness of such criticisms ranging across the diverse positions taken up by a variety of scholars from Spivak to Chandravarkar. But the latter's critique is a good example of the central thrust of such positions: 'Historians have been led on this terrain towards a preoccupation with a close reading of texts . . . with the often Eurocentric question of colonial discourse . . . overly concerned with how colonial discourse and its hegemonized agents represented their subjects, and seeking to liberate themselves from this discursive trap, scholars, rather like colonial ideologues, have increasingly assumed the mantle of representing the natives.' Chandravarkar, *Imperial Power*, 22.

[54] See Guha *Dominance*, pref. p. xii. Thus, for Guha, 'paradox' is the very condition of the colonial society: 'The consequence of this paradox for the political culture of colonial India was to generate an original alloy . . . which has been witness to the historic failure of capital to realise its universalising tendency under colonial conditions, and the corresponding failure of the metropolitan bourgeois culture to dissolve or assimilate fully the indigenous culture of south Asia.'

cultural representation of these practices could talk about reforming criminals, the colonial police often ended up promoting the kind of coercion that the 'reformers' claimed they were eradicating in India.[55] For instance, by using the so-called tools of 'discipline' to preserve and promote forced and non-paid labour, the colonial state in fact preserved and innovated on feudal practices that were at odds with the 'reformist' rhetoric of colonialism. For Guha, this is clearly linked to the peculiar role of capital in the colony:

In colonial India, where the role of capital was still marginal in the mode of production and the authority of the State structured as an autocracy that did not recognise any citizenship or rule of law, power simply stood for a series of inequalities between the rulers and the ruled as well as between classes, strata and individuals.[56]

That is why it is impossible to apply the Foucauldian model of 'discipline' without extensive qualifications in the context of the colonial state.

As I have indicated, Guha's thesis has not been without its critics. Still, his insights on the deep-seated contradictions of the colonial state remain valid. However, I would qualify his conclusions about the colonial ruling classes by focusing on the very contradictions that he theorizes about:

there were the metropolitan bourgeoisie who professed and practised democracy at home, but *were quite happy* to conduct the government of their Indian empire as an autocracy . . . Their antagonism to feudal values and institutions in their own society made little difference . . . to their *vast tolerance* of pre-capitalist values and institutions in Indian society. (emphasis added)[57]

I would venture to state, in fact, that happiness and contentment were not the most prominent feature of either the British ruling classes in the colony, or those at home. The contradictory nature of the colonialist ideology, where the 'fiction' of order and progress was constantly exposed by the actual brutal and autocratic practice of the colonial state, also constantly made the real nature of colonialism visible. For people operating within the matrices of such an ideology, such increased visibility of the ruthless interests of the state could only lead to a constant agitation and awareness of the *emptiness* of the moral norms they attempted to live by. From the

---

[55] Ibid. 25–7.   [56] Ibid. 20.   [57] Ibid. 4–5.

earliest humble private letters of men in trading outposts to the later sophistication of the works of Conrad and Kipling, the effect of this awareness of ideological contradiction, the awareness of the 'manufactured' nature of the so-called civilized norms, is only too discernible.

I do not mean to suggest that the members of a ruthless foreign regime that aimed (and mostly achieved) at a maximum exploitation of India lived in a constant state of mental agony about their moral hypocrisy. Most of them shrilly emphasized the validity of their superiority. But I will suggest that the heightened *awareness* of the contradictions of their ideology prepared a ground where incessant and sometimes radical questioning of the authority of the state could take root. And this critique of the authority of the colonial rulership could seldom be kept separate from the critique of the larger entity—the state of Britain itself. I will try to show that it was fiction that took the fullest advantage of the fractured nature of the rhetoric of crime to facilitate this critique of the ideological claims of nineteenth-century Britain.[58]

---

[58] I have been using the term 'fiction of crime' not only to signify particular kinds of genres like novels, or sub-genres like Detective fiction, but, like Jon Thompson, 'to denote all the genres and sub-genres that concern themselves with violation of the law'. Thompson, *Fiction, Crime and Empire*, 3.

2

The 'Criminal' Colony before the New Police

CRIME AND COLONIZING HISTORY

Seventeen years before India's independence, Cecil Walsh found himself describing the 'nature' of the overwhelming majority of the Indian subjects of the Raj

> My object has been . . . to present some sort of picture of the mentality, the duplicity and the cunning, the indifference to human life, the callous indulgence in false evidence and false charges, and the lack of moral fibre which daily manifest themselves amongst the millions of cultivators whom we govern, and of whom the Englishmen at home know so little.[1]

With a few strokes of his powerful pen, one of the colonial masters here imagines the colony as a penitentiary, teeming with cheating, perjuring, murderous criminals whose 'real' nature must be exposed to the British people (specifically, British men), some of whom had consistently and worryingly showed a misplaced sympathy for those wretches. Walsh's narrative was remarkable only in its typical rendition of the story of a 'criminal India' governed (and reformed) by enlightened British rule that had circulated since the late eighteenth century.[2] By no means was this the only image of India that was produced, but it did have a peculiar importance. Indeed, Cecil Walsh would be scarcely surprised at the analogy between India and a criminal underworld. For him, 'ordering' this

[1] Cecil Walsh, *Crime in India* (London: Ernest Beam, 1930), 9.
[2] This period exactly coincides with the rise of what John Bender has called the penal architecture of the mind in England. See Bender, *Imagining the Penitentiary*. On the surveillant mode of knowledge in the colony, see Bernard S. Cohn, *Colonialism and its Forms of Knowledge* (Princeton: Princeton University Press, 1996), 9.

lawless territory would have been an integral part of British imperial and national prestige.

How did this rhetoric of 'criminal India' come to permeate the various narratives of the Raj? How did it inform the British diaries and memoirs, histories of India, ethnographic studies, and, crucially, fiction? An imperial mythology of crime seems to have developed along a line that connected the 'Black Hole' of Calcutta to the 'Well' at Kanpur and to memoirs such as the one produced by Cecil Walsh. Kate Teltscher, among others, has observed how the account of the 'Black Hole' incident was fashioned into a narrative of crime and punishment to justify the subsequent British aggression in Bengal and beyond.[3]

As hinted above, we cannot begin to look at the fiction of crime without situating it in the context of the large volume of non-fictional narratives that formed the discourse of British empire. In this chapter, we will examine how the rhetoric of crime became a crucial, perhaps a dominant strain in the British representations of India from the mid- to late eighteenth century onward. At the same time, we will be able to notice how *inconsistent* and *contested* this representation of criminal India was from virtually the initial moments of colonial paramountcy in India. Setting out to tell the story of British attempts to introduce order into chaos, the narratives seem to argue against each other and often against themselves, seemingly bearing out the accounts of ambiguity and discursive disturbances that post-colonialist critics have attributed to colonialist discourses.[4] However, in the next chapter, we will attempt to move away from an exclusively discursive explanation of colonialist ambiguity to a more historically charged one by excavating the formation of the ideas and practices of 'criminality', 'justice',

---

[3] See Kate Teltscher, 'The Fearful Name of the Black Hole: Fashioning an Imperial Myth', in Bart Moore-Gilbert (ed.), *Writing India: 1757–1990* (Manchester: Manchester University Press, 1996).

[4] Moore-Gilbert's introduction is an example of this critical commonplace: 'ambivalence in the psychic economy of colonialism is largely the product of an unresolved conflict between recognition and disavowal of the "Other" on both sides of the colonial relationship. On the coloniser's side, its effects are registered principally in varieties of discursive disturbances which haunt colonial narratives of all kinds—legal, literary, political, evangelical'. In Moore-Gilbert (ed.), *Writing India*, 6. For the evolution of this theoretical position see Bhabha, *The Location of Culture* and Abdul JanMohammed, *Manichean Aesthetics: The Politics of Literature in Colonial Africa* (Amherst: University of Massachusetts Press, 1983).

and 'punishment' in Britain. We will try to see how the contests and fractures built within these crucial implements of power at 'home' provided the distinctive flavour of ambiguity to colonial authority in India.

First, however, we might try to see whether the rhetoric of crime did in fact come to play a widely pervasive role in the narratives of the Raj. The numerous British histories of India produced throughout this period provide a suitable ground to begin our survey. Bernard Cohn reminds us that 'In British India, this [the historiographic] modality is the most complex, pervasive, and powerful, underlying a number of other more specific modalities. . . . History in its broadest sense was a zone of debate over the ends and means of their [the British] relationship in India.'[5] A number of these early British historians of India had considerable personal investment in the expansionist policies of the East India Company. Alexander Dow was an officer in the Bengal army. Robert Orme was a member of the Madras Council, a close friend of Robert Clive, and the official historiographer of the East India Company, and John Holwell had held the post of the Governor of Bengal. The overall aim of their works was to show the British presence in India as somehow historically inevitable, a part of the inexorable march of progress. It is also precisely this idea of historical progress that these writers alleged to be missing in pre-colonial India, and as such, the country was shown to be without history itself. Thus the economic and political aggression of the Company was in fact presented as the arrival of history in India, and invested with a unique moral authority. If Britain was shown to be the harbinger of history, the most visible sign of this momentous event was held to be the arrival of order, justice, and legality. Conversely, if India was a country without history, the manifestation of this lack was to be found in the 'naturally' criminal inclination of the native inhabitants. While this explains the dominance of the 'historical mode' in the making of colonial knowledge, the existence of contradictions within it becomes even more interesting.

J. Z. Holwell begun his career as a medical officer in Calcutta and went on to become the owner of the twenty-four pargannas— a vast swathe of land stretching from Calcutta to the Bay of Bengal. He later served as the temporary Governor of Bengal in 1760 on

---

5 Cohn, *Colonialism*, 5.

the strength of his conduct during the crisis of 1756 when the British settlement in Calcutta was razed by the Indian ruler of the province (Siraj-ud-Daulah). As such, his narrative of Siraj's attack is a good place to begin the story of Indian criminality. After all, Holwell himself became a part of the imperial mythification of the incident that was to play an enduring role in the criminalization of India: the 'Black Hole' of Calcutta. There is certainly the titillating promise of a horror story in the beginning of his account: 'as I believe the annals of the world cannot produce an incident like it in any degree or proportion . . . I cannot allow it to be buried in oblivion.'[6] But this hardly leads to any seemingly unproblematic assertions like Cecil Walsh's conclusions about the criminality of Indians 200 years later. The usual suspects of colonialist representations are certainly there. The author sketches the sadistic pleasures of the Indian guards at the sight of the British prisoners clawing each other to death for water.[7] The sole Englishwoman who survives the night is transferred to that den of oriental vice, the harem, and Bengal's Nawab is compared to the tiger in his heartless cruelty.[8] But only once are these incidents used to formulate a *general* feature of the Indian character. This is when Holwell finds himself a hostage of one of the Bengali ministers: 'I was well convinced I should never have got alive out of the hands of that rapacious harpy, who is a *genuine Hindoo*, in the very worst affectation of the word [emphasis added].'[9]

It was only after the Company's assumption of power in Bengal that British writers would systematically attempt to extract an account of universal Indian criminality from Holwell's writing. Holwell himself was much more focused on the trauma of the incident—the guilt of the defeat and 'unmanning' of British gentlemen. Kate Teltscher has perceptively observed that in his narrative, the criminalization of the Indian guards occurred as a result of the guilt of defeat by the so-called 'lesser race': 'Why are the guards demonised? . . . the desperate captives, when represented as victims of Indian torture, are absolved from responsibility for their actions. An ugly fight for survival is transformed into a less disturbing image.'[10] The narrative is pitched at its most intense in its depiction

[6] J. Z. Holwell, *A Genuine Narrative of the Deplorable Deaths of English Gentlemen* (London: A. Miller, 1758), 2.   [7] Ibid. 19.
[8] Ibid. 48–9.   [9] Ibid. 51.
[10] Teltscher, 'The Fearful Name', 34.

of the 'unmanned' British prisoners, stripped to their skins, licking sweat to kill the thirst, breaking into hysterics and a murderous struggle for air and water. Holwell himself repeatedly fainted and contemplated suicide, thereby deserting the proud standards of British courage.[11] But for a text that lay at the root of the subsequent construction of universal Indian criminality, Holwell's account reveals a startling lack of concern about the criminal essence of India. Instead, it is obsessed with anxiety about the loss of masculine and racial prestige in the colony. The criminality of *certain* Indians emerges only as a cover for this failure of the colonialist nerve, as a disguise for the guilt of defeat. In this context, it is instructive to remember the *date* of Holwell's text. Not only was 1758 before the Company's political domination of India, it also pre-dated the domination of the reformist strategies of producing criminals and new ways of punishment in Britain itself. The writing of crime at 'home' had not yet gathered sufficient strength to universalize the colony as criminal.

This as yet unrealized strength of the systematic and disciplined rhetoric (and practice) of criminalization is again evident in Holwell's subsequent (1766) history of India. In the light of later accounts, it is surprising to find that the so-called momentous 'Black Hole' incident left such a negligible trace in Holwell's writing. In fact, his history began with a refutation of one of the cornerstones of colonialism—British racial and cultural superiority:

ignorance, superstition and partiality to ourselves are too commonly the cause of presumption and contempt of others ... confessing myself amazed that we should so readily believe the people of Indostan a race of stupid idolaters, *when to our cost, in a political and commercial view, we have found them superior to us.* (my emphasis)[12]

British victory at Plassey *is* represented as a 'just' punishment of the erring ruler of Bengal. But, instead of using this example to construct an argument for further expansionism (as his successors would do), Holwell went to the opposite direction of spelling out British culpability in the post-Plassey political chaos in the province: 'A just vengeance and necessity drew the English arms against him

[11] Holwell, *Genuine Narrative*, 20–8.
[12] J. Z. Holwell, *Interesting Historical Events Relative to the Province of Bengal and the Empire of Indostan* (London: T. Becket, 1766), 11.

[Siraj] . . . Necessity again, produced a second revolution . . . a few individuals may benefit by this shifting system; but total ruin to the trade of the provinces . . . must necessarily in the end be the consequence.'[13] In fact, Holwell ended by warning the English of the disastrous consequences of any further territorial advancement into the rich province of Awadh: 'It would be almost cruel to molest these happy people; for in this district are the only vestiges of the beauty, purity, piety, regularity, equity and strictness of the ancient Indian government preserved.'[14]

Although, with the subsequent strengthening of disciplinary discourses in Britain, India was gradually absorbed within the intricate meshes of the new rulership, this early ambiguity of Holwell's narratives would be preserved in almost all the subsequent colonialist writings.[15] Undoubtedly, an important reason for this was the strength of the political and cultural institutions of India itself that could not be easily absorbed by the imported ideological/ cultural strategies of the colonial aggressors. But the contradictions already inherent in the English rhetoric of crime *amplified* the Indian resistance to colonialist assimilation. As the later eighteenth and early nineteenth centuries saw British society become a battleground of conflicting ideological positions on crime, the criminalization of India grew simultaneously stronger and even more riven with contradictions. Alexander Dow's famous history of India (1772) is a perfect example of this. Dow joined as an ensign of the Bengal army in 1760, and within ten years had climbed to the rank of a lieutenant colonel. But for a member of the brutal colonial British army, his account of India seems surprisingly multilinear. On the one hand, Dow criticized British colonialist supremacism because it led to a misreading of Indian culture. On the other hand, he found the essence of India in the corrupt native judicial

---

[13] Holwell, *Interesting Historical Events Relative to the Province of Bengal and the Empire of Indostan*, 179.

[14] Ibid. 198.

[15] For instance, in Robert Orme's subsequent influential history of India, accounts of Siraj's 'oriental' criminal excesses were more than balanced by that of the forgery committed by Robert Clive in the drawing up of the treaty with Umirchand. Written at a time when forgery was still treated as a capital offence under British law, this neutralized any formulaic representation of the legitimacy of the Company's expansionism. See Robert Orme, *A History of the Military Transactions of the British Nation in Indostan* (London: John Nourse, 1795), 148–55.

system.[16] For Dow, this venal justice was an extension of the 'national religion', and this connection between Indian religion and criminality was to become a staple formula of imperial writing:

> A religion which indulges in a crime, at which the rest of humanity shudder, leaves ample room for the cruelty of a prince . . . he becomes habituated to death. He mistakes passion for justice; men are dragged to execution with an abruptness that prevents fear . . . the spectators scarcely heed a circumstance, which frequency has made them to expect.[17]

Dow maintained that Islamic law (practised in most north and central Indian courts) was indulgent towards crime, particularly murder, and this familiarized Indians with violence, legal and illegal. The Indian ruler was seen to make justice contingent on personal feelings, not 'universal' laws.

As will become evident, Dow's was the language of the British reformers of criminal law and debates over punishment that had grown in volume from the latter half of the eighteenth century.[18] His criticism of the spectacular and discretionary Indian justice closely echoed the criticism of public executions and debates over a 'new police' and reformed prisons in Britain. As such, his narrative was an early example of the complex and symbiotic relationship between 'home' and 'colony' in English writing. At a time when the contest between the 'old' and 'new' punishment as a mode of power was still very much hanging in the balance in Britain, the canvassing for the latter could be done by playing off 'criminal' India against the 'just' East India Company in India. In British histories, India could become a convenient testing ground where the propaganda for an emergent ideology could be conducted at a (seemingly) undisturbed representative level.

This advocating of a 'new' kind of imperial policing and justice in India by Dow also coincided with the gradual consolidation of East India Company's power in India. By 1803, the Company was firmly in the political saddle and could afford to distance itself from the Burkean rhetoric of negotiation with the laws and

---

[16] See Alexander Dow, *The History of Hindostan*, i (London: Becket, 1772), pp. i–xix.   [17] Ibid. iii, pp. xv–xvi.

[18] See V. A. C. Gatrell, *The Hanging Tree* (Oxford: Oxford University Press, 1996). Although not his chief objective, Gatrell's study of popular attitudes to public execution fleshes out the Foucauldian thesis of power in modern Europe.

customs of the colonized people.[19] At the same time, however, the criticism of the 'old'/criminalized mode of power could also be used to measure the distance from the disreputable policies of early colonial pioneers like Robert Clive. Bolstered by the shift in fortune and power, British historians could now attempt to contrast the present rule with the 'old' misgovernance, and thus strengthen the logic of colonial rulership:

A barbarous enemy may slay a prostrate foe; but a civilised conqueror can only ruin nations without the sword . . . the embezzlement and fraudulent practices were not so detrimental to the Company's affairs as the general depravity of manners and the oppression which they introduced . . . Justice was totally suspended . . . the distemper of avarice . . . seemed to infect all whom the wrath of God, against a defeated people, had placed in power . . . men who retained some property in spite of the violence of the times, instead of being protected by British laws, found that they had not even the justice of a despot to depend upon.[20]

But this nuanced strategy to invent legitimacy for the 'reformed' colonial government could itself be intensely problematic. Thus, if Dow found the 'old' Company's rule at least as criminal as that of the Indians, this spectre of the 'old' corruption loomed over the narrative of the 'new' enlightened British rule. Although he saw India as essentially criminal, the extension of the stigma of criminality to the pioneers of the East India Company raised doubts about any vision of future 'moral policing'. If a criminal despotism lay at its very roots, could one guarantee a 'reformed' and progressive future for empire-building?[21]

---

[19] See Radhika Singha, *A Despotism of Law* (New Delhi: Oxford University Press, 1998), pp. x–xv, and Jorg Fisch, *Cheap Lives and Dear Limbs* (Wiesbaden: Franz Steiner, 1983), for illuminating accounts of colonial law in India. Singha complements Fisch in showing the shift between the early negotiatory aspect of colonial law and its later more authoritarian character by relating it to the political and cultural context of the Company's fortunes in the country. See Martin Weiner's *Reconstructing the Criminal: Culture, Law and Policy in England 1830–1914* (Cambridge: Cambridge University Press, 1990) to conduct a fruitful comparison between penal reforms in England and India and the interrelated nature of strategies of criminalization in the two countries.

[20] See Dow, *History*, iii. pp. lxxi–cvii.

[21] The ambiguities of Dow's text are a fair indication of the pattern found in most of the contemporary accounts. The strength and consistency of the rhetoric of crime are certainly evident, but so is the unease about the fact that, despite grand universalizing aims, this rhetoric could never reduce the complex reality of the colony into the sign of criminality. Robert Orme followed up his earlier account of Plassey with

These histories of India we have so far looked at were all written from what Mary Pratt has called the 'contact zone' of the
colony.[22] As Britons attempting to write history from within the
socio-cultural arena of India, these historians were particularly
alive to the difficulties of bending the complex colonial reality with
the lever of the rhetoric of crime. Following Pratt, we might reason-
ably expect such a complex response from writers who were in
such troubling proximity with their subjects. But what about those
historians of the empire who were liberally peppering their monu-
mental works with the rhetoric of crime from the comforting
distance of metropolitan Britain? By early nineteenth century, the
evangelical/utilitarian movement for a reform of policing and
punishment in Britain had seemingly gained sufficient strength to
counter this challenge of troubled writing from the 'contact zone'.
This may be seen in two extremely influential histories written
from within this tradition by Charles Grant and James Mill.
However, even these texts, with their more consistent application
of formulae of guilt and punishment and the alignment of colonialism with reform, betrayed ambiguities and tensions, albeit of a
slightly different kind and to a different degree. Why should this be
so, unless the very rhetorical device they employed, that of crime
and legality, contained within it seeds of doubt, of contests and
dispersals that marked the metropolitan historical context itself?

Charles Grant was a member of the evangelical Clapham Sect
who saw active military service in India, and became an important
member of the Company's Bengal Council. He amassed a small

a general history of India where pre-colonial society under the Mughals was seen as
little better than a criminal confederacy: 'The Havildar plunders the villager, and is
himself fleeced by the Zamindar; the Zamindar by the Nabob, or his Duan. The
Duan is the Nabob's head slave. And the Nabob exists on the best terms he can
make with his Sultan, or the throne.' After describing the essence of the Hinduo as
deceit and that of the Muslim as inhuman cruelty, Orme was, however, frankly
puzzled at the concluding image of India: 'where the human race is struggling
through such mighty ills as render its condition scarcely superior to that of the
brutes of the field, shall we not expect throughout Indostan dreary plains, desolated
towns? . . . but on the contrary, we find a people equally if not exceeding in number
the most populous states, such as enjoy the best of governments and the best of
laws.' Orme's frank bewilderment at the failure of his own strategy of criminalization seems to me a particularly good example of colonial 'ambiguity'. See Robert
Orme, *Historical Fragments of the Mogul Empire and of the Morattoes and of the
English Concerns in Indostan* (London: Wingrave, 1782), 402–7.

[22] See Mary Louise Pratt, *Imperial Eyes: Travel Writing and Transculturation*
(London: Routledge, 1992), 1–37.

fortune as the commercial resident of the Bengali town of Malda and was later to serve as the deputy-chairman of the Company's Court of Directors. Grant made a passionate plea in the English Parliament on behalf of the colonial venture in India with a carefully constructed vision of criminal India. He claimed that Bengal was destined to be the seat of the 'British empire in the east' and that the British military operations there were essentially defensive measures against the tyranny of Siraj.[23] Grant glossed over the conduct of Clive and the English 'Nabobs' and laboured to point out that the British were not directly chargeable with any misconduct. He hotly denied colonial responsibility for the great famines of the 1770s in Bengal that had occurred due to the Company's mismanagement of revenue collection.[24]

Instead, Grant's subject was the definitive achievement of the English in Bengal: the establishment of courts of circuit for criminal trials with English judges 'selected from the most experienced of the servants of the Company'. For Grant, it was the meting out of justice that best summed up the Company's role in a country populated by 'a people exceedingly depraved'.[25] The economic and territorial interests of the Company were now represented as the noble desire to bring order to a criminal people through trial and punishment. Grant's exemplar of the essence of India was the Bengalis: 'they want truth, honesty, and good faith, in an extreme, of which Europeans furnishes [sic] no example . . . in the worst part of Europe, there are no doubt great numbers of men who are sincere, upright and conscientious. In Bengal, a man of real veracity and integrity is a great phenomenon.'[26] Grant's strategy displayed an expert understanding of the new discourse about criminals that was already circulating in Britain. There the threat of 'criminal classes' was used to establish a growing network of surveillance that cast its disciplining eye on the marginalized figures unable or unwilling to participate in 'useful' economic activities (useful, that is, to the increasingly dominant middle classes). In

---

[23] Charles Grant, 'Observations on the State of Society among the Asiatic Subjects of Great Britain, Particularly with Respect to Morals and on the Ways of Improving it', *Parliamentary Papers*, 10 (1812–13), 36.

[24] Ibid. 42–6. For an illuminating account of the imperial politics of famine in British India, see Mike Davis, *Late Victorian Holocausts: El Niño Famines and the Making of the Third World* (London: Verso, 2001).

[25] Grant, 'Observations', 55.   [26] Ibid. 56.

India, this could be adapted to criminalize all opposition to the
Company's political/economic interests. One of Grant's lasting
contributions to subsequent English narratives about India was the
formula of the 'naturally criminal castes' in India: 'There are castes
of robbers and thieves, who consider themselves acting in their
proper profession, and train their children to it . . . murder is very
common . . . multitudes of individuals employ themselves in
despoiling their neighbours.'[27]

But Grant's narrative was a reminder, not only of the convergence between metropolitan and colonialist strategies of criminalization, but also of the crucial difference between them. If, in
Britain, the 'criminal classes' were seen as an aberration to the
norms of society, in India their counterparts were seen to sum up
the essence of the society. Criminality seeped out from these castes
and tribes to contaminate the rest of the country and the native
political, judicial, and social systems. The Islamic legal punishments like blinding and mutilations seemed to justify abundantly
the belief that the Indians were 'naturally averse to any tender-
ness'.[28] With gloomy satisfaction, Grant concluded that there were
no sentiments diffused at large through Indian society that attached
shame to criminality. After all, religion, which should be the chief
vehicle for the dissemination of morality in society, was as 'criminal' as everything else in India. Grant found in the multitudes of
Hindu deities 'of both sexes' a source of immorality and abandoned wickedness.[29] He observed with profound horror:
'Representations which abandoned licentiousness daren't hardly
imagine within the most secret recesses of impunity, are held up in
the face of the sun to all mankind . . . they are the objects of religious adoration.'[30] Pre-British India, in this kind of writing, was
seen to celebrate a very visible spectacle of punishment and sexuality. It is this that the colonial 'reformers' would attempt to eradi-
cate through moral policing and imprisonment.[31]

[27] Ibid. 58.
[28] Grant even disagreed with earlier British historians of India on aspects of the
Indian family life, concluding that the family members behaved with indifference
and cruelty towards each other, a further proof of their susceptibility to criminal
urges. Ibid. 59.   [29] Ibid. 94.   [30] Ibid.
[31] See Michel Foucault, *The History of Sexuality*, vol. i (Harmondsworth: Penguin,
1978) for a discussion of 19th-century discourses of sexuality as a part of the 'discrete'
technology of power. In the context of Britain, a rewarding way of studying this
connection may be to see how certain sexual activities were criminalized over this

The strength of the evangelical/utilitarian rhetoric of reform and the precision of the discourse of crime imported from Britain could then be used to produce an effective spectre of an atavistic criminal India. Does this mean Grant was able to avoid any of the ambiguities that we have located as a feature of those discourses that used the rhetoric of crime? On the contrary, his employment of the formula of the criminal colony often meant that the very basis of the propaganda for a 'legal' empire was severely undercut. The chief ideological goal of Grant, both as an evangelist and as a colonialist, was to represent criminal India *in need of* the healing touch of British 'moral' (a shorthand for the whole panoply of administrative, legal, military, medical, educational, religious tools of establishing power) reforms. But in Grant's vision, the criminal Indian was *essentially* different from a British criminal and hence less, if at all, susceptible to reform:

> The dacoits of Bengal are not, like the robbers in England, individuals driven to such desperate courses by sudden wants. They are robbers by profession, and even by birth . . . they are all therefore alike criminals . . . wretches who have placed themselves in a state of declared war with government, and are therefore wholly excluded from every benefit of its laws.[32]

Grant aimed to represent the Company as the embodiment of law and order, both moral and administrative. But if the cornerstone of this strategy, representing 'criminal Indians', resulted in the admission of the impossibility of reforming them, then the carefully constructed myth of colonial law and order was rendered ineffectual. One might as well have argued that 'native justice' (or the misrepresentation of the legal mechanism that the colonial power used to demonize India)—corrupt, bloodthirsty, and decidedly 'unreformed'—was indeed the most suitable for such wretches. The necessary illusion of progress, the ideological staple of colonialist aggression, could no longer be fabricated. This fundamental problem became evident in Grant's abandoning of the idea of prison reforms in India. He argued that imprisonment might hold the highest terror for the 'naturally' energetic Englishman, but for the

period. Besides Weiner, see Leon Radzinowicz, *A History of Criminal Law and its Administration*, vol. v (London: Stevens, 1986) and Clive Emsley, *The English Police: A Political and Social History* (London: Longman, 1996).

[32] Grant, 'Observations', 63.

Criminality fixed nature of Indian (margin annotation)

lethargic and indolent Indian it became an attractive option. Thus, Grant's use of the rhetoric of crime, even from the apparently sterilized distance of metropolitan Britain, contained seeds of contest against the very discourse of reform and empire that he sought to construct.

Echoes of Grant's influential, but paradoxically flawed, propaganda were raised in James Mill's celebrated history of India.[33] As the entry in the *Dictionary of National Biography* notes, despite his association with Bentham and philosophical radicalism, Mill was not prepared to extend his radical political stance to his assessment of British colonialism. His *judging* history, as he called it, produced India as a tabula rasa that could serve as a testing and ultimately empowering ground for Utilitarian legal and social theories.[34] For Mill, from the heights of his judgemental position, Indians were a people without any historical consciousness or the concept of progress. Next, he diagnosed the character of this people as generally criminal and anarchic. Thus the text progresses from wiping out history from India ('This people . . . are perfectly destitute of historical records. Their ancient literature affords not a single production to which the historical character belongs'[35]) to a freezing of the natives as fixed and unchangeable entities distinguished by an endless cycle of violence:

Hindus, at the time of Alexander's invasion, were in a state of manner, society and knowledge, exactly the same with that in which they were discovered by the nations of modern Europe . . . The sudden, violent, and unprepared revolutions incident to barbarians are so much guided by caprice . . . that they disgust us by the uniformity of their appearance.[36]

And then he could reach the third stage of his analysis of Indians—that criminality was the defining feature of their 'fixed' nature: 'Our ancestors . . . though rough, were sincere, but, under the . . .

[33] As Javed Majeed has pointed out, Mill's text became the standard work for East India Company officials, and eventually a set text for candidates for the Indian Civil Service. Macaulay consulted it while drafting the Minute on Education and the Penal Acts for India, and it was reissued during the 1857 Mutiny to explain the events to English officials engaged in the suppression of the Indian masses. See Majeed, 'Orientalism', 113.

[34] 'For Mill, as for Bentham, India provided the opportunity to reveal the inadequacies of the English legal system, and to arrive at a code of laws which was universally applicable'. Ibid.

[35] James Mill, *The History of British India* (London: Baldwin, Craddock & Joy, 1817), 99.   [36] Ibid. 101.

exterior of the Hindu lies a *general* disposition to deceit and perfidy.'[37] If history is brought to the colony, it could only be as the history of a criminal people.

However, even for Mill, India is produced as 'criminal' only at the cost of a radical doubting of the reformist rationale. Javed Majeed has noted that this pessimism was to mark all the colonialist projects of the philosophical radicals:

According to Mill, the main purpose of British rule in India was to perpetrate the power of aristocracy in Britain. This pessimistic view of India, reinforced by the notion of India as the culture of poverty, conflicts with the sense of reforming possibilities available in India for the philosophical radicals . . . the History, far from being a confident text, reveals the contradictions in Mill's philosophy which results in a loss of nerve in dealing with India.[38]

As one progressed from the mid-eighteenth century to the early decades of the nineteenth century, then, British histories of India became more systematic in their application of the rhetoric of crime.[39] This reflected both the dominance of the reformist parties in Britain as well as the political fortunes of the Company in India.

[37] Mill, *The History of British India*, 247.

[38] Majeed, 'Orientalism', 13, 118.

[39] The extent of the diffusion of the new strategies of criminalization may be gauged in the echoes found not only in these histories, but in various other kinds of official narratives, including 'scientific' ones. In 1820, Dr Sherwood published an essay in the prestigious journal *Asiatick Researches* on the 'criminal sect' known as Thugs who were to be immortalized in the colonialist myth of law and progress. Sherwood's narrative showed a precise application of the criminalizing techniques found in the colonial histories: the 'hereditary murderers' were first linked to the Company's greatest Indian opponent, Tippoo Sultan of Mysore; this resulted in the proof of the criminal nature of the entire Indian political organization throughout history; this in turn led to the exposure of the symbiotic relationship between Indian crime and Indian religion (the Thugs were seen as devotees of the goddess Kali). The 'scientific conclusion' of this research was that India must be brought under the reformed surveillance system existing in Britain where 'the absence of even a single person, seldom fails to produce suspicion, with corrective investigation and discovery'. See Dr Sherwood, 'Of the Murderers called Phansigars', *Asiatick Researches*, 13 (Calcutta, 1820), 250–81. Sherwood's conclusions were supported by an extract from an official report by Mr John Shakespeare who stressed the importance of bringing the liminal culture of Indian roads, the travelling religious mendicants, grain dealers, etc. under close observation. This provides us with a glimpse of the economic interest that informed the ideology of 'progress, law, and order'. Any group situated outside the norm of 'useful' economic activities (i.e. those serving the interest of colonial capital) were to be made criminal and 'usefully punished'. See John Shakespeare, 'Observations Regarding Badheks and Thugs', ibid. 282–92.

However, one way or other, this use of the rhetoric of crime resulted in the subversion of the particular ideology through which the East India Company sought to legitimize its expansionism. This was a founding contradiction of the entire discourse of colonialism—that its claim for legitimacy was constructed around the 'criminality' of Indians, which at the same time subverted that claim by showing the task of 'civilizing/reforming' to be, in a number of ways, an impossible one. But this, however, was not the only contradiction. Related to it and growing out of it were also deep misgivings about the morality and legality of the taskmaster's presence in India itself. As we shall see, all these can be linked back to the fundamentally contested and ambiguous nature of the rhetoric of crime itself that grew out of a particular history of metropolitan Britain during this period.

CRIME, TRAVEL WRITING, AND MEMOIRS

Like the histories of India, the personal memoirs and travel writings of the British colonialists provide further evidence of the versatile and pervasive nature of the rhetoric of crime. Writing a personal recollection of his Indian experience, Sir John Malcolm could not resist presenting it as an intimate history of the land. And along with usurping the authority of the historical narrative, Malcolm also adapted the rhetoric of crime that the other British historians used to structure their narratives.

Having joined the colonial army at the age of 13, and fought against both Tippoo Sultan and the Marathas, Malcolm's 'impartial' observations are a telling example of writing crime and writing empire. His observations about Hindu Brahmins—that they were 'from diet, habit, and education . . . avaricious, and often treacherous' were a measure of the considerable resistance faced by the British from both Tippoo and the Maratha armies.[40] The virulence of Malcolm's (and most subsequent British) account of Mysore, Marathas, and the Pindaris was directly proportional to the amount of political and military challenges faced by the British in their bid to 'civilize' and 'order' these territories. In colonialist writing, these kingdoms of India were shown to be ripe for earnest

---

[40] Sir John Malcolm, *A Memoir of Central India* (London: Bentley, 1823), i. 67.

reform: 'Every court has its secret history, and that of several in India, if disclosed, would exhibit strange scenes of intrigue and licentiousness. Nothing could be more wicked and shameless than the daily occurrences.'[41] From this corrupt court, criminality was shown to radiate outward to permeate every strand of society. The perfect crystallization of this criminal essence of India was found in those 'instinctive' robbers, the Pindaris, who 'had risen, like masses of putrefaction in animal matter, out of the corruption of weak and expiring states . . . they had neither the tie of religious, nor of natural feelings. They were men of all lands and all religions.'[42]

Indeed, for Malcolm, memories of India seemingly consisted of little more than a dizzying variety of criminals. Besides the Pindaris, Malcolm went on to list other 'habitual' criminals like Bheels (divided into three classes), Charuns, Bhats, Bheelalahs, Meenahs, and Goojurs. There was also the mention of a tribe of marauding Brahmins called the Thugs![43] Against this panoramic backdrop of criminality, Malcolm wove the central matter of his memoirs—the romance of the British policing of these criminal subjects. Most, if not all, of the descriptions of the areas travelled were introduced with the formulaic chant of how they had been made 'safe' under the Company, in contrast to the recent past when no one could step out for a journey without being robbed or murdered. The suppression of the Pindaris became the touchstone of this tale of spreading justice:

There remains not a spot in India that a Pindary can call his home. They have been hunted like wild beasts; numbers have been killed; all have been ruined . . . With the exception of a few, whom the liberality and consideration of the British government have aided to become *industrious*, [they] are lost in that population, from whose dregs they originally issued. (my emphasis)[44]

This seems a full and confident expression of both the criminality of Indians *and* the possibility of reforming them. Not only were the tribes formulated as 'criminal', Malcolm is also able to celebrate their introduction to economic productivity through the 'useful' punishment of the British regime.[45]

---

[41] Malcolm, *A Memoir of Central India*, 289.   [42] Ibid. 431.
[43] Ibid. 426–520; ii. 110–82.   [44] Ibid. i. 461–2.
[45] Similarly, Malcolm's description of the 'criminal' tribe of the Bheels exuded a reformer's confidence: 'their robberies are upon a very limited scale . . . and measures are in progress that will . . . soon complete the reformation of a class of

But again, the contradictions in Malcolm's text closely mirrored the paradox and pessimism found in Mill and Grant's narratives. Amidst the constant assertions that the colonial rule was sanctified by its moral and legal intentions there surfaced contradictory statements about the implausibility of the reforming mission and doubts about manifest destiny. Moreover, with his 'contact' perspective, Malcolm was aware that despite his best efforts, even his highly selective representation of Indian history could not be reduced to a history of crime. In the middle of his story of Maratha criminality, he acknowledged the extraordinarily enlightened rule of the Indian princess Alia Bhy.[46] This mixed perspective on crime and punishment, of course, made it impossible for Malcolm to be consistent in his justification for progressive colonial expansion. So, instead of following up the confident prescription of disciplining and punishing criminal India with the expected recommendation of the expansion and entrenchment of British colonial government, Malcolm proposed a curbing and limiting of expansionism. He foresaw Indians 'waking from a dream of terror and admiration' of colonial rule into a 'feeling of disgust and discontent'. He warned that the British had no natural roots in the soil and suggested that any reforming achieved in India would be at the price of an abandonment of the 'real or supposed eminence' of morals.[47] Accompanying this complete reversal of the direction of the narrative of reform and order was also a reversal in the conclusions about the essence of India. Malcolm's summing up of the 'Indian character' flatly contradicted the masses of data about criminality that he had unearthed throughout the narrative: 'I do not know the example of any great population, in similar circumstances preserving . . . so much of virtue and so many good qualities as are to be found in the great proportion of the inhabitants of this country.'[48]

---

men, who, believing themselves doomed to be thieves and plunderers, have been confirmed in their destiny by the oppression and cruelty of neighbouring governments'. Ibid. 525. Malcolm's rhetoric of 'reform and progress' disguised the fact that under the British administration, the Bheels and other hill tribes were more *systematically* criminalized and oppressed through a more efficient policing organization. See Anand Yang (ed.), *Crime and Criminality in British India* (Tucson: University of Arizona Press, 1985), 128–9.

[46] Malcolm, *Memoir*, ii. 194.   [47] Ibid. 281–91.

[48] Ibid. 440. In the appendix, Malcolm emphasized the importance of respecting Indian habits for the maintenance of British rule: 'Almost all . . . are agreed that our power in India rests on the general opinion of the natives of our comparative

Most of Lieutenant-Colonel Fitzclarence's journal of a journey across India, like Malcolm's, can be read as a history of Indian criminality and its 'ordering' by the East India Company. Like Malcolm, Fitzclarence used the Pindari campaign to represent colonialism as the rule of law:

an upright and impartial administration of justice, a security to personal property previously unknown . . . an extirpation of robbery, and a general diffusion of happiness hitherto untested . . . within the last two years these freebooters have been repressed, and the country placed in a state of tranquillity and protection.[49]

Indeed, Fitzclarence declared that he was not willing to tread the path of earlier British histories of India, because of their tendency to dwell on failures or mistakes:

Instead of these glaring and unfavourable views of British domination of India, I should be disposed to assert, that an enthusiastic mind would be justified in picturing to itself, that providence, fatigued with the continued sight of misuse and crime, had . . . brought the British power, with those concomitants of justice and good government.[50]

Despite this bullish tone that presented colonial rule as providential, large portions of the narrative failed to square with this picture of 'criminal India'. Even as Fitzclarence attempted to construct an encomium for the empire, his very drive for authenticity resulted in the recording of fascinating instances of Indian resistance to the implementation of order. An incident that perhaps throws Bhabha's observations on colonial mimicry into fresh light is provided by Fitzclarence's encounter with an alternative Indian view of colonial justice:

these mimics are the worst kind of buffoons . . . I recollect seeing a set when I was in Hindustan in 1815, who, in ridicule of our own cutchery or court of justice, went through a trial in which the judges were supposed to be Europeans. The offender, when about to enter his defence, is interrupted by a servant who announces dinner is ready, and the judge starts up, pronounces the prisoner is guilty, and runs off. . . .

superiority in good faith, wisdom, and strength . . . this impression will be improved by the consideration we shew to their habits . . . and injured by every act that offends their belief.' Ibid. 433. Quite how respecting the belief of Indians could be compatible with reforming them of their superstitious criminality is left unclear.

[49] Lt. Col. Fitzclarence, *Journal of a Route across India* (London: John Murray, 1819), 234.   [50] Ibid. 342.

It is almost needless to remark how little this buffoonery is justified by the actual practice of our courts in India.[51]

The attempt to discredit the validity of this popular critique of colonial justice could not hide the uneasiness about India that ran through the text. How was one to explain away this ludic laughter that threatened to destabilize the author's claim of law bringing peace to a ravaged land? Evidently, Indian opinion of justice could be very different from that of their 'judges' themselves. The colonialist narrative can be seen here struggling to contain a form of popular, oral, and theatrical resistance that escaped (however momentarily) its discursive surveillance and challenged its project of self-legitimization.

Another significant admission of Fitzclarence's text was that there could be more than what met the eye in the apparent success stories of the introduction of 'civilization'—like the great Bengali reformer Ram Mohun Roy. For instance, there could be the problem of admitting that a society that was described in terms of crime and utter depravity could also produce an educated and enlightened Indian. Fitzclarence attempted to negotiate this problem by treating the Bengali as some freak phenomenon, a deviation from the general 'criminal' mass. As he went over the list of Roy's achievements—an astute understanding of European politics, considerable linguistic skills, acquaintance with the philosophy of Locke and Bacon—it became evident that Roy was a challenge to colonialist political, cultural, and racial supremacism.[52] By all accounts he was one of the centrepieces of the colonialist propaganda of progress and order, but, as Fitzclarence realized in his account of Roy's criticism of British militant expansionism, he

[51] Ibid. 189. Of course, the 'hungry Judge' had an established English literary lineage stretching back to the 17th century. He appears in the poetry of Alexander Pope: 'The hungry judges soon the sentence sign / And wretches hang that jury-men may dine', *Rape of the Lock*, iii. 21–2, in *The Rape of the Lock and Other Poems*, ed. Geoffrey Tillotson (London: Methuen, 1940), 168. He was also familiar to Restoration dramatists like William Wycherley who used him in *The Plain Dealer*, 1. i. ll. 452–3: 'You may talk, young lawyer, but I shall no more mind you, than a hungry judge does a cause, after the clock has struck one.' See *The Plays of William Wycherley*, ed. Arthur Friedman (Oxford: Clarendon Press, 1979), 393. The appearance of this 'British' cultural figure within the theatre of resistance performed by the colonized opens up interesting questions about the convergence and divergences between societies' cultural reaction to the operation of law.
[52] Fitzclarence, *Journal*, 106–7.

could also be a dangerous opponent of that propaganda. Fitzclarence could not quite endorse the idea of the Indian who could think for himself and came away from his interview of the Bengali with a distinct inferiority complex.

This was a slightly different kind of pessimism from the other narratives of reform we have looked at so far, but nevertheless a significant one. Unlike Grant and Malcolm, Fitzclarence's problem was not so much that Indians could not be reformed from their innate depravity and criminality. It was the very consequences of the success of the colonialist reform that worried him. For, as the example of Ram Mohun showed, the 'reformed' Indian could no longer be portrayed as criminal and this struck at the very heart of the major colonialist strategies of self-legitimization. If by its own account the aims of the 'civilizing mission' were beginning to be achieved, colonialism could no longer effectively justify its expansionism with the rhetoric of crime. Even the despotic nature of the colonial rule could not endorse the application of the formula of crime and punishment to describe men like Ram Mohun Roy. Thus, at the level of representation in discourses where crime and the colony intersected, Indians had to be forever kept just beyond the threshold of reform and progress. They must, by and large, remain 'criminals' despite the presence of the benign British government. Many of the English narratives of the rest of the nineteenth century would struggle to maintain their balance on this precarious tightrope of reform and criminality.

We shall look at one final example of British narrative from this period. The Reverend Reginald Heber's account of India was among the most sympathetic and perceptive to be written during the nineteenth century, and to that extent it was all the more alive to the contradictions within the discourse of crime and the colony. Throughout the text, Heber challenged and upset the colonialist 'self/Other' binaries. For instance, he inverted the racist aesthetics of the white/black dichotomy frequently used in colonialist writing: 'the deep bronze that is more naturally agreeable to the human eye than the fair skin of Europe . . . while it is well-known that . . . a fair complexion gives the idea of ill-health, and of that sort of deformity which belongs to an albino.'[53]

[53] Revd. Reginald Heber, *Narrative of a Journey through the Upper Provinces of India* (London: John Murray, 1828), i. 3–4.

Despite his misgivings about the civilizing mission and respect for the political and cultural autonomy of India, the rhetoric of crime crept into Heber's narratives: 'there was a great deal of gang robbery, very nearly resembling the riband men of Ireland, but unmixed with any political feelings; in all these provinces . . . these robbers in the day-time follow peaceable professions.'[54] But for Heber, this rhetoric was always inflected with his actual experience with the villagers, and he shunned any totalizing narrative about Indian criminality. He could not reconcile the received ideas of criminality with his observations and was left puzzled at the 'strangeness' of the land. This estrangement, this inability to comprehend and schematize the colony, was a serious challenge to the ethos of surveillance and progress. There were moments when Heber struggled to keep this sense of estrangement at bay by clutching at marks of familiarity and progress such as a British jail in rural Bengal. But these moments rarely led to any sustained formulaic legitimization of colonialism.[55]

Thus, the rhetoric of crime was conspicuous in Heber as much for its ideological contradictions as for its frequency. Each province he visited seemed to throw up fresh instances of uniquely Indian crimes. Heber has stories of Thugs, or of an Indian femme fatale like Begum Sumroo, who buried her maid alive in a vault and had her own bed moved on top of it to seal the unfortunate girl's tomb.[56] But significantly, instead of developing these anecdotes into a coherent discourse of surveillance and colonial justice, Heber compares them to instances of crimes committed by the British community in India. The rhetoric of crime is applied only in order to compare, and hence relativize, the catalogue of colonial and Indian depravity. And for Heber, the volume and the extent of the former were far greater than all the terrible stories of Indian criminality that formed the core of the kind of colonialist narratives we have looked at. What Heber showed, in effect, was how easily the rhetoric of crime could be turned critically against the 'civilizing mission' itself.

In Heber's withering analysis of British aggression in Awadh and Rohilkhand, the colonizers appeared as liars, frauds, and pillagers, little better than the Thugs or Pindaris who seemingly represented the essence of India. He exposed the duplicity of the

[54] Ibid. 163–4.   [55] Ibid. 165.   [56] Ibid. 543.

annexation of the province of Awadh on the pretext of extreme lawlessness by drawing on his own eyewitness accounts to repudiate the myth of the 'habitual' ferociousness of the inhabitants.[57] Heber did not hesitate to portray British expansion into Awadh as an illegitimate and, in effect, a criminal act: 'this wretched country was pillaged under sanction of the British name, and under the terror of Sepoy bayonets . . . the scandal [was] so notorious and so great . . . that a different course was imperiously forced on government.'[58]

In the end, Heber walked a fine line between his compulsion to record scrupulously the complex reality of Indian society and his position within the colonialist system that dictated the choice of the language available for the recording of that experience. His narrative was often literally in two halves, one proposing and the other contesting the criminality of Indians. In a letter to a Mrs Douglas, he made the formulaic connection between Indian religion and crimes: 'In a Christian country I think they could not have happened, and because they *naturally* arise from the genius of a national religion . . . it makes men worse than indifferent to each other. Accordingly, many of the crimes . . . are marked with great cruelty.'[59] At the same time, as he admitted in another letter to R. J. Wilmot well into his cross-country journey: 'I do not by any means assent to the pictures of depravity and general worthlessness which some have drawn of the Hindoos. They are decidedly, by nature, a mild, pleasing and intelligent race.'[60] The most important result of this contradictory movement of the narrative was again, inevitably, a deep scepticism about the ruse of progress and enlightenment through which colonialism legitimized its brutal expansionism. This is best captured in Heber's tone as he examined the law and order situation in the areas 'liberated' by the colonial administration: 'the criminal calendar is generally as full as in Ireland, with gang-robbers, setting fire to buildings . . . I am assured that *there is no grounds whatever for the assertion that people are become less innocent or prosperous under British administration.*'[61] This irony emerged as one the main modes of the British critical narratives about the noble mission of the East India Company.

[57] Heber, *Narrative of a Journey through the Upper Provinces of India*, 384–5, 396.   [58] Ibid. 400.
[59] Ibid. ii. 314.   [60] Ibid. 307.   [61] Ibid. 307–8.

3

Demanding Reform:
From Fielding to Peel

THE DOMESTIC ORIGINS OF THE RHETORIC OF CRIME

What we have seen so far is the extent to which a wide range of British colonialist writing drew on the rhetoric of crime to represent India. However, the very scale of this strategy also seems to have ensured a constant questioning of the ideology it appeared to serve. Historians have often pointed out that the 'ambiguity' of colonialist discourse and practices arose because of the political/cultural complexity of India that could not be easily aligned with the mercenary interests of foreign capital. This contribution of Indian resistance to the fracturing and auto-subversion of the colonialist discourse must necessarily be acknowledged, perhaps to a greater extent than it so far has been. Working within the boundaries of English narratives and strategies of representation, I would like to introduce another kind of history into this debate about colonialist ambiguity. I will repeatedly, perhaps tiresomely, insist that unless the dimension of British 'domestic' historical and cultural practices of rulership (specifically those of crime and policing) are taken into consideration, and blended with those in the colony, any account of colonialist ideology and representative practices will remain incomplete. This is not an attempt to write out the history of Indian resistance to colonialism. Nor is it to assert that the ambiguities of colonialism arose because of some internal semantic disorder of English writing in the nineteenth century. Rather, it is an attempt to contextualize the rhetoric of crime as a register of the ideological ambiguities that arose from a particular history of conflict within British society. It can then be shown how the extensive use of this rhetoric in the service of colonialism in India meant that these inherent ambiguities were amplified many times in the even more conflicted arena there.

As Holwell and others were writing their versions of Indian history, crime became an intensely debated affair that indicated major shifts in the relations between social groups in Britain. Prison reforms, policing, and a 'just measure of pain'—issues used to legitimize the British presence in India—were far from being generally accepted within Britain, and proved to be a site of intense ideological battle. And by the early nineteenth century, it became evident that the new reformist and largely bourgeois demands for surveillance and 'useful punishment' were winning.[1]

This period saw both an unprecedented explosion in technologies of industrial production as well as an intense and proliferating discourse of normalization and policing in Britain. According to reformist propaganda, it was to progress from the 'old' excessive and sanguinary laws to the moral century, holding the hands of the 'new domestic missionaries', as R. D. Storch has called them—the new police.[2] Recent scholarship has established that the history of crime and order in Britain was an extremely troubled one. We shall consider the implications of this finding as we read the narratives of colonial crime. Some critics have pointed out that the discursive representation of the colony converted it into a utopia where the dreams of European power could be realized. But not only does the schematization of imperial voice/colonial silence ignore the subaltern utterances that disputed this utopia, it also ignores the fact that the 'master voice' often croaked at the sound of its own doubts.

The British histories we have seen attempted to write India as a territory engulfed by criminal anarchy. This was derived from a

---

[1] The new emphasis on surveillance was neatly summed up in a parliamentary report leading up to Peel's Bill: 'no check so effectual can be devised upon the evil designs of those who gain their livelihood by habitual plunder, *as an impression that they are under the vigilant inspection of persons who are acquainted with their persons and characters*, and are at hand to defeat their purposes.' See 'Report of the Select Committee', *Parliamentary Papers*, 4 (1822), 99.

[2] As Storch suggests, 'these police functions must be viewed as a direct complement to the attempts of urban middle-class elites—by means of sabbath, educational, temperance and recreational reform—to mould a labouring class amenable to the new disciplines of both work and leisure—the other side of the coin of middle-class voluntaristic moral and social reform . . . was the policeman's truncheon'. R. D. Storch, 'The Policeman as Domestic Missionary', *Social History*, 9 (1976), 481–96.

very similar hydraulic image of the rising tide of crime that gathered strength in Britain over the second half of the eighteenth century. The numerous descriptions of criminal India could be easily adapted from equally numerous descriptions of a lawless Britain, like this one written by Henry Fielding: 'If I am to be assaulted and pillaged, and plundered; If I can neither sleep in my own home, nor walk the streets, nor travel in safety, is not my condition almost equally bad whether licensed or unlicensed rogue ... be the person who assaults me?'[3] For Fielding, this tide of pillage, assault, and robbery could be attributed to a specific social group—what he called the 'commonality'—that had apparently become opinionated, proud, and insolent as a result of their 'material prosperity'.[4] In other words, Fielding saw crime as an instrument used by the lower classes in their war against the 'polite' (chiefly) middle classes. It was this feature of the rhetoric of crime that would eventually be translated to the colony in the representation of Indians, potentially capable of robbing the imperial masters of their rightful property. In Britain, this propaganda about the criminal classes often produced a version of the metropolis that was as strange and 'exotic' as its oriental counterparts:

Whoever indeed considers the cities of London and Westminster with the ... great irregularity of their buildings, the immense number of their lanes ... must think that, had they been intended for the very purpose of concealment, they could scarce have been better contrived ... the whole appears as a vast wood or forest in which a thief may harbour with as great security, as wild beasts do in the deserts of Africa or Arabia.[5]

The entanglement of the metropolis and the 'orient', as made explicit in the last line here, is an apt expression of the symbiotic nature of the colonialist and domestic discourses of power. It hints at the interest that the 'polite classes' had in the policing of both territories.

Perhaps the most famous of the late eighteenth-century apologies for 'new' policing was Patrick Colquhoun's treatise of 1796. Like Fielding, Colquhoun saw the spectre of rising criminality as a war on property made by a 'dreaded criminal confederacy'.[6] But he

[3] Henry Fielding, *An Enquiry into the Causes of the Late Increase of Robberies* (London: A. Miller, 1751), 3.   [4] Ibid. pp. xxiii–2.
[5] Ibid. 116–17.
[6] Patrick Colquhoun, *A Treatise on the Police of the Metropolis* (London: W. Fry, 1796), p. iv.

was much more rigorous in linking this perceived rise in crime to 'old' or unreformed punishment. He called for the replacement of this less enlightened system with a regular and 'preventive' surveillance: 'in the execution of a criminal code, so sanguine in its issue, little penetration is required to see that it must . . . defeat the ends which were meant to be attained, namely, the prevention of crime.'[7] Colquhoun's critique of 'old' British justice would again be echoed in the colonialist criticism of Indian law.

The crux of Colquhoun's proposal was to replace the 'old' punishment with a system that would make the criminal useful to the state; would make punishment proportional, not excessive.[8] It is obvious how exactly the stress on utility and proportion mirrored the propaganda about the virtues of the market opened up by both new technology and colonial expansionism. Even in the extreme case of death sentences, the manner of execution must now be solemn, regulated, and economical, not the scaffold carnival that had previously legitimized the power of an agrarian, chiefly domestic market-oriented aristocracy. A network of preventive surveillance lay at the heart of Colquhoun's proposed reforms. And the bulk of this surveillance duty would fall on a band of law-keepers distinguished from their predecessors—'a correct and energetic system of police'.[9] Practically all of Colquhoun's proposed reforms were adopted by colonialist writers in their representation of India, and both the writing of British crime and that of their empire grew in strength from the nineteenth century onwards.[10]

One of the crucial problems of the propagandists of reform was to reconcile the demands for heightened surveillance with the concept of individual liberty. The extension of the mechanism of increased surveillance had to be paradoxically conducted in the

[7] Colquhoun, *A Treatise on the Police of the Metropolis*, 10–13.

[8] Ibid. 12.

[9] As Gatrell points out, 'From Bentham to Colquhoun in the 1780s to the businessmen petitioning for penal reform after 1811 . . . the appeal to rational and efficient punishment always sounded out more loudly than the appeal to humanity did'. Gatrell, *The Hanging Tree*, 18.

[10] From the late 18th century onwards, the reformist agenda was supported by the rapidly proliferating numbers of monthly journals. Many articles made explicit connections between new policing and the national prestige of England that had already become a staple of colonialist writings. Often, the exhortation to reform was based on the ground that Britain was losing face to its continental neighbours for the numerous executions and severity of its penal laws. See Anon., 'Colquhoun on the Police of the Metropolis', *Monthly Review*, 32 (1800), 349–50.

name of achieving freedom from the despotic stranglehold of the landed aristocracy. At the same time, this 'freedom' had, above all, to serve the interest of the respectable property-holders against that of the disenfranchised classes.[11] This issue of liberty would crop up in surveillance debates right up to the passing of Robert Peel's 1829 Bill and beyond. On the very eve of the proposal of the Bill, a staunchly pro-reform article in the *Quarterly Review* felt it had to address this problem:

If too much power is given to Ministers of Justice . . . both liberty and innocence are endangered: if too little power is delegated to them . . . then is public security equally endangered from impunity . . . the great difficulty in all the branches of police, is, to determine the true limits of its power, for the attainment of its great object, protection.[12]

The solution to the problem, it was felt, could only lie in a rigorous reformation of both the criminal law and the police. In fact, the new police must not only be in the charge of the new punishment, but also of the flourishing of liberty:

Police . . . when rightly understood . . . is the base on which men's liberties, properties, and social existence repose . . . the instant the preventive has failed to interpose itself between the imagining and the execution of the act, the detective steps in, and its service is of a three-fold kind; first, to secure the offenders . . . to find out and collect the scattered pieces of evidence . . . to search for and procure the stolen property.[13]

It was on these ideals of new policing that claims of 'civilizing' India were often premissed. Reading the constant evocations of to law and order in British writings on India, it is easy to believe that the vast Asian subcontinent was being taken over by a department of the new police as much as it was by the East India Company.

Robert Peel's 1829 Bill was a fairly accurate summing up of the reformist demands. Peel spoke of the spectre of the rising tide of crime, the need for 'useful' punishment, and, above all, the need for

---

[11] Even supporters of Colquhoun's proposals realized that they must grapple with this problem of heightened surveillance versus individual liberty. The solution they preferred was the idea of regulated freedom where a balance would be struck between liberty and ownership: 'it is indisputable that liberty itself is a blessing of subordinate value, when unaccompanied by those regulations which protect property and life from the violations to which both are liable in society.' Ibid. 351.

[12] J. Hardwick, 'Police', *Quarterly Review*, 37 (1828), 494–5.

[13] Ibid. 495–6.

extensive and dispersed policing. A centralized and organized police force was the keynote of his Bill.[14] In the amended version, it empowered the police to prosecute all 'loose, idle and disorderly persons' who refused to participate in the regime 'of useful orde'.[15] Again, the exhortation to live lawfully neatly overlapped with the exhortation to participate in the incessant productivity of the market. In his parliamentary speech, Peel warned about the pitfalls of progress, pointing out that the 'great mechanical ingenuity of the times' also made it harder to apprehend criminals.[16] Law must keep up with technological progress, because as Peel reminded the House, they were dealing with 'a band of trained and hardened profligates' who were constantly incited to crime by the 'present lax system of police held out to them'. He claimed that this plague of crime could only be prevented by a centralized police system where all 'the parochial police was concentrated under one responsible and efficient head'.[17] In the House of Lords, Peel was supported by the Duke of Wellington, who spoke of the prevalent desire in the courts of law to diminish capital punishment and promote preventive police.[18] Every single element of this reformist rhetoric of crime had a precise parallel in the colonialist representation of India. The legitimacy of colonial expansionism was achieved by equating Indian subjects with a 'criminal underclass' and Indian legal and political organizations with the 'old despotism'. Like pre-reform Britain, India was represented as a scene of an ever-escalating crime rate, infested by confederacies of hardened criminals. If the colonialists claimed to bring progress to reform this land, then, according to Peel's logic, 'new' policing was doubly relevant to India. First, it would sweep away the existing benighted criminality of the colonized. And then it would prevent these 'subjects', like their counterparts in London, from misusing the benefits of progress for their own depraved needs. Thus, the narrative of the new police produced British territorial and commercial aggression as the enlightening of the 'black hole' that was India.

If this was the scope of the entanglement of the narratives of crime and empire, we must now survey the inherent instabilities

---

[14] 'A Bill for Improving the Police in and near the Metropolis', *Parliamentary Papers*, 1 (1829), 425.   [15] Ibid. 450.
[16] 'April 15, House of Commons Debate', *Hansard*, 21 (1829), 869.
[17] Ibid. 872.   [18] 'June 5, House of Lords Debate', ibid. 1751.

that opposed their dominant ideological aims. A survey of the considerable British opposition to Peel's Bill will show us the extent to which the representation of criminals and concepts like justice and punishment were riddled with ambiguities within Britain itself. As we have seen, even staunch reformist voices had to deal with the questions of liberty and the limits of police power. But liberty was merely one of the contested points of new policing. David Taylor points out:

This Whiggish view of police history . . . fails to take into account the diversity and legitimacy of opinion that existed among the opponents and proponents of police reform . . . [it] exaggerates the contrast between the 'old' and the 'new' police . . . the persistence of varied and often violent response to the new police has been central to the revisionist school of thought.[19]

Taylor himself is in favour of a 'sceptical synthetic' model which would take into account the localized and varied response to new policing, thus avoiding the rigid application of the revisionist view of the new police as exclusively 'class warriors' and instead seeing it as a 'multi-faceted institution used by Englishmen of all classes to oppose each other'.[20] Following Taylor's account, one may see the history of the coming of the new police and the surveillant regime as a complex phenomenon where competing models and practices of policing coexisted and challenged each other.[21] What this meant was that even as the contests, negotiations, and coercions of the new regime were being incorporated into the socio-political practices of the period, they were also being registered in the language through which criminality was represented and indeed, produced.

The 'rising tide of criminality' that reformers from Fielding to Peel talked about had no claims to any universal truth. Gatrell points out that: 'between 1805 and 1815 felony prosecutions . . . increased by seventy percent in England and Wales . . . from the 4605 prosecuted in 1805 to the 18,107 in 1830, the increase was nearly 300 percent.'[22] But this increase in prosecution was not necessarily an index of the actual rise in criminal offence. It could simply mean a rise in intolerance of what had been tolerated before, of criminalization of acts that had been so recently permitted that

---

[19] Taylor, *The New Police*, 2.   [20] Ibid. 4.
[21] Ibid. 12.   [22] Gatrell, *The Hanging Tree*, 19.

the people did not yet register the 'new morality'. As Ruth Paley shows,

If, by 1829, the public had become predisposed toward an acceptance of new policing methods (and it is by no means clear that this was so), it may have been a rising tide of *order* rather than disorder that had brought about the transformation. . . . With rising standards of public order . . . comes an increasing intolerance of criminality, violence and riotous protest.[23]

Similarly, the representation of 'old' justice as a decayed, ineffective, and irregular system bore little resemblance to reality. The vicious criticisms of the Bow Street runners and the watchmen often concealed the equally vociferous criticisms of the supposedly more effective new police. Paley argues that

One of the main reasons for parochial opposition to the Metropolitan Police was that the service offered was so poor . . . In most cases this was an increase in terms of daylight patrols, but it was a major cut in night patrols. In 1828, some 1700 watchmen were employed . . . in 1829, they were replaced by some 900 police constables—only a quarter of whom were on patrol at any time.[24]

The 'old' police, rooted in the community and with a flexible organization, could evidently command significant popularity. In 1829, Londoners often referred to Peel's force as an occupying army. *Blackwood's Magazine* denounced them as 'general spies', and a respectable jury acquitted a man who killed a police constable in a riot.[25] The sentiment that had led to the Earl of Dudley's (in)famous assertion that he would rather half-a-dozen throats should be cut in Ratcliffe highway every three or four years than be subjected to 'domiciliary visits and spies' seems to have had a popular appeal, even among those whose throats were much more likely to be cut than his.[26] As Clive Emsley sums up: 'policing in pre-1829 London was more dynamic, more efficient and less venal than suggested by supporters of Peel's Police Bill . . . It is difficult to see the new police

---

[23] Paley, 'An Imperfect, Inadequate and Wretched System', 96–7. As Clive Emsley points out in her support: 'It is extremely difficult to measure any increase in the levels of crime and disorder . . . whether the incidents of crime were actually increasing is of far less importance than the contemporary belief that it was necessary.' Emsley, *The English Police*, 15–17.

[24] Paley, 'An Imperfect, Inadequate and Wretched System', 115.

[25] Ibid. 118–20.   [26] See Emsley, *The English Police*, 19.

simply as a response to the failures of the old system.'[27] The contemporary rhetoric of crime absorbed and embodied this popular and elite opposition to police reform, and competing notions of justice, punishment, and policing jostled with each other. Among other things, this ensured that there could be no homogeneous representations of the categories of crime and punishment.

Ruth Paley has called Peel's Bill an example of coercive reform from above. In view of the resistance it provoked from both the 'aristocrats' and the 'underclasses' it may be more correct to call it coercive reform from the 'middle'. We will see that it was the cultural form associated most closely with the 'middle' classes—the novel—that best represented the contradictions inherent in the rhetoric of order and deviance. However, the novel (or fiction in general) did not achieve its insight into the existing contradictions and paradoxes in a vacuum. Rather, it gave a coherent and popular shape to those fractures and contests already inherent in various non-fictional narratives. Before going on to look at the fiction of crime, we will look at two such non-fictional narratives and examine their potential for embodying contradictions in the very process of promoting consensus.

The reports of the parliamentary Select Committees were sensitive registers of the debate over surveillance. It may be something of a surprise to find that there was not only very little consensus in the epicentre of British political power about reforms, but also a sustained criticism of each key point of the 'reformist' demands. In 1818, the committee criticized plans for centralizing the police forces and the diffusion of surveillance techniques on the grounds that they would make policing less accountable to the public and increase the coercive power of the state.[28] The same committee was also wary of taking up the war cry against the watch system and acknowledged that often, 'through the meritorious exertion of individual residents', it functioned well. This hesitation and suspicion of the new policing had always been a feature of the parliamentary committee reports. As early as 1812 the committee had vigorously argued against changing the old system:

Had they found the defects in this part of the system of our police to have been such . . . as to have demanded the immediate interposition of the

---

[27] Ibid.
[28] 'Third Report from the Committee', *Parliamentary Papers*, 2 (1818), 23.

legislature, they would have hastened to have made an early report; but they had the satisfaction of observing, that the apprehension which had been excited had produced such a degree of activity and vigilance in many parishes and districts . . . that all immediate alarms on this head had been in a great measure removed.[29]

One could expect that this bias for the 'old' would be replaced by stronger demands for the 'new' the closer one got to 1829. Instead, it appears that most of the committee reports retained this opposition right up to the actual passing of the Bill. The committee of 1822 had hastened to point out that the old system was by no means obstructive to justice—'certainly not to the degree which would warrant them in recommending any fundamental changes to it'.[30] It concluded with a strong objection to the extension of the coercive power of policing:

it is no doubt true, that to prevent crime is better than to punish it; but the difficulty is not in the end but the means, and though your committee could imagine a system of police that might arrive at the object sought for; *yet, in a free country . . . such a system would of necessity be odious and repulsive, and one which no government could be able to carry into execution . . . among a free people, the very proposal would be rejected with abhorrence; it would be a plan which would make every servant of every house a spy on the actions of his master, and all the classes of society spies on each other.* (my emphasis)[31]

In the light of this continuous objection in the parliamentary circles to the establishment of the network of surveillance, any claim to consensus about reform looks deliberately blinkered. As late as 1828, the committee refused to recommend any wholesale changes, reporting that they had 'obtained no information which justifies them in reporting further than a recommendation of moral remedial measures and to give vigour and constancy to the existing police structure'.[32] From this to Peel's pronouncement of the necessity of a new police to protect property from a confederacy of criminals was quite a leap.

Thus, even the official writings that made up the core of both

---

[29] 'The Committee Appointed to Examine into the State of the Nightly Watch in the Metropolis', *Parliamentary Papers*, 2 (1812), 23.
[30] 'Report of the Select Committee', *Parliamentary Papers*, 4 (1822), 99.
[31] Ibid. 32–3.
[32] 'Report from the Select Committee', *Parliamentary Papers*, 6 (1828), 9.

metropolitan and colonialist propaganda for reform did not offer any unproblematic representation of crime and punishment. The rhetoric of crime emerged more as a register of conflicting positions than as a catalyst in the construction of a unifying ideology. But of course, it was not only the official narratives that testified to the lack of consensus about policing.

The *Newgate Calendars* that appeared in the last half of the eighteenth century have been seen as 'respectable' attempts to contain the liminal oral energy of the popular scaffold culture of gossips, penny-gaff melodramas, and 'that most transgressive of folk heroes and lords of misrule—Mr Punch'.[33] The *Calendars* sought to moralize the ludic oral energy into ordered and printed forms suitable for the consumption of the middle classes.[34] But the sanitization of the scaffold carnival was not an easy task. Sandwiched between the moralizing reformist rhetoric and expensive covers were tales of gore, public executions, and other rites of 'old' power. This often resulted in interestingly ambiguous rhetorical constructions of crime and punishment. For instance, William Jackson often insisted on highlighting his *Calendar's* commitment to moral order: 'we have thrown the whole into the form of a narrative, and at the end of each life, deduced such practical influences, as cannot fail to make a lasting impression on the minds of the readers.'[35]

But such pious declarations were often clever dressing that served a titillating dish of the 'old' excesses. Jackson offered a tentative apology for the rough language, 'cant, thievish phrases', that crept into the narratives, but excused it on the grounds of historical veracity. But the attempt to package the tales of 'old' punishment within the framework of the 'new' morality resulted in irresolvable contradictions. For instance, how could the story of the crime and punishment of Revd Thomas Hunter be consistent with Jackson's declared reformist motives? The *Calendar* vividly described how the priest lured his two young pupils for a walk and

---

[33] Gatrell, *The Hanging Tree*, 114–19.

[34] Gatrell writes: 'Most Calendars ran to several hundred pages per volume and six volumes per edition by the end of the eighteenth century. Often finely engraved with criminal portraits or execution scenes, they were expensive productions beyond the reach of the common people.' Ibid. 114.

[35] William Jackson, *The New and Complete Newgate Calendar*, vol. i (London: Alex Hogg, 1795), 6–7.

then pinned them on the ground, and cut their throats one after the other. His punishment had little of the sombre usefulness demanded by the reformers: 'previous to his execution, his right hand shall be cut off with a hatchet, near the wrist . . . then he should be drawn up to the gibbet . . . hung in chains between Edinburgh and Leith, the knife with which he committed the murder being stuck through his hand.'[36] It was precisely this kind of punishment—theatrical, excessive, and, as Foucault would argue, marking the monarch's personal ownership of the subject's body—that the reformers were aiming to moralize away.[37] The detailed, indeed celebratory, accounts of old punishment found in texts setting out to illustrate the 'new' morality showed both the keen business acumen of the editor as well as the problematic nature of the reform project.

Indeed, if the prison was the centrepiece in the call for reform, the *Calendars* were at best extremely ambiguous vehicles for propagating its value. The prison often came off worse than the gallows in these stories of crime, and the tale of Jack Sheppard's repeated escapes from the various jails was reprinted in great detail in almost every issue. Thus was retained the 'old' appeal of the criminal as a culture hero. Indeed, the Newgate novels would transform Sheppard into a romantic symbol of old punishment against the new order of things. Subsequent issues of the *Calendar* seem to have maintained this split between the professed commitment to the reformist agenda and the problematic eulogy of 'old' punishment. If propagating 'instructive tales of punishment' was the *Calendars'* self-declared intention, one was bound to wonder how serious those intentions were. They frequently reproduced, without editorial amendments, the 'gallows speeches' of the condemned criminals that traditionally challenged the state's claim to justice, through declarations of innocence. In fact, at several points, the editor supported these claims of the criminals, thereby providing a popular platform for dissent.[38]

---

[36] Jackson, *The New and Complete Newgate Calendar*, 34.

[37] See Foucault, *Discipline and Punish*, 3.

[38] For instance, see the narrative of the trial and conviction of Thomas Muir in William Jackson, *The New and Complete Newgate Calendar* (London: Alex Hogg, 1818), 145–6. The editor was clearly sympathetic to Muir's claim of innocence in the scaffold speech, and hinted that it was Muir's radical politics that led to his framing by government spies.

Besides the 'voices' of the accused that often challenged the state's authority, there were tales of acquittals that directly contradicted the reformist morals of crime and punishment. The trial of Robert Watt and Thomas Hardy, for instance, quickly became a tale of triumphant acquittal rather than one of exemplary punishment:

> The jury withdrew . . . and returned with a verdict of 'not guilty'. The populace, who, notwithstanding the wetness of the day, filled the streets adjacent to the court-house, received the news of his acquittal with the loudest exclamation of joy . . . They followed the coach . . . and turning the horses from it, drew him [Hardy] to different parts of the town.[39]

When one remembers the importance of this acquittal to the formation of working-class resistance to authority in future years, one can begin to understand the troubled nature of the *Calendar's* disciplinary credentials.[40] How could the account of an incident of seminal importance to the contest against, among other things, new policing find a place in publications professing 'reformed' morals, without testifying to the essential ambivalence of the rhetoric of crime?[41]

The narratives of British 'domestic' crime, from Fielding to Peel, were marked by the jostling of ideas and contradictions, and this had significant consequences for colonialist writing. We have already seen the extent to which colonialist narratives used the rhetoric of crime. If the socio-political complexity of Indian society

---

[39] Ibid. 333.

[40] See E. P. Thompson, *The Making of the English Working Class* (Harmondsworth: Penguin, 1970), 19–203. Thompson gives an account of the trial of Hardy and Watt and the importance of the London Corresponding Society in the formation of the English working-class resistance.

[41] Jackson was embarrassed enough to apologize for his text's failure to be consistent: 'the original plan of this work was to give faithful accounts of malefactors who had suffered for their offences; but some extraordinary cases of persons who have been acquitted, and of others who have been pardoned, are occasionally introduced.' Jackson, *Calendar* (1818), viii. p. vi. Although the later editions of the *Calendar*, especially the 1824 one edited by Knapp and Baldwin, were much stronger in their reformist tone, this ambivalence remained the central feature. For example, the 1824 edition began with the stereotypical reformist argument against public execution and frequent capital punishment, that 'by being often repeated, the minds of the multitude are rendered callous to the dreadful example'. Yet, the rest of the text, in the sheer volume of tales about public execution and the 'scaffold speeches' that opposed the state's right to punish, completely contradicted this initial assertion. See A. Knapp and W. Baldwin (eds.), *The New and Complete Newgate Calendar* (London: Robins, 1824), p. iii.

mpossible to totalize India as a criminal space, the use of a
that was already a site of contests and contradictions
doomed it to subvert constantly the stereotypes it aimed to produce.

CRIME AND THE 'MORAL' PURPOSE OF COLONIALISM

Ranajit Guha points out in his introduction to Bernard Cohn's
important work:

Law was the site where the indigenous culture of dominance and subordination . . . came into contact with the political culture of colonialism articulated, at the level of the state, in the judicial apparatus and the legal
procedures of the Raj . . . The study of law thus leads Cohn to the historic
paradox of colonialism—the paradox that law, intended to serve as a basic
defining principle of colonial rule, indeed as a primary signifier of British
dominance in the subcontinent corresponding in function and structure to
the hegemonic signifier of Rule of Law in metropolitan Britain, became
itself an instrument of misunderstanding about the very nature of that
dominance . . . the two constituents of colonial power relationship would
henceforth simply go on reciprocating a mutual misrecognition.[42]

The rhetorical construction of a 'criminal' India was an important
part of this colonialist misrecognition.[43] But paradoxically, law
also formed the site where the contradictions of and resistances to
the colonial state and its ideology were most powerfully articulated. As Fisch has shown, British law was in constant negotiation
with the well-entrenched Indian legal tradition:

The new law was . . . not the English criminal law of the time . . . it was a
kind of dialectical consequence of it (Islamic law). The Islamic law was in
many respects excessively mild . . . the purpose of British legislation was to
limit this mildness. But at the same time the original mildness was a check
to the new law being too harsh.[44]

The production of 'criminal' India made the denunciation of the
country's existing legal practices necessary. But at the same time,

---

[42] Ranajit Guha, 'Introduction', in Bernard Cohn, *An Anthropologist among the
Historians* (New Delhi: Oxford University Press, 1987), pp. xviii–xix.

[43] The production of criminal India went hand in hand with this misrecognition
of the nature of Indian judicial system. For instance, the colonial reduction of various and flexible Indian legal systems to a monolithic 'Hindu' law paved the way for
representing the same law as irregular, sanguinary, and corrupt. See ibid. 465.

[44] Fisch, *Cheap Lives*, 7.

the inability to exorcize the influence of those very Indian laws that they claimed to be replacing made colonial law-making a distinctly hybrid process. As Singha points out, hybridity and inconsistency were features of even the spearhead of Macaulay's reformist programme, the Indian Penal Code.[45] How could British colonialism be written as purgation and transformation of 'old' India, if it persisted in the very fabric of the 'new' laws? Not only would dissident Indian voices show up the reality behind the claims of colonial rule—'fining and killing and hanging and maiming and confining people'—but dissidence was built into the fabric of Anglo-Indian legal discourse itself.[46]

For instance, at the very moment when the British historians were attempting to mythologize India as a land of 'criminal' tyranny, legal experts were criticizing Indian law as well, but for being excessively mild! In a letter written in 1773, Warren Hastings defended his administrative measures by comparing Islamic and British legal traditions: 'the Mohammedan law is founded on the most lenient principles, and an abhorrence to bloodshed. This often obliges the sovereign to interpose, and by his mandate to correct the imperfections of the sentence.'[47] Hastings was cleverly writing himself into Indian history by comparing his role in India with that of the traditional monarch and thus justifying his own 'interposing'. But in the process, he also showed Indian law to be exactly the reverse of the draconian nightmare that colonial propagandists frequently claimed it was.[48] The pressure of misrecognizing the complex Indian legal system as chaotic and 'criminal' thus often threw colonialist rhetoric into contradiction.[49] As for the claims of

[45] As Singha reminds us, even that centrepiece of Macaulay's programme for reforming India, the Penal Code of 1837, had to 'build some discursive bridges with the religious and social norms of the subject population'. See Singha, *Despotism*, p. viii.   [46] Ibid. 1.
[47] Fisch, *Cheap Lives*, 68.
[48] The various Indian legal systems were much milder and of finer calibration and sensitivity. For example, European law could measure guilt only by the extreme alternatives of 'guilty' or 'not guilty' whereas Islamic law knew various intermediary stages. If guilt could not be established, acquittal was not the inevitable consequence. See Singha, *Despotism*, 36–79.
[49] With the strengthening of the position of the East India Company and the 'reformist' demands in Britain, the contradictory nature of the British legal discourse became even more apparent. On the one hand, legal experts like J. Neave and J. D. Erskine thought the Islamic codes had been 'happily transformed by British clemency'. On the other hand, as late as 1832, a parliamentary report

British 'impartial' justice, anecdotes like the following unearthed by Cohn provide us with a glimpse of the reality behind them:

> George Wyatt, a deputy collector in Benaras ... may not have been completely joking when he said an impartial judge in India made his decision in court on the basis of counting flies on the punkah ... an even number being taken for a verdict of guilty and an odd number for a verdict of innocent.[50]

It was the very effort of converting this reality into the 'fiction' of enlightened rule of law that ensured persistent contradiction within colonialist ideology. Added to this was the fact of the deep-seated fractures within the British rhetoric of crime that originated in its 'domestic' context.

Given this perhaps fatally paradoxical ideological investment in the rhetoric of crime, it is hardly surprising that the majority of the British narratives about India evoked the issues of law and order. Critics like Miller and Bender have shown that prose fiction in general, and the novel in particular, played the key role in the establishment of a new British (and west European) political order in the late eighteenth and early nineteenth centuries. We will focus on the novel of colonial crime to show how it also conducted an interrogation of the order of things. In later chapters, we will develop a series of conjunctions between these novels and those dealing with 'criminal' Britain to show that prose fiction's opposition to the ruses of authority was equally perceptible at the very heart of the metropolis itself.

William Hockley entered the East India Company's service in 1813 and was a Judge by the 1820s. In an interesting twist of the 'criminal' India phenomenon, he was dismissed from his post for receiving bribes, and, after a protracted and unsuccessful bid to clear his name, was 'retired' with a pension in 1824. No doubt drawing on this substantial experience of crime and punishment, Hockley published his first novel, *Pandurang Hari*, in 1826. The novel began with an editorial note containing strongly expressed and, by then, increasingly familiar ridicule of 'men of talent' who

---

contradicted this by pointing out the excessive mildness of Indian legal codes. Any study of colonial law-making must ultimately take into account these ever-present contradictions and the equally persistent efforts to twist them into 'fictions' of Indian criminality. See ibid. 91–169.

    [50] Cohn, *Anthropologist*, 476.

have been duped by the Indians into believing that they were a 'pure, virtuous, open, generous people'.[51] This editorial 'I' functions as the panoptic eye of the text, securing, organizing, and presenting the confession of a 'real Hindoo', bringing the hidden essence of the subject population to metropolitan knowledge. As such, the novel was one of the early instances of what we may call the technique of colonial ventriloquizing—an 'Indian' narrator whose 'confessions' reinforce all the colonialist stereotyping of a subject people. An 'Indian' memoir was almost always a detailed presentation of the criminality and corruption that allegedly pervaded all layers of Indian society. It was to be a favoured technique of the novelists of the British empire.

The confessions of Hockley's 'Indian' hero, Hari, methodically expose each 'criminal' layer of Indian life. Growing up as the adopted son of a Brahmin, Hari soon finds himself in a minor clerical position in the Maratha court. It proves to be a convenient position to observe and criminalize the statecraft of one of the staunchest rivals of the East India Company, and the place is soon shown to be plagued with extortion and oppression.[52] Hari is soon expressing opinions remarkably like the British reformers, likening India to 'old' England: 'Their justice was regulated, as it is in most countries, by individual caprice or expediency, instead of certain immutable principle, which should make it the same everywhere.'[53] To help his opinions appear respectable, the editorial interventions constantly remind the reader that it was the 'immutable principles' of British justice that had since replaced this immoral Indian system. The process of colonization is presented as an extension of the rule of reformed law.[54]

Hari is also particularly vehement about those Indian social groups that roamed the borders of 'respectable' society, and have been described by one historian as constituting a 'vibrant culture of the road'. The novel singles out the various wandering Indian mendicants as a group that demanded special policing. Gabbagee

---

[51] W. Hockley, *Pandurang Hari*, 3 vols. (London: Whittaker, 1826), i. pp. xi–xiii.   [52] Ibid. 11–13.   [53] Ibid. 24–5.

[54] One of the central images of the novel is Hari's comparing and contrasting of the corrupt Indian courts with their British counterparts: 'The Court at Broach consisted of a judge, a registrar, and an assistant registrar—all Englishmen . . . everything was done with the greatest order and regularity: no confessions, no squabbling, or pulling off turbans, or coarse abuse was allowed. All had equal access to the judge.' Ibid. iii. 63–7.

Gosla, the arch criminal, is a member of the Gossain sect of the Hindu religious order, and comes to symbolize the murderous nature of all Indian religions. In fact, so recognizably criminal are the Hindu priests that whenever Hari wants to commit crime with impunity, he disguises himself as a priest. This is an endorsement of the propaganda that Indian religions offered little more than theological justifications for a criminal career. Hockley's priests act as go-betweens of Indian rulers and the Thugs and Pindaris, roving bands of murderers and robbers. It is they who forge the criminal link that holds the whole of Indian society together.

Hari's confessions implicate India's political leaders as well as its religious ones. Again, the novel closely reproduces the arguments presented in many colonialist narratives of the Pindari wars and Thug 'suppressions'—that Indian society was comprised largely of gangs of organized criminals protected by heads of states. This, of course, made the Indian monarchs little more than criminals themselves, as Hari shows with the help of the 'confession' of a Pindari robber: 'As to honourable . . . what is the practice of all our Rajahs and Peshwas . . . do they not call themselves the fountains of all justice!—rob, cheat, tyrannise over and murder whomsoever they please . . . are not we acting under their immediate sanction?'[55] Liaising between the king and the Thug, the priests become the true demons of the land: 'The sanyasee was indeed a strange being. He seemed a living skeleton, without teeth, and bent double from age and hardship . . . his nails were as long as the talons of a bird of prey, and his toes were bowed inwards . . . a character not belonging to the race of men.'[56] And an Indian ruler, when not murdering his way to tyranny, can only be a fugitive from British law: 'poor Badjerow is like a hunted hare. He never sleeps two nights in the same place. The very idea of the Toope Wallas being near him, makes him issue orders for marching.'[57]

The novel shows its awareness of the role played by the rhetoric of crime in colonial propaganda by establishing a causal link between colonial 'justice' and British military victories. It presents the conquests as the result, not of superior military technology and a series of eminently dishonourable intrigues, but of the instinctive recognition by the Indian troops of the justness of the British cause

---

[55] Hockley, *Pandurang Hari*, i. 305–6.
[56] Ibid. 315–16.   [57] Ibid. 225.

and the criminality of their own leaders. The Company's army thus perfectly reflects the 'order' of the British criminal courts, while the Indian troops are as irregular and squabbling a bunch as the 'native' pleaders thronging Indian courts. Armed with this power of criminalizing the colony, the novel shows the British forces as an agent of a universal law that operates to save India from itself.

But this story of Indian criminality and British justice is not the only one that Hari narrates. A parallel and equally significant story emerges through his 'confessions' where the British moral claims are rigorously re-examined. A number of episodes in the novel challenge its own careful construction of the colonizers as embodiments of noble justice. The civilian officer for whom Hari carries messages is as brutal as the Indian rajas: 'The Toope Walla seldom spoke to me, and when he did, it was as if he was addressing a dog . . . he darted from his seat upon me like a tiger would upon his prey . . . kicking me out of the tent.'[58] This scene of colonial arrogance perfectly illustrates Singha's observations about the consequences of legal reforms from around 1817: 'Paternalism was imbricated in the fabric of Anglo-Indian domestic life, the common contention was that Indian servants preferred to be whipped, cuffed or kicked rather than dismissed.'[59]

Perhaps the most daring and damaging example of the novel's subversion of the claims of colonial justice came from the glimpses of the corrupt legal machinery. After numerous contrasts between the 'criminal' Indian and the 'enlightened' colonial rule, the novel chooses to support its claim with this illustration:

The magistrate of the place surrounded the prison with troops . . . No great mischief had been done by the frolics of the prisoners . . . the doors were blown open with a six-pounder, and a whole corps was commanded to put the unresisting prisoners to death! I could not conceive such a dreadful example would have been made by those who pride themselves upon their humanity, as the Toope Wallas are accustomed to do. The poor, naked, defenceless men crouched up in one corner . . . were fired upon from a distance of few yards only, as they were begging for mercy . . . those in the authority were very well-pleased with the civil officer's conduct . . . the Toope Wallas boast of their desire to do justice, but never take notice of the complaints against their agents . . . *How the magistrate would have been able to justify himself to the government, I cannot tell* . . .

[58] Ibid. 117–19.   [59] Singha, *Despotism*, 152.

perhaps the silence may be attributed to the known modesty of our conquerors, who never indulge themselves in anything like a boasting, even of their most valiant acts. (my emphasis)[60]

The irony and the bitter mocking with which this example of justice is presented successfully negates all other favourable representations of the colonial court. For an instant, the authorial control over the ventriloquist strategy of colonialism is relinquished and the recording and confessing 'eye' constitutes a 'native' view of the colonial regime. The passage shows the colonial prison not as a site of reform, but of brutal dehumanization and massacre. Like a chameleon, the colonial novel approximates a subaltern confession, and the story it tells is startlingly juxtaposed against the dominant narrative of justice.

If *Pandurang Hari's* ambiguity lies in its simultaneous legitimization *and* subversion of colonialist ideology, Hockley's next novel, *The Zenana* (1827), is ambiguous for taking up a distinctly anti-reformist position on pre-colonial or 'old' India. The narrative is again presented as the discovery of an 'authentic' Indian voice by the editor—a British civil servant. Coupled with this power of textual discovery of 'Indianness' is the editorial presentation of the 'zenana' as a site of unnatural sexuality and criminal intrigues: 'replete with deceits and intrigues of women, both immoral and improper . . . ample information respecting the infidelity of Asiatic women is already before the public in a work lately published, entitled the "New Arabian Night's Entertainments".'[61] These framing devices seemingly prepare the reader for a tale of the licentious criminality and intrigues of 'native' Indian courts.[62] The narrative, however, turns out to be nothing of the sort, and takes a stand diametrically opposed to that of the reformist history of India as seen, for example, in Mill's writing. Although despots are given to bursts of capricious anger, Indian rulers are shown to be extremely able administrators—'pure and impartial, his [the ruler's] justice checked the tyranny of the rich, whilst it shielded and protected the rights of the poor . . . like the water of Noorshevan that spread

---

[60] Hockley, *Pandurang Hari*, iii. 389–94.

[61] William Hockley, *The Zenana* (London: Sanders & Otley, 1827), i. p. vii.

[62] The novel's subject also corresponded to the increasing of the authority of the colonial state over the sexual behaviour of its subjects. See Singha, *Despotism*, on the legal changes brought about after 1817 that criminalized certain sexual acts.

blessings all around him.'[63] Surat, where most of the action takes place, shows no signs of the criminal chaos that is supposed to have marked Indian cities before the arrival of colonial law:

> many years before the British appeared on the Indian stage in the charac- ter of rulers, the city of Surat . . . preserved its extensive commerce, being considered as a port of the greatest consequence in India . . . this part of the city was crowded from sunrise to midnight, by men of all nations . . . whose business, through the means of a regular and well-organised police was translated without discord or confusion.[64]

This representation of a pre-British India governed with a regular and well-organized police force harks back to the early 'orientalist' phase of colonial imagining that persisted during the aggressive 'reformist' days of the nineteenth century. In the 1770s, both Hastings and Cornwallis had claimed that they were restoring India's ancient glory that had decayed because of the incompetence of regional rulers.[65] This representation of the Company as the rightful heirs of a glorious Indian past no doubt played a part in establishing its ideological credentials. But during the early nine- teenth century, in the teeth of the dominant reformist representa- tions of 'criminal' India, this version could often serve as a challenge to the rhetorical construction of colonial authority.

In Hockley's novel, the 'zenana' is distinctly different from the site of unnatural licentiousness of the *New Arabian Nights*. Despite the editor's claim of it being the seat of oriental deviance, it is shown to have a well-defined position in the ordered governance of the state. It provides a space for heroines like Mehtab to have an independent voice, as well as to feminize the potentially despotic nature of the ruler and make him more malleable to the operation of justice. Her resistance to the Nawab's overtures is also a witty education in the rights of the subject that the ruler has to undergo before he can gain consent. The 'zenana' becomes a necessary, and even an originary site for the establishment of just rule in India.

The only Europeans who appear in the novel, the Portuguese, introduce disturbance and disorder among this ordered prosperity of the country. This may have served to highlight the 'liberal' British rule against its Catholic and continental (and by this time

---

[63] Hockley, *The Zenana*, ii. 6.
[64] Ibid. i. 3–5.
[65] See Singha, *Despotism*, 2.

largely defeated) rivals. But when one remembers the demonization of Indian religions and the role played by the missionaries in the establishment of European power, the description of the terror unleashed by the Portuguese certainly tilts the balance back in favour of Hinduism against Christian practices.

A common narrative strategy of the reformist histories of India was to make a distinction between the unprincipled early phase of the Company's rule (the nabobs like Clive and the impeached Hastings) and the enlightened latter phase where commercial interest had been apparently replaced by the desire to bring civilization to India. What these histories left unresolved were the problems that surfaced when the rhetoric of crime was applied within the parameters of this strategy. As we saw in the writings of Grant and Mill, criminalization was indispensable to the colonizers, for it was against 'criminal' India that the propaganda for the civilizing mission took shape. On the other hand, once the rhetoric of crime was extended to the 'old' Company rule, an element of critical doubt was introduced within the body of colonialist representation of India. The universalist assumption of essential differences between 'criminal' India and 'just' Britain could no longer be maintained. What guarantee was there that this new 'enlightened' colonialism would not regress back to its criminal older version? If the pioneers could be as 'criminal' as Indians, then the construction of the difference between the races that justified the colonialist conquests was already jeopardized. The historical narratives mostly tried to hide this unease under the cant of progress. It was the novel that chose to meet this problem head on by articulating it clearly.

Walter Scott's *The Surgeon's Daughter* (1827) examines the propaganda about the reforming mission by employing a schematic distinction between the 'old' and 'new' colonialism. In the novel, Richard Middlemas represents the freebooting 'nabobs', and Adam Hartley the 'new' moral reformers of India. The novel then makes any formulaic allocation of virtues impossible by applying the rhetoric of crime to the colonizers and that of justice to the Indians. As a result, the whole reformist cant of progress in the colony is now critically re-examined. As the narrator confesses, by denying the 'natural conclusion' to the Adam Hartley–Menie Grey romance plot, the novel refuses to indulge in another crucial colonial fantasy where British masculine anxieties are happily resolved in the charmed arena of India.

Richard Middlemas is born out of wedlock to a Portuguese-Jewish mother who had eloped with Richard Tresham, a Catholic Jacobite nobleman. Thus, Middlemas arrives in the novel under the signs of disinheritance and crime. He is seen as suspiciously foreign to the solid morality of provincial Scotland where he is brought up. Typically, Richard feels alienated and frustrated and sees India as the theatre where his stigma will be washed away in the orgy of conquest:

O Delhi! O Golconda! . . . India, where gold is won by steel; where a brave man cannot pitch his desire for fame and wealth so high that, but that he may realise it . . . Methinks I have a natural turn for India. . . . My father was a soldier, my mother's father was a rich trafficker . . . this petty two hundred a year, with its miserable and precarious possibilities . . . seems in the ears of one like me, who has the world for the winning, and a sword to cut my way through it, like something little better than a decent kind of beggary.[66]

Thus the 'old' steel-and-gold brand of colonialism is shown to originate in impulses 'foreign' to moral Britain. This concurs with those histories like Mill's which concluded that the early colonial expansion in India was carried on by undesirable aristocratic elements with dubious morals. But crucially, Scott's novel refuses to set up any 'reformed' colonialism as a counterpoint to this earlier expansionist phase.

Richard's ambition to become a 'nabob or a Rajapoot' takes him away from Menie Grey, the 'surgeon's daughter' of the novel. In this betrayal of the British domestic ideal, he is assisted by an agent of the East India Company. In fact, Scott goes on to show that the Company could be both dishonourable as well as 'criminal', a startling revision of the image of the merchant-princes of the eighteenth century. Tom Hillary, the agent, entices Richard with fantasies of war against cowardly 'black rascals', the plundering of their temples and even their dead bodies as they are said always to carry 'mines of gold' on them.[67] This lure of material conquest is blended with the sexual, as Tom describes Indian women as enchantresses of 'peculiar beauty' who perform their 'voluptuous eastern dances for the pleasure of the haughty English conquerors'.[68] These fevered fantasies are quickly shown to be

---

[66] Walter Scott, *The Surgeon's Daughter* (1827; repr. London: Penny Pocket Library, 1893), 19.   [67] Ibid. 21.   [68] Ibid.

allied to a 'criminality', as Hillary turns out to be engaged in the illegal kidnapping of men to serve as the Company's cadets: 'Indeed, the practice of kidnapping, or crimping, as it is technically called, was at that time general ... there was not only much villainy committed in the direct prosecution of the trade, but it gave rise incidentally to remarkable cases of robbery and even murder.'[69] From this very lowest of organizational rungs, the 'honourable' company is shown to be mired in shady activities. Its Madras factory is run by an unscrupulous British manager and a sinister Indian Brahmin, 'a master-councillor of dark projects, an oriental Machiavel'. The novel makes it clear that although this priest confirms to the stereotype of the 'criminal' Indian, he is encouraged and patronized by his British superiors for their own political interest.[70] Unsurprisingly, in this atmosphere of moral decay the inherent criminal impulses of Richard flourish. He promptly absconds from his post at Fort St George and takes up the service of the Company's biggest enemy, Hyder Ali, the ruler of Mysore. There, his cruelty to British prisoners acquires legendary proportions and he becomes the lover of another European 'gone native', the formidable Mrs Montreville, a commander of a detachment of Hyder's troops.

In Mrs Montreville, Scott reverses the colonial stereotyping of Indian female sexuality, and attaches those signs to the European woman. Far from being a space where British male fantasies of economic and sexual domination are fulfilled, the colony becomes a potentially dangerous area where European women may become 'unsexed'. This is made amply clear in Mrs Montreville's contemptuous reminder to Richard about his position in her household:

Slave and son of slave! Since you wear the dress of my household, you shall obey me as carefully as the rest of them, otherwise—whips, fetters . . . the gallows, murderer . . . dost thou dare to reflect on the abyss of misery from whence I raised thee, to share my wealth and affection? I am a woman, renegade, but one who wears a dagger, and despises alike thy strength and thy courage. I am a woman who has looked upon more dying men than thou hast killed deer and antelopes.[71]

Realizing that in this subordinate position neither his dreams of looting gold, nor of being entertained by voluptuous Indian

---

[69] Scott, *The Surgeon's Daughter*, 29.
[70] Ibid. 50.   [71] Ibid.

women, are likely to be fulfilled, Richard tries to win back the favour of the Company by turning into a spy and betraying Tippoo, Hyder Ali's son, to the British. In the moral economy of the novel, this is a criminal act of treachery (as his friend Adam Hartley comments) and can only merit punishment. This is achieved when he is caught by Hyder himself, who is shown to be an extremely able ruler. Hyder is also generous and even-handed in his dispensation of justice, and all his qualities are contrasted with the crimes of Richard and the Company. The scene of Richard's execution is finally a judgement on the criminal duplicity of the British company. If Richard is described as the 'ill-fated European' whose life and crimes are crushed to death under the foot of the royal elephant, Hyder's final words also clearly indicate that the Company itself deserved the same kind of annihilation:

You have brought to me words of peace, while your masters meditated a treacherous war . . . tell that kaffir, Paupiah and his unworthy master, that Hyder Ali sees too clearly to suffer to be lost by treason the advantages he has gained by war. Hitherto I have made inroads as a compassionate and merciful conqueror . . . in future I will be a destroying tempest.[72]

In linking criminality to the early expansionism of the Company, Scott followed some reformist histories. However, he took this to an uncomfortable extreme by allocating justice and the power of punishment to the Indian Hyder Ali. This clear reversal of the colonialist strategy is also consistent with the denial of any satisfactory resolution to the story of the 'reformist' colonizer, Adam Hartley. In the novel, Hartley is defined as the opposite of Richard. While Richard is dark and reflects his aristocratic breeding in his sense of dressing, Hartley is described as capable of being slovenly but physically fair with an honest countenance. While Richard goes to India fired by the fantasies of wealth and sexual conquest, Hartley goes there as a man of medicine, restoring the British and Indians alike to health.

Healing aside, Hartley's other virtues also mark him out as a morally stern reformer. He becomes an expert in oriental languages, and his tolerance and appreciation of the Indian religions enable him to gain a vital understanding of the native courts where priests act as informers and spies. In short, whereas Scott

---

[72] Ibid. 59.

shows Richard's gory conquest belonging to the 'old' colonialist era, Hartley's mapping of India through medicine and language belongs to its 'new' and humane phase. The apparent moral superiority of this 'new' colonialism is made evident in Hartley's refusal of material reward for the curing of an Indian mendicant—who turns out to be the disguised Hyder Ali himself. Not only do the proponents of 'reformed' colonialism use peaceful weapons like medicine and language, they also appear to be uninterested in any material profit. Thus their presence in India can be explained in terms of humanitarian interest.

In the novel, the full endorsement of the ideological validity of this 'new' colonialism is projected to be achieved in the union of Hartley with the heroine—Menie Grey. A paragon of British domestic/feminine virtue, Menie stands at the opposite pole to the Semiramis-like figure of Mrs Montreville. The betrayal of her love by Middlemas is one of the key components in the novel's negative representation of 'old' colonialism. Consequently, Scott sets up her rescue and marriage with the virtuous hero Hartley as the final seal of approval on the humane European presence in India. But as the narrator points out, this colonialist romance does not quite proceed as planned: 'it might be thought a natural conclusion to the history of Menie Grey, that she should have married Hartley . . . but she returned to Britain, unmarried though wealthy, and, settling in her native village, appeared to find her only pleasure in acts of benevolence.'[73]

It may be possible to explain this deliberate refusal to bring the story of 'humane colonialism' in India to a happy ending by seeing it as consistent with the novel's problematic reversal of the criminal/justice stereotypes. Despite its apparent alignment with the reformist British histories of India, Scott's novel maintains a subtle but crucial distance from them. It does oppose the 'old' colonialism of Richard Middlemas, but in allocating justice to the Indian ruler Hyder Ali, it stops short of empowering the proponent of 'new' colonialism—Hartley. Moreover, the novel sets up a parallel disempowerment of 'domestic' Britain. For Scott, the 'domestic' problem (historically, that of forcing open new markets for British capital) figures as the marriage of Menie Grey. Like idle money, Menie must find a suitable master/husband who will deploy her

---

[73] Scott, *The Surgeon's Daughter*, 59.

'usefully'. The reckless Middlemas is deemed too unsuitable to perform this task with prudence, and by transporting Menie to the colony and into the arms of the virtuous Hartley, Scott seems to set up the classic colonialist solution to all domestic problems. But the novel's refusal to plot India and Hyder Ali as criminal produces a uniquely disempowered hero in Hartley. Despite all his virtues, he cannot (unlike Meadows Taylor's hero, as we shall see) achieve the required union with Menie, who is left to return to Britain. Without the power to criminalize the colony, the 'new' ruler is also sexually disempowered. He cannot use capital, be it human or monetary, towards any reproductive effect.

The novels we have looked at in this chapter preserve the contests and contradictions found in the contemporary British non-fictional writings of crime. Like the colonial histories of India and the Company's legal reforms, their use of the problematic rhetoric of crime results in the destabilization of the messages of British moral and ideological supremacy. Of course, colonialist writings are everywhere marked with this ambiguity and fracture. What marks out these novels is their deliberate and methodical display of the awareness of the subversive possibilities of the rhetoric of crime. Through corrosive irony, knowing nods and winks, and a laughter that belied its earnest civil-servant façades, the genre could register an opposition against its own seemingly dominant agenda. This feature, already displayed in the early colonial novels dealing with 'criminal' India, enabled it to use the same strategy to test the 'condition of England' in the later decades. Using stereotypes of Indian criminality, it would show the interdependence of British colonial and domestic authority and find both wanting. Moreover, it was also this feature of the fiction of crime that Wilkie Collins used in his critique of the 'domestic' surveillant regime in what is still popularly called the 'first English detective novel'. So far, we have looked at a prehistory of this fiction of crime, where criminals, both domestic and colonial, challenged dominant norms of crime and punishment.

4

Resisting the New Police

CONTESTING THE MAKING OF THE 'CRIMINAL'

The decades after 1829 proved to be even more troubled for the new police. The reformers, arguing for improvement of the prisons, stronger surveillance, and 'useful' sentences, gradually became dominant. Yet, the voices that questioned all these fundamental reformist axioms could not be silenced: 'Differing models of policing (and all that that implied in constitutional and financial terms) vied with one another. Different options were explored in a period of unprecedented experimentation.'[1] Predictably, the representation of criminals and indeed, the whole discourse of crime remained significantly fissured.

For India, these were the decades crucial to the entrenchment of the myth of 'enlightened' colonial policing. They saw Sleeman's suppression of thuggee and Macaulay's drafting of the Penal Code. Historians have noticed the significant difference between the strengths of the respective reformist positions in India and Britain during this period. What was a struggle to establish the 'new' agenda of criminalization at 'home' could often be transformed into unchallenged policy-making in the colony, thanks to the despotic powers of the Company.[2] But did not these contests inherent in British domestic policing also affect the rulership in the colony?

Singha has noted that although from the 1830s colonial officials attempted to implement a uniform way of formulating Indian criminals, they struggled to 'anchor such projects within acceptable

---

[1] See Taylor, *The New Police*, 25. Also Emsley, *The English Police*, 43: 'As the 1840's dawned, there was no single model of policing dominant in England . . . the London model was not suitable for everyone.'
[2] See Majeed, 'Orientalism'.

social and cultural forms'.[3] Guha and Cohn have viewed this struggle to implement British 'reformed' penal policy in India as a part of the attempt to entrench the colonial state. But a significant cause of the virtual impossibility of making colonialism 'legal' lay in the contradictions within the discourse of crime that originated from within the British 'domestic' context. Before we examine the role of fiction in this problematic production of criminals and making empires in this period, we will have to review briefly the debates over policing in contemporary Britain.

The Select Committee report of 1834 was self-congratulatory in its assessment of the police reforms: 'The result has been ... a successful commencement of a methodised system of police, first for the prevention, and secondly for the detection of crime.'[4] However, the 1834 report was also very much alive to the oppositions faced by the new police. It noted a number of complaints brought against the police, about the general rowdy conduct of the men and the deliberate undermanning of police stations.[5] The committee hastened to add that these abuses of power had been infrequent, and promptly dealt with. But in noting both the success of and opposition to new policing, their report may be taken as symptomatic of the divided nature of the time.

It is certainly possible to chart a 'Whiggish' view of the progress of British law and order from the official reports that monitored the pace of the police reform. In 1839, a Bill resolved to add 'any parishes, townships, precincts and places in the counties of Middlesex, Surrey, Hertford, Essex and Kent within twelve miles of Charing Cross' to the Metropolitan Police district.[6] The legal powers of the constables were considerably increased, and steps taken to ensure the collection of the unpopular Police Tax.[7] Not only urban, but rural and agricultural areas were also slowly infiltrated by these

---

[3] Singha, *Despotism*, xvi.

[4] 'The Select Committee Report to Inquire into the State of the Police', *Parliamentary Papers*, 16 (1834), 4. The report went on to note that the number of violent offences had decreased due to both police vigilance and a 'well-regulated prison discipline', see ibid. 8. This coupling of the themes of policing and 'well-regulated' punishment thrived in the reformist language of the period. See Victor Bailey (ed.), *Policing and Punishment in Nineteenth-Century Britain* (London: Croom Helm, 1981), 11.   [5] 'Select Committee Report' (1834), 8.

[6] 'A Bill for Further Improving the Police in and near the Metropolis', *Parliamentary Papers*, 4 (1839), 414.

[7] 'A Bill for the Improvement of Police in Birmingham', ibid. 445–6.

'domestic missionaries'. Still in 1839, a Bill sought to appoint additional county and district constables where 'ordinary officers appointed for preserving the peace are not sufficient'.[8] The justices of the peace were asked to prepare a detailed report to determine the area, number, and available police force of the counties and then assess the number of constables needed per area. This statistical bend was also to be a feature of the British attempts to break down the complexity of India into understandable and administrable units.[9] The drive to absorb rural Britain within the gaze of the new police would only culminate with the passing of a series of Bills in 1856–7.[10]

Some of the most influential cultural figures of the time helped in this 'disciplining' of Britain. Charles Dickens's articles in *Household Words* were easily more trimphalist than the contemporary parliamentary reports. For Dickens, 'thief-taking' had been elevated to the heights of a refined science by the new Metropolitan Detective Department which 'consisted of only forty-two individuals, whose duty it is to wear no uniforms and perform the most difficult of operations of their craft'.[11] These detectives were the very embodiments of the panoptic gaze that lay at the heart of new policing: 'Every clue seems cut off; but the experience of the detective guides him into tracks quite invisible to other eyes . . . so thoroughly acquainted with these men are the detective officers . . . that they frequently tell what they have been about by the expression of their eyes.'[12] Elsewhere, Dickens contrasted the 'systematic and well-trained' new police with the old watchmen: 'We are not by any means devout believers in the Old Bow Street police. To say the truth, we think there was a vast amount of humbug about those worthies . . . Far too much in the habit of concerting with thieves . . . they never lost a public occasion of jobbing.'[13] This apparent

<hr />

[8] 'A Bill for the Establishment of County and District Constables', *Parliamentary Papers*, 2 (1839), 533.   [9] See Cohn, *Colonialism*.
    [10] See 'Rules for Establishing Uniform System for Government', *Parliamentary Papers*, 1 (1856). The Bill called for the establishment of identical police constabularies in every county.
    [11] Charles Dickens, 'The Modern Science of Thief-Taking', *Household Words*, 1 (1850), 368.   [12] Ibid. 369–71.
    [13] Charles Dickens, 'A Detective Police Party I', *Household Words*, 18 (1850), 409. Dickens's assessment of the new police had considerable currency. For instance, writing in 1852, W. O'Brien would celebrate the new surveillance by comparing it to a strong and intricate web spun and watched over by the spider-like police inspector. O'Brien imagined the whole of London contained in this network

triumph of new policing, as we have seen, was accompanied by a sustained propaganda against public executions, but also increasingly against the death penalty itself.[14] In 1831, the *Edinburgh Review* saw capital punishment as counter-productive: 'In most cases capital punishments are found to frustrate themselves . . . The feelings of mankind are apt to run against the punishment . . . the frequent spectacle of blood, tends of itself to harden the hearts, and corrupt the nature of the people.'[15] Moreover, capital punishment was found to be too inexact. Only a fraction of those sentenced to death actually suffered punishment. The rest were thrown back as an unwelcome burden on society.[16] It was also argued that capital punishment was self-defeating because it did not take into account the moral principle in man:

Whatever law deviates from this principle, will always meet with a resistance, which must ultimately destroy it . . . The same feeling that, elevated . . . animates the patriot to resist civil tyranny . . . when it is perverted . . . goads on the convict to arraign the justice of the system, to rebel against those who execute it.[17]

If Dickens's propaganda for new policing was influential, his fellow novelist Thackeray's opposition to capital punishment was also memorable. Using his meticulous eye for details, Thackeray sketched a scene of public execution that skilfully articulated the specific politics of the opposition to the gallows carnival. Thackeray correctly discerned in the theatre of public execution a celebration of the paternalist power of the 'old' aristocracy. In his article for the *Fraser's Magazine* he described the scene of a public hanging as a tableau of power. This consisted of the mob, always

of order, where information of the slightest criminal deviation would radiate along the web without any loss of time. See his 'The Police System of London', *Edinburgh Review*, 96 (1852), 8.

[14] The historical shift away from capital punishment in western Europe must be put in the context of the entrenchment of industrial capitalism. As Foucault explains: 'the political investment of the body is bound up, in accordance with complex reciprocal relations, with its economic use . . . largely as a force of production . . . it is caught up in a system of subjection . . . the body becomes a useful force only if it is both a productive body and a subjected body.' Foucault, *Discipline and Punish*, 26. On the history of the decline of public execution, also see Gatrell, *The Hanging Tree*.

[15] Henry Brougham, 'Anti-Draco; Or Reasons for Abolishing the Punishment of Death', *Edinburgh Review*, 52 (1831), 402.   [16] Ibid. 403.

[17] Anon., 'Punishment of Death', *Westminster Review*, 27 (1832), 53–4.

turbulent and dangerous because of its indecipherable nature: 'Chiefly blackguards and boys . . . who saluted the policemen on their appearance with a volley of jokes and ribaldry.'[18] The presiding lord of this riot is a shown to be a perfumed 'degenerate aristocrat', who, like the mob, signals his political allegiance when he joins in the taunting of the policeman.[19] For Thackeray, this carnivalesque atmosphere at the gallows defeated the very aim of punishment, as the 'awful majesty of law' was reduced to a joke.[20]

Thackeray's final words on 'old' punishment articulate the rationale of the opposition to public execution: 'Blood demands blood . . . does it? . . . where is the reason for the practice? Revenge is not only evil, but *useless*.'[21] He is not so much troubled by the fate of the condemned people as by the callous wastage of the opportunity to make the criminal body 'productive'. For Thackeray, this wasteful behaviour by the state encouraged a corresponding recklessness in the people. To avoid the calamity of a violent social upsurge, he advocates the implanting of a morality that would control the mob's excessive and violent impulses. And this morality could only come into existence when 'new' forms of imprisonment accompanied the 'new' police to replace the gallows carnival. He would have the mob cheer and not abuse the policemen.[22]

But before prisons could replace the hanging tree, the British legal system would also have to change its inexact nature.[23] A parliamentary report of 1834 called for the establishment of a definite scale of punishment, with strict correspondence between the different degrees of criminality and punishment.[24] Throughout this

[18] W. M. Thackeray, 'Going to See a Man Hanged', *Fraser's Magazine*, 22 (1840), 154.   [19] Ibid. 155.   [20] Ibid.
[21] Ibid. 158.
[22] Gatrell explains the rise of 'new punishment' in terms of the threat felt by the middle classes from the 'old ritual' of public execution: 'New penal attitudes accommodated unambiguous hostility to aristocratic values . . . generated a provincial "urban renaissance" and a heady tradition of aristocratic dissent.' See Gatrell, *The Hanging Tree*, 232.
[23] The irregular nature of British criminal law became a favourite target of the reformers. As *Fraser's Magazine*, complained, 'in the same day, and for a like crime, one man will be sentenced to transportation for life, while another may be let off with a month's imprisonment, and yet both equally bad characters'. See Charles Wall, 'The Schoolmaster's Experience in Newgate', *Fraser's Magazine*, 5 (1832), 527.
[24] 'First Report from His Majesty's Commissioners on Criminal Law', *Parliamentary Papers*, 26 (1834), 119–77.

period, reports on criminal law recommended replacing the death penalty with longer terms of imprisonment, and differentiating between the various degrees of crime: 'The more heinous of such offences as were not capital should subject the offender to long terms of imprisonment . . . a scale of punishment should be established by which the different gradations of crime should be more distinctly marked, and settled according to an uniform system.'[25]

As more and more criminals were produced by these legal refinements, it also became imperative to reform the prison that was going to accommodate them. A report in 1837 advocated the use of the 'separate' system to control the inmates and discarded the old 'silent' system as cumbersome and inadequate.[26] The whole emphasis of punishment shifted to reclaiming the 'ingenious villains and finished hypocrites'.[27] Hence, the prisons were to be restructured by the building of separate cells for the implementation of a standardized and uniform prison discipline. The report ended by aligning this prison reform with the civilizing process:

Whatever be the obstacles against which the system will have to contend, we are satisfied that they must yield to the force of . . . the power of truth. Other nations, less enlightened and powerful . . . are adopting the effective system of prison discipline. We must ensure that England will not incur the reproach of being outstripped in the race of social improvement.[28]

Like the 'new' police force, the 'new' jails had to resemble each other in their minutest details throughout Britain. A Select Committee report in 1850 noted with annoyance that while many

[25] 'Second Report from His Majesty's Commission on Criminal Law', *Parliamentary Papers*, 36 (1836), 210–11. This 'refinement' of law was accompanied by an increasing attention to the implanting of morality in the criminal. This was the period that saw the growth of an opposition to transportation on the grounds that in letting the criminals avoid the regime of the prison, it did not sufficiently reform them. Increasingly, transportation was being seen as a boon to the offender. See M. Heather Tomlinson, 'Penal Servitude 1846–65: A System in Evolution', in Bailey (ed.), *Policing and Punishment*.
[26] 'Second Report of the Inspectors of the Prisons in Great Britain', *Parliamentary Papers*, 32 (1837), 5.
[27] The report pointed out that it was physically impossible for the prison guards to maintain the 'equable and uninterrupted maintenance' of their vigilance under the then current spatial division of the prison. See ibid. 7.
[28] Ibid. 24. Not only was the physical separation of the prisoners ensured by the reforms, the prisoners were also to be classified according to gender, age, and health to facilitate greater supervision. See 'A Bill for the Better Ordering of Prisons', *Parliamentary Papers*, 4 (1839), 3.

prisons had been rebuilt and materially altered since 1835, a 'great variety of constructions and discipline still exists . . . such a variety is a great evil . . . the legislative should entrust increased power to some central authority of enforcing uniform adherence to rules'.[29]

Along with new prisons and new policing, the third major theme that grew in strength in the discourse of crime of the period was that of the criminal classes/tribes. This concept had always been a part of the propaganda about the 'tidal wave' of criminality, but now, with the organization of penal practices reaching new heights, it assumed significant proportions: 'There is a distinct body of thieves, whose life and business it is to follow up a determined warfare against the constituted authorities, by living a life of idleness and plunder.'[30] The gaze of the new police could convert entire social groups to criminality from the study of a single individual: 'The character of one is the character of the whole class; and their manners and notions are all of one pattern and mould . . . they have a peculiar look of the eye . . . the development of their features is strongly marked with animal propensities.'[31] This universalising power would reach its apex in colonies like India, but even in the domestic context, its political utility was clear. Taylor notes that over this period, 'The working classes were being subjected to an unprecedented degree of scrutiny . . . the police were expected to maintain a constant, unceasing pressure of surveillance upon all facets of life in the working class communities.'[32] With this new strategy of statecraft, any organized dissent could be represented as yet another sign of rising criminality, for official language had already produced the labouring classes as 'dangerously criminal'. In 1844, *Blackwood's Magazine* placed the burden of an 'astonishing increase in human depravity during a time of unprecedented progress' squarely on the 'labouring classes'.[33] Significantly, the justification of the surveillance and repression of these classes was derived from the example of the pacification of the colonies through extensive policing:

[29] 'Report from the Select Committee on Prison Discipline', *Parliamentary Papers*, 17 (1850), 5.
[30] Wall, 'The Schoolmaster's Experience', 522.   [31] Ibid.
[32] Taylor, *The New Police*, 90.
[33] 'Destitution, profligacy, sensuality and crime, advance with unheard of rapidity in the manufacturing districts, and the dangerous classes massed together combine every three, four years in one general insurrection.' Archibald Alison, 'Causes of the Increase of Crime II', *Blackwood's Magazine*, 56 (1844), 1–2.

And for decisive evidence that the new establishment of a police force is not the cause of the prodigious increase of crime ... we refer to the contemporary examples of two other countries, in which a police force on a far more important scale has been established ... In Hindoostan a most extensive and admirably organised system of police has been found absolutely indispensable to repress the endless robberies.[34]

This is a telling example of how new policing could demonize subaltern and liminal groups in both Britain and the colony. The strategy of producing a criminal class (figured as caste) would be carried to its hilt in India. At the same time, the policing success there could justify the criminalization of the restive British labourers in the era of Chartism.[35]

Increased police surveillance, a refinement of the prison regime, and the production of 'criminal classes/castes'—these may then be said to be the three chief strategies employed in the writing of crime in the decades that followed Peel's Bill in 1829. But to conclude from the above evidence that consent or homogeneity had anything to do with 'new policing' would be to ignore deliberately the massed evidence of contests and contradictions that marked the decades of the supposed eminence of Peel's reforms. Each feature of this new criminalization was contested both in writing and in practice and popular voices continued to be raised against the reformers. An article in the *Poor Man's Guardian* exhorted the citizens to 'exercise their strength to put down this blue-bottle force, or this country will soon be like Venice . . . a man could not talk to his neighbours without one of these devils listening'.[36] The 6 June, 1840 edition of the *Northern Star* recorded the defiance of a weaver: 'Who sent for the police? The middle class. The middle class chose the men who conceived and passed the laws empowering the police.'[37] In Hull and Manchester, soldiers and the mob rioted together against what they called the 'blue locusts'. Perhaps

[34] Archibald Alison, 'Causes of the Increase of Crime I', *Blackwood's Magazine*, 55 (1844), 538.

[35] Immense efforts were taken to identify the members of these 'dangerous classes'. In his influential treatise in 1849, J. C. Symons noted that not only did criminals and paupers make up this 'obnoxious body', but also those labouring classes 'who are within reach of its contagion, and continually swell its numbers'. Symons suggested it was the 'moral disease' of wanting high wages that led to criminal acts. See J. C. Symons, *Tactics for the Times as Regards the Condition and Treatment of the Dangerous Classes* (London: John Oliver, 1849), 1–18.

[36] Quoted in Storch, 'The Policeman', 60.   [37] Ibid. 71.

the most famous instance of popular anti-police rioting took place in mid-April 1840, at Coine, where the police were repeatedly driven from the station and out of the town by a series of well-planned and well-executed attacks. As Storch has observed: 'The events at Coine from April through August 1840 were not so much riots . . . as a bitter war of attrition against the New Police.'[38] Nor was the widespread resistance to the new police limited to the Chartist years. The 1850s, the so-called 'age of equipoise', offers us the spectacle of great riots in the West Riding, pointing to the general crisis in the maintenance of order.[39] Storch's conclusions about the consolidating years of new policing is instructive:

One must conclude from the example of Yorkshire in 1857 that the imposition of a modern, uniformed police called forth a bitter and often violent response, and that this reflex took place despite the general state of economy or the level of political and social tension . . . If one of the functions of the 'new police' was to act as a 'domestic missionary', translating and mediating bourgeois values in the working class communities, they were not successful in that task.[40]

Again, it was the fiction of crime that most profitably tapped into this culture of dissent against the new police. But the strength of this opposition and debate about the new police was also registered in the official narratives and reformist rhetoric even as they attempted to entrench their own positions. Sometimes, the fracture between the official claim of successful policing and evidence against it became so wide that the coercive and oppressive nature of policing became startlingly clear. In 1833, a parliamentary Select Committee met to discuss the petition by one Frederick Young, who accused policeman Popay of infiltrating his workers' union as an agent provocateur. No amount of cross-questioning could reduce the union to a criminal organization. Shem Shelly, for example, simply answered: 'I am not much of a political man, they [the union] were for the protection of ourselves, equal rights and equal

---

[38] Storch, 'The Policeman', 79.

[39] See Taylor, *The New Police* (1997), 37.

[40] Storch, 'The Policeman', 90. The opposition to the new police was hardly limited to the industrial centres. David Jones has shown in his study of Suffolk and East Anglia that the attacks on policemen and their families were an important part of the farmers protest against the erosion of their traditional rights. See David Jones, *Crime, Protest, Community and Police in Nineteenth-Century Britain* (London: Routledge & Kegan Paul, 1982), 44–5.

laws is what we want . . . not to be oppressed quite so much as we are . . . it is poverty that brought people together.'[41] Young's petition itself rang out with sincere indignation and the belief that justice would be done against the new police.[42] Faced with this evidence, the committee was forced to conclude that the conduct of Popay had been highly reprehensible, although they qualified this by attributing Popay's misconduct to his 'misjudging zeal'.[43] They categorically refused to condemn the practice of employing plain-clothed policemen for infiltration and surveillance, but a crucial aspect of the exchange was the strength of the voices opposing surveillance.

In the same year, another parliamentary committee again struggled unsuccessfully to contain popular outrage against police brutality in Cold Bath Fields. Evidence upon evidence piled up to disturb the official accounts of the 'exemplary' action of the police force:

They levelled everybody without any sort of distinction whatever, men, women and children. . . . They did nothing but knock them down, break their hands . . . I begged of some persons to interfere, and two gentlemen went out of my balcony on purpose to assist one particular woman, whom they were beating in the most shameful manner.[44]

When, in the face of this evidence, the committee concluded that no blame could be attached to the conduct of the police and that the 'actual dispersion of the meeting was not attended with greater violence than was occasioned by the resistance', it could only point to the radical divergence in the vested interests of social groups.

As on the issue of police surveillance, there was no consensus on the reformist attacks on the 'old' bloody code in favour of the penal regime. Capital punishment could often be prescribed by the very people who were staunchly in favour of other reformist measures. If *Blackwood's Magazine* could theorize about the 'criminal classes', it could also take up a resolutely anti-reformist position by advocating the 'old' punishment and blame the rise in crime rate on the 'new' penology:

[41] 'Minutes of Evidence', *Parliamentary Papers*, 13 (1833), 445.

[42] 'Reports of the Select Committee on the Petition of Frederick Young', ibid. 411.   [43] Ibid. 409.

[44] 'Report of the Select Committee on Cold Bath Fields Meeting', ibid. 25.

In consequence of the relaxation of the severity of our criminal code, the astonishing increase of serious crimes cannot be passed over . . . The executions in Great Britain now range from twenty-five to thirty-five only a year . . . Has the promised and expected diminution of crime taken place? . . . quite the reverse.[45]

J. C. Symons, whose 'tactics' were resolutely based on the reformist idea of a criminal tribe/class, could argue for the divine sanction of capital punishment and saw it as the only effective deterrent.[46]

Similarly, most writers appeared to agree that the industrial and agricultural labourers and 'professional' criminals composed the residuum that engaged in war against legitimate society. Yet they were far from consistent in this application. An article in *Fraser's Magazine* compared the manufacturing poor to ferocious savages, 'human beings without humanity'. A few lines later, however, it reversed its representation of the industrial poor in an astonishing indictment of the 'bourgeoisie':

We hate tyranny in every disguise. We are too much ruled by the spirit of the bourgeoisie . . . our unequal taxation, our class legislations, our unnatural distinction among ranks, all attest to this. . . . The refinement of our police enables us to adopt milder punishments. But although the form may be more mild, the spirit may be the same. Think you that by substituting for a sanguinary punishment the series of laws . . . We have made any advance in the direction of clemency and justice? . . . we should be glad to see this indirect and cowardly mode of punishment discontinued, now that the universal voice of mankind has pronounced that opinion shall not be punished at all.[47]

The 'mixed' nature of these writings is not so much an indication of inconsistent editorial practices of the journals, but of the essentially contradictory nature of the rhetoric of crime, indeed, of the very concept of the 'criminal' itself. The lack of consensus on new policing resulted in the strengthening of the fractures that had been

---

[45] Alison, 'Causes of the Increase of Crime I', 539–40.

[46] Symons, *Tactics for The Times*, 77. There were, of course, earlier examples of famous opposition to 'new punishment'. In 1830, an article in the normally reformist *Fraser's Magazine* argued against the very basis of the new penology: 'the maxim that it is not the intensity of the punishment, but its duration, which makes the greatest impression on the human kind . . . will be found in direct opposition to all experience.' See William Hazlitt, 'On the Punishment of Death', *Fraser's Magazine*, 2 (1830–31), 666.

[47] Hazlitt, 'On the Punishment of Death', 586.

present in the writing of crime from the earliest reformist days. And since the British colonial regime continued the attempts to empower itself by making extensive use of the rhetoric of crime, it also faced a radical questioning of its legitimacy that grew from the potential for opposition that was inherent in that very rhetoric. There is no better indicator of the scope of this opposition than the fiction of domestic crime that developed in conjunction with the rise of the new police.

NEWGATE FICTION AND THE NOVEL'S DISSENT

But the law is vindictive, cowardly, mean and ignorant. It is vindictive because its punishments are more severe than the offences, and because its officers descend to any dirtiness in order to obtain a conviction. It is cowardly, because it cuts off from the world those men whose disposition it fears to undertake to curb. It is mean because it is all in the favour of the wealthy, and reserves its thunder for the poor and the obscure . . . and it is ignorant because it erects the gibbet where its should rear the cross.[48]

This statement from 1846 could have easily made at one of the numerous meetings like the one held at Cold Bath Fields. The fact that it came from a very successful novel gives us some idea of the oppositional role fiction could play throughout the era of the new police.

Recent critics have explored the role played by the novel in nine-teenth-century British rulership. D. A. Miller has described the genre as a 'discrete and supplementary' weapon of a state that had made significant investment in surveillance. Following Foucault, and to an extent Althusser's theory of the plural and dispersed nature of the state's repressive apparatus, Miller sharply distin-guishes the cultural power of the novel from the coercive power of the police.[49] If the new police and the penal regime were 'visible and explicit tools' of the British state, then the novel was the supremely disguised cultural agent that carried the task of implant-ing disciplinary regulations in its readers. Miller shows that the genre often criticized police practices to create the illusion of its rapidly expanding readership that they were somehow beyond

---

[48] G. W. M. Reynolds, *The Mysteries of London*, i (London: Vickers, 1846), 101.
[49] Miller, *The Novel*, 17.

surveillance, all the while instilling disciplinary norms through the very practice of reading: 'While the Novel censures police power, it has already reinvented it, in the very practice of novelistic representation.'[50] The kind of reading demanded by the novel, Miller argues, reproduces the panoptic act of vigilance that disciplines the reader:

The panopticism of the novel thus coincides with what Mikhail Bakhtin has called its monologism: the working of an implied master-voice whose accents have already unified the world in a single interpretative centre . . . The feat is possible because nineteenth century narrative is usually conceived as a genesis: a linear, cumulative time of evolution. Such a genesis secures duration against the dispersive tendencies that are literally 'brought into line' by it.[51]

Occupying a less extreme position than Miller, and concentrating on only a single kind of novel, Dennis Porter also reads detective fiction as one of the prime agents for the installing of social norms: 'It furnishes a model of narrative art in which the denouement determines the order and causality of the events narrated from the beginning.'[52] As the reader follows the detective to the end of his case, the myth of solving the social problem of crime through the exercise of reason is enacted. This seems to be the lesson of the classical detective fiction.

Valuable as these observations are, perhaps both Miller and Porter have tended to overstate their cases by underplaying the possibilities of resistance that seem to be the defining features of the so-called 'disciplinary' narratives. While formulating his influential reading of nineteenth-century state power, Michel Foucault acknowledged that the strategy of discipline did not preclude the possibilities of contests or inversions: 'They [the technologies of Discipline] are not univocal; they define innumerable points of confrontation, focuses of instability, each of which has its own risks of conflict . . . and of an at least temporary inversion of power relations.'[53] Although Miller and Porter are undoubtedly correct to focus on the ideological component of the novel genre, they propose a too-controlled model of disciplinary strategies. I agree with Porter about the importance of the closure of the detective

[50] Miller, *The Novel*, 20.   [51] Ibid. 25–6.
[52] Porter, *The Pursuit of Crime*, 24.
[53] Foucault, *Discipline and Punish*, 27.

novels, but would argue that not all closures are unproblematic celebrations of surveillance. From the very originary moments of the English detective novel, closures have disturbed as well as enforced 'discipline'. Even more significantly, as we shall see, some of these disturbances in the economy of power at 'home' in metropolitan Britain were created through the figure of the 'criminal' colonial native from India. The fiction of crime, whose progeny detective fiction was, interrogated both colonial and domestic authority and, as Foucault would say, effected temporary inversions of power relations. The linear, cumulative reading that brings all 'dispersals into line' may not apply to all kinds of novels. To take just one example, consider the differences between a 'crime' and a 'detective' novel:

> The Novel is in origin an oppositional, even parodic form . . . we shall find such variations in crime novels, but within the larger frame of what Alastair Fowler calls 'antigenres' . . . antitheses of existing genres. Deviation from the Detective novel is the norm of the Crime novel . . . the central presence of the detective guarantees the rationality of the world and the integrity of the self. But the central and defining feature of the Crime novel is that in itself and the world, guilt and innocence are problematic.[54]

From its very beginning in the 1850s, the detective novel inherited the problematics of the fiction of crime. As we shall see, it was no accident that in the 'first' detective novel, *The Moonstone*, Wilkie Collins problematized guilt and innocence with the help of a recognizable cultural device—the 'criminal' Indian.

Although not involving the 'criminal Indian' figure, one precedent of detective/crime fiction's problematization of criminality is to be found in the genre of 'Newgate fiction' that flourished between 1830 and 1847.[55] We have already seen Gatrell's analysis of the roles played by popular genres such as Flash Ballads and the Penny Dreadfuls in the 'old' economy of power.[56] And although the *Newgate Calendars* were largely 'respectable' incursions into the culture of the gallows, they were themselves profoundly influenced

[54] A. C. Hilfer, *The Crime Novel: A Deviant Genre* (Austin: University of Texas Press, 1990), 1–2.
[55] See Keith Hollingsworth, *The Newgate Novel* (Detroit: Wayne State University Press, 1963), for chronology and other aspects of the genre.
[56] See Gatrell, *The Hanging Tree*, 126–61.

by the gallows literature and their moralizing mission was often superseded by their graphic representation of the whole spectacle of 'old' punishment. The genre fiction that came to be known as 'Newgate novels' maintained this subversive feature of the *Calendars*, and deserves to be more than just a footnote in the story of the crime and empire.

'Newgate novels' preserved the vestiges of the 'old' technology of power—a hagiography of the executed criminals, their 'confessions', and a fatalism that explicitly renounced reformative possibilities. But these were more than the mere repackaging of the 'old' literature of the gallows. They attracted critical hostility precisely because of their unsettling mixture of the 'new' and 'old' ideologies of crime and punishment. Keith Hollingsworth began his study of the genre by asking, 'when the Newgate subject was so old and so familiar, why should it attract a new kind of attention, genuinely hostile, after 1830?'[57] Gary Kelly provides a part of the answer when he identifies the main features of these novels as at once the criticism of the 'old order', the contemporary criminal law reform, the Reform Bill of 1832, and the Poor Law reform of 1834, as well as the depiction of urban lower-class life as being exotic and glamorous, but beyond reform and redemption.[58] This 'mixed' nature of the novels was an extreme version of the official writings, both 'domestic' and 'colonial', where contradictions arose from the contested versions of criminality and legitimacy.[59]

In his preface to the 1840 edition of *Paul Clifford*, Bulwer-Lytton outlined the aims of the novel: 'to draw attention to a vicious prison discipline and a sanguinary criminal code . . . that

[57] Hollingsworth, *The Newgate Novel*, 15.

[58] Gary Kelly, 'Romantic Fiction', in Stuart Curran (ed.), *The Cambridge Companion to British Romanticism* (Cambridge: Cambridge University Press, 1993), 208.

[59] In this context, it is important to remember that the *Newgate Calendars* were still popular enough to be published throughout these decades, carrying tales of crime and punishment that often ran against the grain of new policing. The 1832 edition carried gory descriptions of crimes like those of John Price, who raped and beat a 'minor' girl till her 'eyes were forced out of their sockets'. Editorial comments and the narratives often clamoured for the 'old' public executions of such criminals, arguing that it was the only effective punishment. The edition also continued the printing of the gallows speeches, some of which were extremely subversive. Again, editorial comments, as in the case of the 'unjustly executed' Christopher Slaughterford, did not hesitate to rebuke the state. See Anon., *The Newgate Calendar* (London: T. Werner Laurie, 1832), 1–51.

there is nothing essentially different between the vulgar and fashionable vice—and that the slang of the one circle is but an easy
paraphrase of the cant of the other.'[60] This was a useful indication
of the novel's 'mixed' nature. It showed clear reformist allegiances
in the proposal to attack a 'sanguinary' criminal code. On the other
hand, in the opposition to prison discipline and dispensing with the
notion of a 'criminal class', Bulwer-Lytton problematized some of
the central features of new policing. The novel begins with an
encomium to the British highwayman:

The Hero of the story is an attempt to portray an individual of a species
which the country is now happily rid, but which seems to me to have
possessed as many real properties of romance . . . For my part, I will back
an English highwayman . . . trotting over Hounslow Heath, against the
prettiest rascal the continent ever produced.[61]

With this enlisting of romance and nationalism on the side of
crime, the author begins the interrogation of the reformist agenda
of the novel. In the light of the story, 'happily rid of' can only ring
with an ironic cheer. The idea that crime is predetermined, and
thus beyond all scope of reformative punishment, also makes an
early appearance in the novel. Paul's criminal tendency is coded in
his heredity—his grandfather had been three times transported,
and twice hanged, the first time having been restored to life by the
surgeons ('much to the chagrin of a young anatomist')'.[62] Like
Ainsworth's hero Rookwood, Paul seems to have been doomed to
crime from the very moment of his birth.

Even the discovery of Paul's real father, the judge Brandon, does
nothing to allay the sense of this fatalism. Indeed, this discovery
sets the stage for a subversive equation of crime and authority.
Brandon, the embodiment of law, is also the fountainhead of Paul's
criminal career. His abandoning of the child at his birth is only one
sign of his entire lack of honour. At the dramatic moment of passing judgement, the physical resemblance between father and son
clinches the umbilical link between the state's authority and criminals. 'Law' is no longer distinguishable from 'crime': 'But as alone
conspicuous throughout the motionless and breathless crowd, the
judge and the criminal gazed upon each other . . . a thrilling and

[60] Hollingsworth, *The Newgate Novel*, 66.
[61] E. Bulwer-Lytton, *Paul Clifford* (London: Colburn & Bentley, 1830), i. p. xxi.
[62] Ibid. 17.

electric impression of a powerful likeness between the doomed and the doomer ... struck upon the audience.[63] Along with this subversive reading of criminality, the novel undertakes a sustained criticism of policing. The Britons are a people with a 'prodigious love for punishment'. With the judicial system seen as criminally oppressive, and places like Bridewell a place for extortion and torture, the attractions of a criminal life are 'justified'.[64] The characters intuitively understand that crime and law are manufactured through language, and language always belongs to those in power: 'All crime and all excellence depend upon a good choice of words ... to knock a man on his head is neither virtuous nor guilty, but it depends upon language applied to the action to make it murder or glory.'[65] This demythification of crime then enables the novel to occupy an oppositional site where reform can in turn be seen in its political context

Repent!—that is the idlest word in our language. No,—the moment I repent—that moment I reform ... the older I grow, the more I see of men, and the callings of social life—the more I, an open knave, sicken at the ... covert dishonesty around. I acknowledge no allegiance to society ... openly I war against it ... This may be crime; but it looks right in my eyes, when I go around and survey ... the masked traitors.[66]

This attack on reform is a part of the novel's nostalgia for an 'older' economy of power. Coming from what he claimed to be one of the oldest aristocratic families of Norfolk, Bulwer-Lytton's nostalgia for an agrarian/feudal social organization may have been considerable. Traces of it are seen in the ballads and the gallows song that pepper the novel. Together with a cheerful acceptance of the futility of reform, the songs celebrating the world of the chase, the manor, poaching, and highway robbery formed a part of the celebration of the old order.[67] These ditties could also point towards an alternative reading practice of the novel from that suggested by Miller. A linear model of 'surveillant reading' is eschewed for these achronological ditties that upset the progression

---

[63] E. Bulwer-Lytton, *Paul Clifford*, iii. 295.   [64] Ibid. i. 287.
[65] Ibid. 200–1.   [66] Ibid. 145–6.
[67] Needless to add, this myth of the 'old' order was itself an ideological construct that privileged agrarian aristocracy. For the harsh reality that lay behind the 'romance' of poaching see, for instance, E. P. Thompson, *Whigs and Hunters* (Harmondsworth: Penguin, 1977).

of the story. Also, there are no disguised zones of discipline set up by the criticism of the legal machinery in the text. The 'romance' of the outlaw could only instil the norms of a very different kind of power. It is only fitting that the novel ends with Clifford's exposure of the legal practice: 'Your laws are but of two classes . . . the one makes criminals, the other punishes them . . . the laws themselves cared to break the laws! First, by implanting within me the goading sense of injustice; secondly, by subscribing me to the corruption of example.'[68]

In many ways, Bulwer-Lytton's next novel was calculated to provoke more of the same critical hostility that greeted his first. The *Spectator* observed in disgust that *Eugene Aram* contained no message of social reform and *Fraser's Magazine* went so far as to imply that the author was disreputably close to the criminal community he wrote about.[69] They may have been provoked by the very opening of the novel: 'I have wished to impart to this romance something of the grandeur of tragedy—something of the more transferable of its qualities.'[70] If turning the story of a murderer into a 'romance' was considered deviant, infusing it with tragic grandeur must have smacked of heresy. As in his previous novel, Bulwer-Lytton provides a cover of reformist elements to slip his agenda in. Initially, Aram is identified as a criminal, in the true surveillant fashion, from his physical features: 'Did you note the sly, and yet ferocious eye, like that of some animal, that longs yet fears to spring on you?' But almost immediately, as if mocking this strategy, he derives a very different conclusion about the man's nature from those same features: 'A physiognomist would have loved to look upon, so much did it speak both of refinement and the dignity of intellect.'[71]

This unsettling 'mixed' response to reformist elements remains a central feature of the novel. The peaceful and idyllic rural community where Aram hides is saturated with a disciplinary ethos. Aram is constantly watched in a community that so obsessively polices

---

[68] Bulwer-Lytton, *Paul Clifford*, iii. 277–8. As Hollingsworth has observed, it was this tendency to 'put blame upon society rather than on the criminal' that earned Bulwer-Lytton the sustained hostility of the critics. See Hollingsworth, *The Newgate Novel*, 81.

[69] Hollingsworth, *The Newgate Novel*, 82, 93.

[70] E. Bulwer-Lytton, *Eugene Aram* (London: Colburn & Bentley, 1832), i. pp. x–xi.   [71] Ibid. 45–6.

itself that it has no need of external agencies. He is quickly identified as a man with a past, with depths where dangers may lurk.
Although he struggles against it, Aram knows that he is 'chained to
yonder valleys' and the ever-alert vigilance of the villagers. The
greatest of these watchers, however, is Aram himself. Not only
content with discovering the laws that govern the human soul in his
capacity as a philosopher, as an astronomer he 'watches' the stars
in his quest to discover the universal laws. His 'surveillance' only
affirms the view of individuals as subjects of the immutable laws of
destiny lying beyond the scope of reforms and policing: 'Ye mystic
lights . . . can we look upon you, note your appointed order . . .
and not feel that we are indeed the poorest puppets of an all
pervading and restless destiny . . . the colours of our existence was
doomed before our birth. What then is crime?—fate; what life?—
submission!'[72] Armed with this pre-reformist vision of the individual, Aram can now form a critique of the claims of progress and
the civilizing mission of law

> what are the temptations of the rich to those of the poor? . . . Yet see how
> lenient we are to the crimes of one,—how relentless to those of the other!
> . . . What is civilisation, but an increase of human disparities? The more
> the luxury of the few, the more startling the wants . . . more galling the
> sense of poverty.[73]

In *Aram*, justice is the product of the same inscrutable universal
laws that predetermined men to commit crime: 'What is writ is writ
. . . who can struggle with the invisible and giant hand . . . at whose
decree we hold the dark boon of life and death?'[74] Rowland Lester,
the 'detective' of the novel, finds himself in the grip of this blind
destiny. His exposure of Aram has nothing to do with an abstract,
universal principle of justice, but the jealousy of a defeated rival in
love. It is only later that he attempts to construct legitimacy by
clothing his personal motive with the grand language of universal
morality. In fact, the novel suggests that if there is any morality at
all, it must belong to the murderer Aram. The father Rowland is
determined to avenge turns out to be an alcoholic gambler and
rapist. By killing him, Aram is acting as an extra-legal functionary
of justice. But caught in the grip of fate, it is he who must be

[72] E. Bulwer-Lytton, *Eugene Aram*, 65–6.   [73] Ibid. 27.
[74] Ibid. ii. 139.

punished though the agency of Rowland. Rowland himself realizes that he is a part of an amoral destructive force:

'I have been the mute instrument in bringing you to this awful fate, in destroying the happiness of my own house . . . be merciful, Aram'. . . . In the fire and heat of vengeance he had not recked of this; he had only thought of justice . . . the woe, the horror he was about to inflict on all he most loved—this had not struck him with due force.[75]

The idea that crime is predestined and thus beyond any reformative possibilities was opposed to the essence of dominant nineteenth-century ideas of criminalization. In *Rookwood*, W. H. Ainsworth strengthened this 'deviant' argument by creating the romance of highway robbery through the figure of Dick Turpin, who is presented as

The last of a race which is now altogether extinct . . . with him expired the chivalrous spirit which animated successively the bosom of so many knights of the road . . . the highwaymen, we fear, like their Irish brothers, the Rapparees, went out with the Tories. They were averse to reform, and eschewed emancipation.[76]

By enlisting the romance of lawless life (and the Tories) against reform and emancipation, the novel declared its alignment to the same subversive project present in Bulwer-Lytton's works. While honour and morality were attached to the criminal, 'society' took on the familiar tinge of corruption that Aram had railed against: 'honour . . . where else should you seek it? . . . for it has left all other classes of society. Your highwayman is your only man of honour'.[77] Indeed, the highwayman is seen to preserve a notion of honour uncontaminated by bourgeois 'reforms':

It is as necessary for a man to be a gentleman before he can turn highwayman, as it is a doctor to have his diploma . . . England has reasons to be proud of her highwaymen . . . who are as much before the cut-throat brigand of Italy, the assassin contrabandist of Spain, or the dastard cutpurse of France, as her sailors are before all the rest of the world.[78]

As in other novels of the genre, crime is seen as providential, beyond all reformative possibilities of punishments like imprisonment. Luke Rookwood is condemned to reproduce the criminal

---

[75] Ibid. iii. 224, 129.
[76] W. H. Ainsworth, *Rookwood: A Romance* (London: Bentley, 1834), ii. 307–9.
[77] Ibid. 211.   [78] Ibid. i. 221–3.

features of the generations of the Rookwood nobles who are doomed to murder their wives. It is a fate that cannot be prevented by any policing. Faced with this inheritance, Luke has no choice but to succumb to his fate: 'If fate should guide your hand—if the avenging spirit of your murdered ancestor should point the steel, you could not shun it then.'[79] It is this hereditary sign of criminality that validates Luke's claim to the Rookwood estates. Even his rival and stepmother Eleanor is forced to admit that Luke was literally the reincarnation of the most famous of the Rookwoods—'the profligate and criminal' Sir Reginald. Once this providential view of crime was evoked in the reformist era, the romance of criminality succeeded in violating 'disciplinary' norms. In a world where Luke Rookwood could not be reformed, Dick Turpin's 'noble' crimes validated an ideology diametrically opposed to the surveillant.[80]

In 1840, when Lord William Russell was murdered by his butler, the killer reportedly said that the idea of the crime had come to him upon reading Ainsworth's *Jack Sheppard* .[81] Hollingsworth has commented on the novel's status as an 'extra-literary popular phenomenon'.[82] This popularity of the book, however, was secured against the chorus of disapproval from the guardians of morality. The *Athenaeum* called it a 'bad book' and was puzzled by the 'attempt . . . made to invest Sheppard with good qualities, which are incomprehensible with his character and position.'[83] *Fraser's Magazine* vehemently scolded the author:

With every great regard for Ainsworth . . . we must say that we like not the gutter school of literature . . . the progress of civilisation, and the mutation

---

[79] W. H. Ainsworth, *Rookwood: A Romance*, ii. 254.

[80] Ainsworth regularly baited his readers by using criminal stereotypes not to support, but to subvert the codes of new policing. For instance, from the 1830s onwards vagrant, migratory communities refusing or unable to participate in the regime of 'useful' productivity were increasingly represented as dangerous criminals. This was as true in Britain as it was in India, where the anti-thuggee drive would also serve to wipe out a vibrant culture of the road. Given this norm, Ainsworth's positive representation of the gypsies in his novel was an instance of the oppositional role of the fiction of crime. In the novel, Luke learns of the fundamental values of freedom and collective good from the band of gypsies that befriend him, and other liminal groups like the poachers are described as 'the finest of all boys . . . the only professional sportsmen'. See ibid. i. 99–220.

[81] Hollingsworth, *The Newgate Novel*, 145.

[82] Ibid. 140. Apparently there was a choice of four versions of the book that could be seen on the stage on almost any given night.   [83] Ibid. 142.

of manners, may be traced by the diversities and fluctuations of crime. . . .
The man who undertakes the truly philosophical task . . . ought to be
patient in research . . . calmly discriminating between individual guilt and
a community of errors.[84]

The chief accusation against Ainsworth was that he had yet again
failed to locate the source of crime *inside* the individual, thus negat-
ing the possibility of reforming him through punishment. There
were other reformist maxims that Ainsworth flouted at will in the
novel. Instead of confining Sheppard to the criminal classes,
Ainsworth showed the pervasive and diffused nature of crime
throughout society by making him 'highly born'.[85] Moreover,
Ainsworth was accused of failing to use Sheppard's history from a
reformist perspective. His focus should have fallen, his critics
claimed, on the fact that Sheppard's life exemplified the drawbacks
of the 'old' regime when crime and justice were indistinguishable:

His execution was as criminal as any of his own criminal acts. He was
hanged, on the most wretched evidence . . . under a law directly enacted to
entrap him. . . . Can there be found a more forcible illustration at once of
the brutality and inefficiency of the criminal jurisprudence from the blood-
sucking informer . . . to the jury, selected from those classes in which the
infraction of the rights of property are held to be offences of the deepest
dies . . . to the judge and the lawyer?[86]

But even in *Fraser's Magazine,* it is noticeable how blurred the lines
between the 'old' and 'new' could get once the rhetoric of crime
was evoked. Attacking Ainsworth for the lack of correct historical
perspective, the review's language collapsed (how telling is that
shift to the present tense 'are' in the last sentence) virtually into an
indictment of *all* jurisprudence, including its contemporary manifestation. It was as if in dealing with the bewilderingly 'mixed'
nature of the fiction of crime, the reviewer had been infected with
a subversive perspective that refused to differentiate the 'old' from
the 'new'. This was precisely where the disturbing power of 'gutter
literature' lay.

But for its counter-narrative, the novel could easily have been
read as a purely reformist criticism of the 'old' policing. It was set
in pre-reform London where pockets of 'licensed' criminality, like

---

[84] Anon., 'William Ainsworth and Jack Sheppard', *Fraser's Magazine,* 21 (1840),
227.   [85] Ibid. 236–7.   [86] Ibid. 242.

Southwark, existed as a 'grand receptacle of the superfluous villainy of the metropolis'.[87] Here thrived a criminal subculture that mimicked high society and its norms to create a disturbing mirror image. The inhabitants of this world zealously guarded their liberty like any 'free' citizens.[88] The text makes it clear that there is little to choose between this criminal subculture and 'normal' society with its gangs of aristocratic hoodlums like the Mohocks, led by the Marquis of Slaughterford. The link between these two social halves is maintained by 'thief-takers' like Jonathan Wild, who embodied the arbitrary and oppressive power of the state to make and punish criminals.

Of course, the reason why Ainsworth's novel provoked such hostility was its refusal to see this 'criminal' jurisprudence as a thing of the past. Instead, it remained ambivalent in its attempted distinction between the 'old' and 'new' techniques of producing and punishing criminals. Wild, the epitome of old corrupt policing, employs identical surveillant methods to those followed by the 'new' police—a meticulous mapping and dividing of London into beats, manned by a disciplined body of watchers: 'He was the Napoleon of knavery, and established an uncontrolled empire over all the practitioners of crime . . . he it was who formed the grand design of a robber corporation . . . divided London into districts; appointed a gang to each district, and a leader to each gang.'[89] If this recognisably 'new policing' strategy could be employed to construct a criminal network, the uneasy feeling that the lines between not merely old and new policing, but between new policing and crime, were very blurred indeed, was confirmed by the novel.

As in other Newgate fiction, fatalism further contributed to the critique of the surveillant agenda. Jonathan Wild may have had his own plans for Jack's doom, but Sheppard had already been marked by an overbearing fate even before his birth. He is born in a room adorned with copies of the gallows speech and confessions of his father Tom, himself a victim of Wild. This fatalism is closely allied to the 'old' view of punishment. The novel, like the *Newgate Calendars* we have seen, abounded in graphic descriptions of gory violence, and as in the *Calendars*, detailed descriptions of violent

---

[87] W. H. Ainsworth, *Jack Sheppard* (London: Bentley, 1839), i. 28.
[88] Ibid. 42.   [89] Ibid. ii. 64–5.

crimes are used to reinforce the 'blood for blood' code. Jack is publicly executed, and his death affirms the notion of a popular justice and a paternalism that was fostered by the gallows carnival. The novel ends in a riot where the mob claims his body and he is enshrined as a culture hero: 'a thousand eager assistants pressed behind him. Jack's body was caught, and passed from hand to hand over a thousand heads, till it was far from the fatal tree.'[90]

Perhaps what shocked 'respectable' critics most was the repeated and detailed description of Jack's escapes from jails. His escape from Newgate, especially, is described in glowing terms of heroic exploits by a listing of the obstacles he had to surmount: 'The windows which were about nine feet from the floor, had no glass; but were secured by thick iron bars, and an oaken beam. Along the floor ran an iron bar to which Jack's chain was attached.'[91] Instead of an instrument of effective containment of criminality, Jack's escapades converted the prison into a site of celebration of the workmanship of a criminal. It was this celebration of the anti-carceral in the era that held the prison as an icon of progress which provoked the sustained critical hostility against the 'Newgate novel'.

[90] Ibid. iii. 310–11.   [91] Ibid. ii. 160–5.

5

New Policing, India, and Thuggee

A MYTH OF LAW IN THE COLONY

Our brief look at the 'domestic' fiction of crime in the two decades after 1830 has shown its capacity to interrogate normative myths about crime and punishment. It was this same oppositional impulse that would surface in the fiction of colonial crime set in India, where the power of the regime was rhetorically constructed through the language of legality.

In 1826, the British Parliament passed a Bill to regulate the appointment of juries in India and bring the management of the affairs of the Company in line with that of Europe.[1] Two years later, another Bill was passed for improving the administration of Indian criminal justice, which proposed to introduce in the 'East Indies some of the wholesome alterations made in the criminal laws of England'.[2] India had become an important testing ground for the 'new' strategies of surveillance and rulership. But again, one cannot read the history of colonial India between 1829 and 1857 as an unchallenged triumph of new policing. Some historians have suggested that the British paramountcy in India provided a tabula rasa where the imperial fantasy of reform could be carried on virtually unopposed. This is at best only partially true. As Sandria Freitag has pointed out, 'the authoritarian and not the libertarian side of utilitarianism reigned . . . The British never forgot that the Indian context did not merely provide a hothouse environment in

---

[1] 'A Bill to Regulate the Appointment of Juries in East India', *Parliamentary Papers*, 1 (1826), 93.
[2] 'A Bill for Improving the Administration of Criminal Justice in India', *Parliamentary Papers*, 2 (1828), 463.

which to conduct Benthamite experiments, but what was more frequently a hotbed of challenges to their authority.'[3] If the very nature of the colonial paramountcy demanded the authoritarian face of reform, this was achieved against a backdrop of constant challenges and protests that often forced the regime to negotiate. As we have seen, the 'new' strategies of surveillance that were now being applied in the colony were already marked by deep contests arising out of the domestic context. In India, these were amplified as they brushed against a firmly entrenched and radically different concept of power:

The concept of authority for the British was an exclusive one, encompassing both power . . . and moral influence, in the sense of providing the ultimate source for norms . . . But Indians had practised a divisible, or perhaps more accurately, a 'discrete' perception of authority . . . each discrete social unit had its locus of moral authority which in turn . . . owed at least symbolic obeisance to outside powerholders.[4]

Although it was during this period of establishing new police at home and paramountcy in India that British authority gradually attempted to jettison the negotiatory aspects of rulership, there was to be no smooth grafting of the new techniques of power onto the body of the colony.

In 1829, the year of Peel's Bill, new policing began in earnest in India with the inception of the anti-thuggee campaign.[5] Throughout the next decades, a number of legislations would be passed to implement new policing techniques in India that also paradoxically underlined the mixed nature of the colonial rule. For example, even as Macaulay was drafting the Indian Penal Code, colonial authorities were resorting to 'pre-reform' measures like public group hangings to terrify the colonized into obedience. This, of course, flew in the face of the 'progressive' claims of the reformers who had been arguing precisely against such examples of wasteful punishment in Britain. Again, a perfect example of such

---

[3] Sandria B. Freitag, 'Collective Crime and Authority in North India', in Yang (ed.), *Crime and Criminality*, 145–6.   [4] Ibid. 142.

[5] Singha writes: 'A communication for Chief Secretary Swinton of 23 October 1829 was afterwards cited as the official declaration of a new initiative . . . Sleeman hailed this letter as establishing the principle that the paramount power had assumed a responsibility for the trial of thugs in the Indian states, and that a recognised judicial terrain had been opened up under the aegis of the political department.' Singha, *Despotism*, 203–4.

unsettlingly mixed rulership in the colony is provided by the penology that became central to the regime's 'rule of law'. David Arnold has shown that although the showpiece of British legal reforms in the colony, the prison was never recognized by the British as the only instrument of punishment. Capital punishment became a far more common punitive measure.[6] Moreover, instead of being the site of 'useful punishment', the prison was a porous entity that highlighted the negotiatory aspect of the colonial rule:

The colonial prison was, in many respects, a remarkably permeable institution, connected to the outside world through venal warders and communal identities ... the colonial authorities felt obliged to recognise a continuum between the prison and the wider community and so abandoned any pretence at individualizing or reforming prisoners.[7]

This was, of course, a very different model of the relationship between prisoners and their social and spatial configurations from the one being practised in contemporary Britain. At the same time, however, and in line with the aims of new surveillance, the prison remained a critical site for the acquisition of colonial knowledge, and a more 'narrowly state-centred enterprise' in India than in Europe.[8] What the unique nature of the colonial prison pointed to was the heightened instability of the strategy of criminalization that underwrote the rhetoric of British authority in the colony.

Macaulay's Minutes of the parliamentary debate over Indian legal reform, containing as they did a clear articulation of the reformist position on India, had a number of central contradictions. Macaulay began by asserting the universality of all subjects under British law. But he soon admitted that this essential condition of the reform could not actually be employed in India, as in Calcutta public opinion was a shorthand for the voice of '500 people without any interest, feeling, or taste in common with the 50 million among whom they live'. Thus the cherished British principle of liberty actually operated as a repressive measure there, since it stood for 'the strong objection which the 500 feel to every measure which can prevent them from acting as they choose to the 500 million'.[9] Macaulay realized that this meant that the British

[6] Arnold, 'The Colonial Prison', 150.   [7] Ibid. 171–2.
[8] Ibid. 148.
[9] 'Copy of the Minutes of the Supreme Government of India, on the Subject of Act xi of 1836', *Parliamentary Papers*, 41 (1837–8), 221.

government could only play at being an impartial lawgiver, while in reality it would remain a despotic authority.[10] This recognition also meant the virtual admission of the fictive nature of the British claims about establishing the rule of law. As Arnold notes:

Certainly, the language of the report and many of its recommendations echoed Bentham and the spirit of Prison reform . . . But no less striking is the frequency with which the committee and its critics departed from western precedent to stress the impracticality of simply exporting the British model into India.[11]

Thus, new policing, in the Indian context, was always an unsettling mixture of the old and the new, of the carceral and the spectacular, and perhaps even more so than in Britain, it is impossible to glean from it a narrative of the progression of enlightened rule of law. As late as 1854–5, a committee appointed to investigate allegations of torture carried out by the Madras police force found that:

The whole police is underpaid, notoriously corrupt, and without any of the moral restraint and self-respect which education ordinarily engenders . . . the character of the native when in power displays itself in the form of rapacity, cruelty and tyranny, at least as much as its main features are subservience, timidity, and trickery, when the Hindoo is a mere private individual.[12]

An article in 1852 assessed the history of the British anti-thuggee drive and found that far from illustrating the principles of the colonial 'rule of law', Sleeman's success had been achieved by abandoning all the vaunted new policing strategies.[13] As a matter of fact, contrary to all British claims, it was the native states that were seen as having the better and more effective administration against the Thugs: 'In the native states, the thugs and dacoits were not so much unmolested as with us; they were much more likely to be, without any particular accusation, stopped and searched . . . dreadful punishment was wrecked [*sic*] on them . . . But, under us they shared the general liberty of the subjects.'[14] The implication was

---

[10] Ibid.   [11] Arnold, 'The Colonial Prison', 152.
[12] 'Inquiry and Report, with Reference to the Statement of Mr. Theobald, as to the Employment of Torture by the Police', *Parliamentary Papers*, 40 (1854–5), 618.
[13] The article pointed out the peculiar despotic powers given to Sleeman's anti-thuggee squad, including the power to convict men without any particular charge. This was rightly considered to be a departure from the enlightened claims of colonial new policing. See William Empson, 'The Thugs, Dacoits and the Police of India', *Edinburgh Review*, 96 (1852), 35.   [14] Ibid. 34.

that in a country as rooted in the 'old' view of power and statecraft as India, reformed or new policing was not only ineffective, but also anachronistic.

How did this admission, often unacknowledged, that new policing in India was at best a negotiation with the older techniques of governance, and at worst despotic beyond all recognition, affect the representation of Indians as criminals during this period?[15] How was the colonialist propaganda of progress and civilization maintained when one of its chief strategies, that of producing criminals, was fraught with contradictions? If one of the consequences of this was a relapse into the representation of the Indians as intrinsically unredeemable from their criminality, how was that squared with the propaganda about colonial 'useful' punishment? The contradiction between the universality of the colonialist claims of reform and its practice was too glaring not to be registered in its discourse. We shall briefly turn to the narratives of the thuggee campaign to examine this. This will also serve as an introduction to the next section where we shall look at the fictional Thugs as signs of criminal India.

Thugs, the talismanic exemplars of Indian criminality, were publicly hung in large groups at Jabbalpore and Sagar to 'give the populace a forceful sense of the reshaping of order'. These executions were phased out in favour of life imprisonment only after reports hinted that 'in comparison with the penal practices of the Indian rulers, the paramount power seemed to be undertaking its mission of benevolence in too bloody a fashion'.[16] Singha has analysed the political purpose that the manufacturing of the 'Thug crisis' served in establishing British paramountcy. Like the drive against the 'dangerous classes' during the Chartist years, this had little to do with a rising tide of criminality:

Nor is it clear that special measures were required because the crime of thuggee had reached crisis proportions. Official reports stress the discovery of the ramifications of thuggee rather than its escalation . . . There was no clamour from the Indian subjects for measures against thuggee; the

---

[15] Another example of the contradictory nature of colonial criminalization can be found in the regime's approach to corporal punishment in India. Although William Bentinck officially replaced them with imprisonment in 1834, branding and public flogging were carried on at least till 1850. This mixture of the 'old' and the 'reformed' punishment in the colony undermined the regime's reformist pretensions. See Singha, *Despotism*, 250–3.   [16] Ibid. 211.

major complaint of the officials was the difficulty of working through layers of collusion.[17]

The phenomenon that came to be known as thuggee was manufactured for the extension of colonial knowledge and power. It was one of the ways of representing India that could justify the massive incursion of the colonialist administrative panoply in the name of constructing an archival 'knowledge' about the essence of the country. Thus, even when faced with contradictory evidence, the British officials insisted on streamlining this in a manner that would facilitate the representation of the Thugs as hereditary criminals.[18] What was also glossed over in this rereading of the evidence was the contribution made by the colonial administration to the rise in thuggee and other road crimes.[19] Thus, the 'thuggee crisis' could powerfully construct an official typology of 'criminal' India and then legalize the pacification of the thriving liminal culture of India: 'groups which seemed to elude the reach of taxation and policing; their way of life was considered motley and suspect . . . the thuggee campaign reinforced this latent suspicion about the wandering profession.'[20]

Once the Thugs had been constructed as hereditary criminals, the next step was to find in them the true essence of India or even the 'orient'. In 1833, the *New Monthly Magazine* declared, 'The Thugs form a perfectly distinct class of persons, who subsist almost entirely upon the produce of murders they are in the habit of committing.'[21] Four years later, thuggee was being shown to be growing out of a peculiar 'eastern' human nature: 'Conscience in the East is neither very delicate, nor very enlightened, and if any scruples arose, the countervailing profit would more than balance them.'[22] Thuggee was seen as deeply embedded in the mainstream Indian culture and religion:

The dark and cheerless night of superstitions, which has long clouded the moral vision of India, has given rise to institutions and practices so horrible and fantastic that . . . their existence could not be conceived by minds

[17] Ibid. 171.   [18] See ibid. 183.   [19] Ibid. 188.
[20] Ibid. 186–7.
[21] Philip Meadows Taylor, 'On the Thugs', *New Monthly Magazine*, 38 (1833), 277.
[22] E. Thornton, *Illustrations of the History and Practice of the Thugs* (London: W. H. Allen, 1837), 4.

trained under happier circumstances . . . A trade of assassination, is sufficiently horrible: but when it is added that their occupation is sanctified by
the national religion . . . we must be struck by the reflection, that we have
opened a page in the history of man, fearful and humiliating beyond the
ordinary records of iniquity.[23]

The eastern/Indian character was thus summarized in the figure of
the Thug. Using it as a rubric, the colonial rulers could draw
conclusions about the 'Indian mind' that would serve every administrator of that country: 'Few things are more difficult to a native
of India than to tell the truth and the confessions of the criminals
. . . may be expected to contain a mixture of truth and false-
hood.'[24]

In 1841, *Blackwood's Magazine* saw thuggee not only as a sign
of criminal India, but as a central feature of the entire Asian civilization: 'the thread of those secret and murderous societies, which
. . . had exercised an influence immutable as the decree of fate . . .
over all the kingdoms of Asia.'[25] By aligning the Thugs to the so-
called sect of the Assassins of Alamut, they were also seen as
successors of medieval marginalized Islamic groups like the
Ismailies and the Abbasides. Thus, the entire history of Asia was
shown as turning on the hinges of murders and assassinations, and
the continent itself as ripe for the thrust of British reforms.

The close links between the production of domestic and colonial
criminality also became clear in some of these writings. In an 1840
article, a degenerate 'East' was linked to deviant groups closer to
home through the Thug motif:

Nor is this a truth predicable only of our eastern fellow-subjects. What is
ribandism . . . but a species of political thuggee, in which the conspirators
are of one religion, and bind themselves by an oath of blood, to the extermination of all from whom opposition to their evil design may be appre-
hended? . . . the system of Irish thuggee is political as well as religious. It
is by acting upon the temporal power, that it is enabled to accomplish its
ecclesiastical objects.[26]

[23] E. Thornton, *Illustrations of the History and Practice of the Thugs*, 20.
[24] Ibid. 43–4.
[25] Frederick Holme, 'The Secret Societies of Asia: The Assassins and the Thugs',
Blackwood's Magazine, 49 (1841), 229.
[26] Samuel O'Sullivan, 'Thuggee in India and Ribandism in Ireland Compared',
Dublin University Magazine, 15 (1840), 59–60. The power of the 'Thug' metaphor
in the construction of colonialist authority was demonstrated in its use in the 1857

But precisely because thuggee was such a major component in the strategy of criminalization of India during this period, its rhetoric was also riddled with contradictions. The reports of the master campaigner, Colonel Sleeman himself, carried tales of miscarried justice like that of the three men who had escaped a Thug attack and were then imprisoned for three years by the 'benevolent' power after reporting to the nearest police station![27] Even more significantly, Sleeman himself often steered clear of the official strategy of reading India through the lens of thuggee. For Sleeman, the existence of thugs did not automatically lead to conclusions about the 'criminal' nature of India and the moral superiority of British civilization:

I do not exactly know what is meant by civilising the people of India . . . if unrivalled manufactories . . . establishments of schools for reading and writing . . . a scrupulous respect and delicacy towards the female sect are amongst points that denote civilised people . . . then the Hindoos are not inferior in civilisation to the people of Europe.[28]

Far from being the natural liars who constantly betray a criminal propensity, Sleeman saw Indians of all classes as an intelligent and polite people. For him, thuggee emerged not as the norm of this culture, but as an inexplicable deviation from it. Neither was it in any way aligned to the central current of the national religion,

Mutiny. In that year of the most concerted military challenge to the British colonial regime, James Hutton published a detailed account of thuggee in order to remind his readers about the 'natural criminality' of Indians. Thus, the Thug and the 'rebel' became indistinguishable in the colonial imagination, and the Mutiny was represented as merely another manifestation of latent Indian criminality. Hutton traced the history of the suppression of Thugs, which in his writing figured as the reforming of natural criminals into productive workers, best exemplified in the 'school of industry' in Jubbulpore. Also, the victory over thuggee was shown to prefigure the eventual victory over the rebels. From this rhetoric of criminalization was derived the legitimacy of colonization: 'Let British supremacy cease when it will, the suppression of thuggee will ever remain a glorious monument to the zeal, energy and judgement of the civil and military servants of the East India Company. It is easy to direct epigram and innuendo against the idea of a body of merchants ruling a vast empire with enlightened and disinterested beneficence. But the impartial student of Anglo-Indian history can readily adduce many such examples . . . in order to prove that the merchants were really princes'. James Hutton, *A Popular Account of the Thugs and Dacoits of India* (London: W. M. Allen, 1857), 97.

[27] Philip Meadows Taylor, 'State of Thuggee in India', *British and Foreign Review*, 15 (1843), 267.

[28] W. H. Sleeman, *Rambles and Recollections of an Indian Official* (London: J. Hatchard, 1844), i. 4.

which he saw being as beneficial to Indians as the civil code was to the British.

This approached a cultural relativism that ran against the myth of British racial superiority. If the native states were living examples of misrule and oppression, then Sleeman did not shrink from making a subversive comparison between them and Britain. He gave the example of press-ganging in the Royal Navy to highlight the despotic practices that were carried on at the heart of 'civilization' itself.[29] After this, his conclusion—'We give to India what India never had before our rule, and never could have without it, the assurance that there will always be at the head of the government a sensible ruler trained up to office in the best school in the world'—has the ring of a conclusion reached despite the evidence about it.[30] Sleeman's account of the Thugs thus not only frequently ran against any totalizing vision of a criminal India, but also hinted at the scale at which fiction would be able to use the conflicts and contradictions of the ideologies of crime and empire to take up a dissident position.

NOVELS AND THE PROBLEM OF THE CRIMINAL COLONY

As the case of the Newgate novels demonstrated, the fiction of 'domestic' crime was perfectly capable of interrogating the norms of British domestic authority. It could hardly fail to do the same in the context of its colonies. During the very period that the novel was instilling discipline among its readers, it also formed a site from where challenges to that disciplinary authority could be mounted. Ignoring this fact leads to a fantastic account of power and culture that does not acknowledge any possibilities of resistance.

Kate Teltscher, among others, has found 'contention and doubt' to be a central feature of European discourses about India.[31] In

---

[29] W. H. Sleeman, *Rambles and Recollections of an Indian Official*, 237.

[30] Ibid. ii. 12. Similarly, Sleeman's reports of the Pindari campaign differed significantly from the majority of the official accounts in the criminalization of India. He could admire the intelligence and integrity of demonized liminal figures like the religious fanatic 'Byragee' and the courage of heroic Indian defenders against the Company's aggression like that of Buldeo, the chief of Bharatpore. See ibid. 77.

[31] Kate Teltscher, *India Inscribed: European and British Writing on India* (New Delhi: Oxford Univeristy Press, 1995), 2.

fact, Teltscher argues that there was a significant increase in the disturbances in colonial self-representation as British paramountcy over India was established:

> But with the accession to the diwani in 1765, the British adopt the titles and structures of the Mughal power themselves. What happens when the Self takes on the guise of the Other? The confident narratives of national identity continue to be told, but are now haunted by anxieties and instabilities . . . The assumption of colonial power marks the emergence of a much more precarious sense of self.[32]

Thus, British literature from the late eighteenth century onward saw a sustained outburst against the East India Company. Richard Clarke wrote in 1773:

> Concerns it you who plunder in the East,
> In blood a tyrant, and in lust a beast?
> When ills are distant, are they less your own?
> Saws't thou their tears, or heards't thou the oppressed groan?[33]

In poetry, the mock-heroic style seemed peculiarly suited to the questioning of British conduct in India:

> Where rage and av'rice jointly strive
> Sits the Nabob, plundering C-ve
> In jaghirs to his countless store
> See Asia's golden tide runs o'er!
> Still his ran'crous looks breathe murder;
> Sure with such a scowling yawn,
> Twas he who murdered Ali Cawn.[34]

In the parodic 'The Grandmaster, or Adventures of Qui Hai', the voice of the colonized is evoked not to sing the praise of British rule, but to lay bare its oppressiveness:

> Hearken, sahib, before you go,
> To a sad tale of Hindoo woe
> We gave them ev'ry thing they wanted,
> E'en leave to build a house was granted . . .
> They rul'd us with an iron rod,
> Trod down the temples of our God,
> Plac'd cannon on the sacred ground,

---

[32] Ibid. 7.   [33] Quoted ibid. 174.
[34] Quoted in Amal Chatterjee, *Representations of India 1740–1840* (Basingstoke: Macmillan, 1998), 57.

> And shook the Ganges with the sound . . .
> Our money and our land
> The merchant holds at their command.[35]

Clearly, the interrogation of British colonial conduct was not limited to prose fiction. But perhaps more than other genres, the novel displayed an understanding of both the importance and vulnerability of the rhetoric of law and crime in the establishment of domestic and colonial authority. We will now see how even as the Newgate novels interrogated new policing at home, the fiction of Indian criminality contested British colonialist authority abroad.

The talismanic nature of the anti-thuggee campaign makes the fictional response to it an appropriate place to begin. At 18 years of age, Philip Meadows Taylor found himself policing a million people in a district over 250 miles in length.[36] It was the stuff of colonial fantasies of power and in his memoirs Meadows Taylor repeatedly celebrated the near 'divine' status of the colonial administrator over a subject people. Recalling a mission to capture a dangerous bandit chief, Meadows Taylor registers his surprise at the ease with which he was simply able to ride alone to the criminal's den and ask him to come along.[37] On another occasion, he apprehends the member of a 'dangerous class'—a Beydur—who had assaulted his servant: 'I met him on the main street, and ordered him to give up his sword, which strangely enough he did at once (I had only a slight riding whip in my hand).'[38] Again, Taylor's rhetorical strategy is to strike a note of surprise at his seeming omnipotence and, by doing so, modestly highlight the absolute power that colonialism supposedly infused its agents with. It was around this time that Taylor claims to have made the first European contact with the thuggee phenomenon.[39] Later on, he was to muse how, if he had been allowed to remain at his post, it would have been he, and not Sleeman, who would have 'first disclosed the horrible crime of thuggee to the world'.[40]

Philip Meadows Taylor then, in his avatar of the colonial lawgiver, had a more than usual interest in the thuggee phenomenon. His autobiography, written in the 1870s, was steeped in colonialist

[35] Amal Chatterjee, *Representations of India 1740–1840*, 66.
[36] Philip Meadows Taylor, *The Story of my Life* (Edinburgh: W. Blackwood, 1878), 40.   [37] Ibid. 49–50.   [38] Ibid. 147.
[39] Ibid. 54–5.   [40] Ibid. 57.

sensibility. He saw the Mutiny of 1857 as a product of the same savagery that had led to thuggee.[41] British rule in India is compared with that of Charlemagne's over the Saxons—'a great struggle between light and darkness'.[42] However, at the same time, this reminiscence also contradicted the assertions he made about the 'criminal essence' of India. How, for example, is one to take this sentence after Taylor's description of the land of Thugs, mutineers and corrupt princes? '[T]he people among whom I have been living were highly civilised and in many ways resembled ourselves.'[43] It was this tension between the criminalization and privileging of India recorded here that emerged as the most prominent feature of Meadows Taylor's fiction.

His first novel, aptly called the *Confessions of a Thug* (1839), was extremely successful. The author proudly recorded that Queen Victoria herself had ordered the publishers to send her the sheets as they were being revised, because she could not wait for them to be published.[44] The novel went through two editions in the first four months, and more than fifty years later was still selling so well that it was reprinted four times between 1887 and 1897. This popularity was no doubt due to the fact that the novel seemed to produce a version of India that privileged the fantasy of colonialist rulership. But this success may also be attributed to the novel's exploration of the unease that many felt about the propaganda of criminality and the colony. Brantlinger has called the work a model of Benthamite surveillance where the patiently listening and recording sahib 'is the perfect policeman and ideal figure of imperial discipline and punishment . . . when every detail of one's supposedly secret life can be penetrated, known from a myriad hidden sources of imperial authorities, there seems no alternative but to co-operate and confess.'[45] As the 'sahib' approximates the position of the judge, the text becomes a court where Indian criminality is put on trial. However, the authorial/judgemental silence of the recording

[41] Ibid. 348.   [42] Ibid. 340.   [43] Ibid., p. xii.

[44] David Finkelstein, *Philip Meadows Taylor* (St Lucia: University of Queensland Victorian Research Unit, 1990), 9.

[45] Patrick Brantlinger, *Rule of Darkness: British Literature and Imperialism* (Ithaca, NY: Cornell Univerisity Press, 1988), 88–9. The 'recording sahib' certainly closely corresponded to the reformer's ideal of the judge after the passing of the Prisoner's Council Act of 1836, where instead of being the feeder of emotion into the trial procedure, he was supposed to monitor against it. See Weiner, *Reconstructing the Criminal*, 66.

sahib also contributes to the subversion of the process of criminal-izing the Indian body in the novel. As the criminal native is allowed to 'confess' without being checked or directed by moralistic inter-ventions, it often manages to construct a narrative that contests the authority of the editorial framing device, or at least holds it in balance.

The novel begins by employing a number of new policing strate-gies. Criminality is shown to arise from the social organization of India itself: 'the greatest facilities of disguise among thieves and Thugs exist in the endless division of the people into tribes, castes, and professions.'[46] Thus, it becomes the duty of the colonialist authority to suspect everyone in the colony, for all are potentially disguised criminals in the pay of the native rulers.[47] The 'false reli-gion' of the land is yet another source of sustenance for crimes like thuggee, as the religious vagrants and mendicants who throng every village are shown to liaise with the Thugs.[48] It is this whole network of criminality from the Himalayas to Cape Comorin that the imperial policeman has to control. All these, we have seen in the previous chapters, were elements that were common to the language of British domestic as well as colonial authority by the 1830s.

But these rhetorical strategies of the novel are made problematic by the narrative voice of Ameer Ali. For example, by citing the diverse class/caste composition of the Thug gangs, he can conjure up a picture of honourable brotherhood that is remarkably close to that of the highwaymen found in the Newgate novelists of the period

among them, bad faith is never known . . . For where on this earth will you find true faith to exist, except among us? . . . From the lowest to the high-est among us, all are animated with the same zeal; go where we will, we find homes open to us, and a welcome greeting among tribes of whose language we are ignorant.[49]

In both cases, the deviant groups are seen to possess a morality that is conspicuously absent from the 'policing' society. Thugs and highwaymen are also connected in their fatalist belief in an inscrutable destiny. Like Dick Turpin or Sheppard, Ameer Ali

---

[46] Philip Meadows Taylor, *Confessions of a Thug* (London: Bentley, 1839), i. p. ix.   [47] Ibid.   [48] Ibid. p. x.
[49] Ibid. 39.

repeatedly questions the wisdom of fighting fate with reformative policing.[50] If the ideological work of the novel of crime is allegedly the insertion of disciplinary norms, then Taylor's novel also constantly flaunts the possibilities of questioning those norms.

For example, Ameer's narrative provides an alternative to the 'official' interpretations of the military encounters with groups like the Marathas and the Pindaris, who were resisting the extension of British power in southern and western India. A constructive political motive is now assigned to the exploits of the so-called lawless Pindaris. Cheetoo, the Pindari chief, explains that the aim of his expeditions was to keep the British in a state of perpetual distraction and provide the Marathas with an opportunity to organize a revolt.[51] Ameer Ali remains defiantly proud of his campaigns on behalf of the Pindaris and the Maratha warriors.[52] Like the Newgate criminals, he defies the power of British law: 'thuggee, capable of exciting the mind so strongly, will not, cannot be annihilated. Look at the hundreds who have suffered for this profession; does the number of your prisoners decrease?'[53]

If the novel aimed to criminalize Indians, it certainly did not deny a code of morality and honour to them. Yet, this is not a morality that leads to disciplining, as the Thug remains unrepentant about his craft. In defiance of the official version of 'criminal Indians', Ameer Ali emerges as a moral being: 'Have I not ever been a kind husband and a faithful friend? Did I not love my children and wife . . . have I ever broken a social tie? Ever failed in my duty as host? Ever neglected a rite or ceremony of my religion?'[54] The policeman's answering silence is also a sign of the novel's refusal to plot Ameer Ali according to conventions of representing the 'criminal' Indian.

This 'Indian' point of view of the novel slants a different light on the British assumption of paramountcy. The linking of Thugs to Marathas and Tippoo does not lead to a narrative of 'just' British victory over criminal Indian forces. Instead, the Thugs emerge as participants in a proto-nationalist struggle against colonization: 'The times of fair fighting are passing away, and the inventions of Europeans are fast supplanting the bravery of the men of Hind . . .

---

[50] Ibid. ii. 179–80.   [51] Ibid. iii. 57–8.
[52] Ibid. i. 2.   [53] Ibid.
[54] Ibid. ii. 186.

one or the other must be beaten. . . . Then will be the time of the believers to rouse themselves, and free their country from the yoke.'[55] The British conquerors are now shown to be the stealthy usurpers whose intrigues have taken them beyond the modest confines of their Bombay fort till 'they have upset the Maratha empire'.[56] In this reading of Anglo-Indian history, the 'criminal' Indian confederacy is transformed into the moral and just party. Cheetoo, usually a talismanic evocation of the deviant colony, can now be described as 'A fine looking man, and a gallant leader . . . no man that ever led a Lubhar was juster in his division of plunder; no one was ever more attentive to the words and complaint of those under him than was Cheetoo Pindhari.'[57] The Thugs become heroes who fall defending their homes against the systematic and destructive advance of the British forces.[58] In the end, when Ameer Ali describes the heroism of the Thugs on the gallows, fearlessly putting the ropes around their necks and plunging to death shouting their defiance, like the highwayman, their 'criminal' activity becomes a part of the culture of dissent. Singha has shown how the suppression of thuggee constituted a departure from the new policing practices. For example, officials argued that it was justified to arrest not only the Thugs, but their entire families. And throughout the early stages of the operation, the supposedly reformed and enlightened police force resorted to 'old' punishments like public group hangings. Taylor grasped the fact that these 'enlightened practices' opened colonialism to an unsettling critique. These were the fissures through which the phenomenon of thuggee could emerge as resistance, not criminality; as dissent, not deviance. The confessions of Taylor's Thug, like the countless gallows confessions in front of Newgate, licensed a defiance of policing that sought to discipline the colony as well as the metropolis.

As the brief reference to him in the *Confessions* had shown, Tippoo Sultan of Mysore remained an icon of Indian criminality in the colonialist imagination even more than three decades after his death. By the time Taylor published his novel about him in 1840, the dominant view of Tippoo was that of the perfectly criminal oriental ruler, marked by cruelty, despotism, and 'unnatural' vices. But those British narratives about Tippoo that recorded the actual

[55] Philip Meadows Taylor, *Confessions of a Thug*, i. 186.
[56] Ibid. iii. 164.   [57] Ibid. ii. 329.   [58] Ibid. 324.

encounters with him often told a slightly different story. As Taylor made extensive use of these 'mixed' or unstable representations of Tippoo, we shall briefly look at some of them before we discuss the novel itself.

Perhaps the most interesting and representative accounts of the British experiences of Tippoo were provided by the several 'captivity narratives' of the prisoners taken by him in the Mysore wars. These were marked by the trauma of defeat felt by men often well versed in the myth of racial superiority. For James Bristow, this trauma found its expression as a quasi-sexual violation of manhood. Bristow minutely described the forced circumcision of the British prisoners, making little effort to distinguish it from the ultimate loss of honour—castration.[59] Having been forcibly deprived of their 'manhood', the prisoners of Bristow's narrative become slaves or effeminate dancers who are shown as victims of the 'unnatural' vices of the ruler of Mysore.[60] Captured British women suffer similar racial and sexual abuse as they are parcelled out among black slaves and 'abominable Abyssinians'. Besides being a sexual aggressor, Tippoo is shown to be a thief and a cheat who short-changed his own followers: 'the army is neither well-paid, nor well satisfied, and . . . nothing but fear, and lack of unanimity and bold leaders . . . prevents them from revolting.'[61] A detested and unpopular figure, Tippoo can cling to power only because of the patience and indolence, the abject tameness of the Indians.[62]

But accounts like Bristow's were disputed in every detail by other narratives like Edward Moor's. Moor's Tippoo was very far from being the tyrant whose army followed him out of fear. Instead, he admired the troops of Mysore who, despite a series of defeats and unfortunate reverses, carried on fighting out of devotion to their able leader.[63] Instead of the usual colonialist harangue

[59] James Bristow, *A Narrative of the Sufferings of James Bristow* (London: J. Murray, 1793), 39–40.   [60] Ibid. 53–6.

[61] Ibid. 96–7.

[62] It is interesting to see how even Bristow's meticulously detailed propaganda worked at least partially against its own agenda by his dismissal of one of the most enduring anti-Tippoo myths—that he murdered the captive British Colonel Bailey with poison: 'for what I have been able to collect then, as well as since, I have no right to believe that his demise was actually brought on by mortal drugs', Ibid. 59–60.

[63] Edward Moor, *A Narrative of the Operation of Captain Little's Detachment* (London: Woodfal, 1794), 197–9.

against his oppression, Moor applauded Tippoo's administrative prowess: 'His government, though strict and arbitrary, was the despotism of a politic and able sovereign, who nourishes, not oppresses, the subjects who are to be the means of his future aggrandisement.'[64] Nor did Moor bring charges of criminal cruelty and bloodlust against Tippoo by citing the public execution of the criminals in Mysore. He perceptively concluded that this method of punishment grew out of a different kind of political sensibility from that of the British, but not necessarily an inferior one:

It should be recollected, that in governments, like that of Mysore, unlimitedly monarchical, the mandate of the sovereign is the law . . . the summary mode of punishment sometimes practised in the East, has an appearance much more irreconcilable than the forms of the process established in Europe; but divested of national and local prejudices, it is of little consequence whether . . . the body be gibbeted, anatomised, given to the worms of the earth.[65]

In Moor's account, it was the British colonial army, not Tippoo's, that emerged as discontented, troubled by desertions and arguments about pay.[66] He avoided any moral justification of the British victories, but put them down to superior firepower and unlimited greed.[67] The signs of criminality, in Moor's account, were attached to the colonizers and not to the Sultan of Mysore.

At first glance, Innes Munro's series of letters appear to be closer in spirit to Bristow's narrative than to Moor's. He begins with the familiar account of the 'natural' criminality of the Indians—a result of exposure to a deviant religion from childhood.[68] But Munro quickly qualifies this by warning that making any generalizations about the Indians from these examples would be like judging London by its beggars and criminals. The refusal to generalize about the essence of India from the allegedly criminal particulars places Munro outside the dominant parameters of British colonial sensibilities after paramountcy had been achieved in India. Instead, his narrative (like several others) serves to maintain links with those earlier eighteenth-century accounts of the East India Company that questioned British dominance in India and the negative stereotyping

---

[64] Moor, *A Narrative of the Operation of Captain Little's Detachment*, 202.
[65] Ibid. 194–5.   [66] Ibid. 105.   [67] Ibid. 120.
[68] Innes Munro, *A Narrative of the Military Operations on the Coromondal Coast* (London: T. Bensley, 1789), 26.

of Indians. Echoes of these earlier writings are clearly present in his description of the conquest of India:

After obtaining, however, a thorough knowledge of the meek and pusil-lanimous nature of these unfortunate natives, the inexhaustible wealth of their country . . . they were soon induced, by such rapacious considera-tions to blend war with commerce . . . until they had, by the most dishon-ourable acts of injustice and oppression, rendered the British more odious in all the Indian courts.[69]

Munro is unambiguous about casting the Indian rulers as the wronged party in the hands of the avaricious administrators of Bombay. The generosity of the Indian princes like Scindia and Hyder Ali is repeatedly contrasted with 'criminal' breaches of faith by the British governors.[70]

Similarly, in his descriptions of Tippoo and Mysore, Munro refuses to employ the rhetoric of crime. Tippoo's father, Hyder Ali, is compared to Frederick II for his sagacious rule, and the Mysore wars held up as examples of the laudable spirit of patriotism of the Indians.[71] Munro also demolishes the myth of the 'just' British campaign by describing the motives of military leaders like General Mathews

Nay, such was the intoxication of this man's mind, and so unbounded were its rapacious desires . . . General Mathews did so disgust his officers and men, by his sordid and unfair distribution of plunder . . . that Colonels Macleod and Humberton . . . were deputed by the army to lay their griev-ances in person before the governor.[72]

But while Munro's and Murray's narratives ignored colonialist rhetoric of crime, others like those by Major Dirom and James Scurry reinforced it. For Dirom, the campaign against Tippoo is nothing short of an attempt to bring a murderer to justice.[73] And in James Scurry's captivity tale, Tippoo is the bloodthirsty criminal whose real nature is seen in acts like his pitiless murdering of Bailey's outnumbered regiment and treatment of his Christian and other minority subjects: 'Their noses, ears, and upper lips were cut off . . . [There was] a wooden horse, curiously and infernally

---

[69] Ibid. 100–1.   [70] Ibid. 112.   [71] Ibid. 123.
[72] Ibid. 313–14.
[73] Major Dirom, *A Narrative of the Campaign in India* (London: W. Bulmer, 1793), 33–4.

contrived, on the saddle of which were nine rows of sharp spikes
. . . as soon as the culprit mounted, the horse . . . would rear on its
hind legs . . . the spikes would enter the posterior of the riders.'[74]

These contradictory representations of Tippoo were what
Meadows Taylor drew on while writing his second novel. Although
belonging firmly to the period of paramountcy and new policing,
this novel (like his first) preserved rather than resolved the tension
found in the earlier non-fictional narratives. The propaganda of
British justice is made problematic through the Indian hero,
Kaseem Ali. Like the Thug Ameer Ali, Kaseem's defining action is
the betrayal of his community by showing the advancing colonial
army a secret entrance to Tippoo's fortress at Srirangapatnam. The
novel can thus raise questions about the moral dimension of colonialist military venture by showing British victory as being contingent upon the profoundly immoral action of betrayal. If the war
against Tippoo is a justified attempt to bring a criminal to justice,
why does it need an act like that of Kaseem to defeat and capture
him? Nor is this the only betrayal of Kaseem. An essential plot
ingredient of the novel is the romance between Kaseem and
Ameena, whom he succeeds in marrying against overwhelming
odds. But this feat, like his martial exploits, is only possible
through betrayal. For Ameena is the wife of his benefactor, the old
Khan, under whom he serves in Tippoo's army. Kaseem himself
realizes this in the beginning: 'This passion is nothing short of criminal; and shall the son of Noor-ud-Deen . . . disgrace his home by
treachery with whom he hath exercised hospitality? . . . better that
I should perish than hold such thought.'[75]

Yet Kaseem can only emerge as the 'good native' in the novel
precisely by indulging in this criminal passion and treachery, and his
reward at the hands of the British authorities in the end suggests that
the moral rhetoric of colonialism is merely a disguise for greed and
ambition. To Tippoo, in whose service he gains his reputation as a
fighter, Kaseem swears undying loyalty. And yet, immediately after
this he enters the service of the British expedition force and leads the
assault on Srirangapatnam. Thus, his boastful declaration to his new
masters—'I have fulfilled my promise; I am faithful to the salt I eat;

[74] James Scurry, The Captivity, Sufferings and Escape of James Scurry (London:
Henry Fisher, 1824), 104, 112.
[75] Philip Meadows Taylor, Tippoo Sultaun (London: Bentley, 1840), i. 56.

thou wilt testify to that?'—can only highlight the novel's ironic portrayal of British colonialists and their loyal native creature.

This ironic treatment of the hero is also a signal of the novel's exposure of the propaganda of 'just' war against Tippoo. Instead, the sultan is seen as the aggrieved party, a victim of the conspiracy hatched by the British and his rival Indian rulers.[76] The avenging British army is far more interested in looting than in any abstract concepts like justice:

> wealth unbounded, the sack of towns . . . only awaited their coming to fall into their possession . . . Now, indeed, shone out the true spirit of many a one whom Herbert . . . had even respected hitherto; and they saw rapacity and lust possessing them, to the extinction of every moral feeling, which unbridled revelry, habitual disregard of temperance, and indulgence in excess, hurried many to their graves.[77]

In its unflinching description of the looting of the victors, the novel echoes some of the earlier narratives of the campaign.[78] After taking Srirangapatnam through Kaseem's treachery, the British troops sack the city, looting and raping on their way, and the ironical voice of the text again emerges through the contradiction between the 'official' and 'alternative' renditions of the events: 'The morning broke gloomily after that fearful day and night; for during the latter there had been appalling alarms, shots . . . violated women . . . the moderation of the English in their victory, their justice, and protection of all, is yet sung and said throughout the country by wandering minstrels.'[79]

But Taylor's problematic representation of British 'morality' is balanced by his portrayal of Tippoo as the very essence of 'oriental/Indian' criminality. The ruler is surrounded by courtiers who have sprung from the lowest of the 'criminal classes' and are identified by their pathological hatred of the foreigners.[80] The walls of his capital shout out his innate cruelty to the world, splashed as they are with gaudy paintings of British prisoners being tortured, executed, or fed to the tigers.[81] The sultan's favourite pastime is slaying calves and daubing Brahmins, who hold the animal sacred, with their blood.[82] Out on a hunt, Tippoo's murderous nature is demonstrated in his slow torture of an elephant calf

[76] Ibid. iii. 369.   [77] Ibid. ii. 7–9.   [78] Ibid. 77.
[79] Ibid. iii. 391.   [80] Ibid. i. 228–9.   [81] Ibid. ii. 116.
[82] Ibid. 292.

Instantly, it appeared to Kaseem that his eye lighted up with the same cruel expression he had once or twice noticed . . . a shudder at the cruelty of the act ran around the circle and the Hindoos present trembled at the impiety . . . it screamed with pain. Almost human was that scream . . . the human tiger, sated for that day with blood, hunted no more.[83]

Besides this pathological cruelty, Taylor's Tippoo also closely resembles the sexual deviant of the 'captivity' narratives. Taylor only hints at his pleasure in circumcising British prisoners, but his 'unnatural' love for effeminate boy dancers evokes colonialist fears of being unmanned in the colony:

Around Tippoo . . . were a number of fair and youthful creatures, whose ruddy or pale cheeks showed their origin to have been in the cold and distant climate of the west. They were all dressed sumptuously as women, they had been instructed in the arts of music and dancing. Some boys were young . . . These took pride in their gorgeous dresses and moved about to display them.[84]

Yet, in keeping with the novel's problematic tone, the criminal-ization of Tippoo is never consistent or complete. Alongside hints of his deviant sexuality, he is shown to be a good father and husband. He is capable of the noblest and loftiest sentiments of honour and displays this in his treatment of Kaseem Ali. Moreover, much like the Newgate novels, Taylor accepts the notion of predes-tination. Tippoo's defeat is seen not so much as a reformative punishment, but as the work of a destiny that had determined this particular course of history.[85] The British, like Rowland Lester in *Eugene Aram*, are no more in control of this blind force than Tippoo himself. If this plots colonialism as an unavoidable turn in India's history, it also takes away from it notions of progress, direc-tion, and civilizing process. Colonial aggression becomes yet another random factor, and its moral rhetoric of conquest and progress is shown to be empty.

The novel ends with deliberately ambiguous conclusions about Tippoo. A man whose bloodlust has motored much of the narra-tive is also seen to inspire hysterical love and devotion among his subjects: 'Tippoo could endure no more . . . unable to quell the wild tumult within him, he burst into tears . . . men embraced one

---

[83] Philip Meadows Taylor, *Tippoo Sultaun*, ii. 299–300.
[84] Ibid. iii. 110–11.   [85] Ibid. iii. 201.

another, and swore to die side by side . . . they determined to retreat upon the city, and to fight under its walls to death.'[86] The murderer of young boys is also characterized thus by the 'loyal' Kaseem Ali: 'he was a great man—such a one as Hind will never see again. He had great ambitions, wonderful ability . . . the art of leading men's hearts more than they were aware of . . . he was brave, and died like a soldier . . . a steady friend to those he loved.'[87] Taylor's novel, in its contradictory and uneven criminal-ization of Tippoo and contesting of the propaganda about British 'justice', maintained a link with the earlier historical narratives about one of the major military and political conflicts of colonial India. It is interesting to see how this in turn played upon the unease about colonialism and the rhetoric of crime that permeated Meadows Taylor's Britain. A contemporary review of the novel in fact criticized the unsympathetic treatment of Tippoo by Taylor: 'Tippoo Sultan, though not portrayed by Captain Taylor as the monster, with whom it was the fashion some fifty years ago to terrify old women and children, is yet drawn with darker shades than reality will justify.'[88] A further proof, if needed, of the deeply ambivalent nature of criminalization and colonization in nine-teenth-century Britain.

Meadows Taylor was not alone in this using of fiction to fore-ground the fissures within the dominant ideologies of the period. We have already looked at the novels of William Hockley that were written in the 1820s. He followed these up with *The Memoirs of a Brahmin* in 1843, well after colonial new policing became estab-lished in India. Like Pandurang Hari and Ameer Ali, Hockley's hero Bapoo is again used in a case of 'colonial ventriloquism', where the 'Indian' voice is used to construct a representation of the true essence of the country, which in turn appears to legitimize colonialist presence there. Bapoo declares that his memoirs, consisting of the most minute incidents of a Brahmin's life, would help form a 'just estimate' of India.[89] This, as it turns out, is a continuous criminalization of Indian politics, culture, religion, and people. The Brahmin cannot understand the British tolerance of his

---

[86] Ibid. 375.   [87] Ibid. 407.
[88] Anon., 'Review of Tippoo Sultan', *Athenaeum* (23 Jan, 1841), 73.
[89] W. Hockley, *The Memoirs of a Brahmin* (London: Newby & Boone, 1843), i. 211.

own monstrous religion. He candidly confesses his lust for gold and goes on to find this criminal impulse deeply embedded in Indian society where 'All were tyrants, all unjust, and all actuated by the same impulse . . . gain, sordid gain . . . wrung, as it might be from the hearts of the poor cultivators of the land.'[90]

The rulers of the land and the lowest of the criminal fraternity are connected through the agency of Brahmin priests. Bapoo spies on the 'special guest' of his Brahmin teachers, who turns out to be nothing less than a famous Thug.[91] The teacher acts as the go-between for the Thug and the Maratha ruler, Peshwa Bajee Rao, thereby emphasizing the criminalization of Indian politics: 'And who could surmise that the Peshwa should wish to screen, rather than execute Naroo the Thug? Pehaps, the Governor's murder was planned by the Peshwa himself, and Naroo was his agent.'[92] Bapoo himself commits a wide variety of 'vices, trick, deceits and murder' and his confession shows how this is absolutely normal for an Indian. His friends congratulate him on his successful criminal career: 'Bapoo, what Maratha would not have done as you have done? . . . you have a right to destroy your enemies in any way you possibly can.'[93]

However, like Taylor, Hockley's Indian 'confessional' is a double-edged weapon that not only produces Indians as criminals, but also their colonial rulers as sham moralists who collude with that criminality to serve their own end. From a murderous Brahmin, Bapoo becomes a member of the colonial police force without any intervening reformatory stage. Indeed, he commits even more murders in his capacity as a policeman than before, and for this he is congratulated by his British superior: 'You represent yourself as a very Shiva, the destroyer of the human race—Thugs, imposters . . . all vanish at your approach.'[94] If disciplining Thugs and other criminals through reformative imprisonment was the chief aim of colonial new policing, then this is not much in evidence in Bapoo's account. Bapoo's murders take on the legal veneer of 'executions' and 'destruction of the race', and in this, he is encouraged by his superiors. Colonial authority is consequently deprived of any moral force and instead shown to be in an opportunistic collusion with the colony it insists on criminalizing.

[90] W. Hockley, *The Memoirs of a Brahmin*, 28–9.   [91] Ibid. 17.
[92] Ibid. 71.   [93] Ibid. ii. 85.   [94] Ibid. iii. 234.

This lack of moral authority is made explicit in the novel's treatment of the 'criminal tribe' of the Bheels. The Bheel episode of the novel is a detailed reworking of the fragment found in Hockley's earlier novel *Pandurang Hari*, and may refer to an incident that left a deep impression on the author in his life as an (allegedly corrupt) British judge. Stewart Gordon has recently exposed the unsavoury side of British 'success' against this mountain tribe: 'With Bhils safely outside society as a "criminal tribe" there could be no moral restraint on attacking and burning Bhil villages, holding a clan responsible for individual robberies, and frequently sentencing them to death and transportation.'[95] It is startling to see this post-colonial historicism anticipated in a nineteenth-century novel ostensibly committed to explaining and justifying the expansion of British power over of the Bheels and other Indians. The episode begins conventionally enough with the tribe being described as 'scarcely human'.[96] Bapoo offers his service to the colonial police force, suggesting that British bravery needed tempering with Maratha cunning in order to control these 'sub-humans'. He receives this mandate from his commanding officer: 'you may shoot as many Bheels as you please . . . if you could bring this renowned chief alive to me.'[97] It is from here onwards that the novel's representation of colonial policing overtly disrupts colonialist ideology. Even as he helps to imprison hundreds of Bheels, Bapoo understands their plight: 'Yet when I considered how this race of men were bound to each other from their very infancy, that the wild, damp, jungles were to them palaces, canopied alone by the vault of heaven . . . was their home, their haven of rest where dwelt father, mother, wives and sisters.'[98] When the desperate Bheels protest against their mass confinement by taking over the prison, the local British administrator marches his army in and opens fire on the defenceless crowd to demonstrate the reality of the rule of law:

It was an awful sight . . . to see cart loads of dead bodies carried from the prison, to be interred in one large hole without the city walls, and many blamed the collector for his severity . . . As long as the collector satisfied his superiors that he had acted right, he cared not for the opinion of the bazaar . . . the whole affair was forgotten in less than seven days.[99]

[95] Stewart Gordon, 'Bhils and the Idea of a Criminal Tribe in Nineteenth-Century India', in Yang (ed.), *Crime and Criminality*, 136.
[96] Hockley, *Memoirs*, ii. 305.   [97] Ibid. ii. 24.
[98] Ibid. 10.   [99] Ibid. 14–15.

The same enlightened policing impulse is seen to be at work when the British commander thinks about setting fire to a whole jungle to burn a tribe of the Bheels to death.[100] In comparison to these civilized rulers, it is the Bheel leader Kundoo who scores all the moral points. When the British tempt one of his followers to treachery, he sends back his severed head with 'traitor' blazoned on it. The novel, instead of commenting on his barbarous nature, applauds him for his moral courage. In his leadership, he exudes a kind of paternalism absent among the colonial rulers: 'the Bheels were many of them wounded, and Kundoo was everywhere attending to his men, like a father.'[101] When, after the extermination of the Bheels, the British officer announces, 'We never execute persons without having most satisfactory proof of their guilt . . . if a link in the chain of evidence is wanting, and the crime cannot be satisfactorily brought home to the person', one suspects the level of irony in the text to be of a considerably higher degree than it at first appears to be.[102] Fittingly the text refuses to privilege Britain as a counterpoint to 'criminal India', and instead of being the site of a civilizing force it is shown to be a 'sink of misery and want, the recital of which, would almost break your heart . . . in England, you will see the rich merchant of today, a beggar tomorrow, a hopeless object of want, with perhaps a broom in his hand'.[103] The novel does not place the ruler and the ruled in an unequal relation of power as demanded by the colonialist ideology.

Though not strictly about 'Indian' criminality, the final novel discussed in this chapter explores the connection between criminalization and colonization with sufficient thoroughness to merit a closer examination. J. W. Kaye served in the Bengal Artillery, but resigned to pursue a literary career in 1841 as editor of the *Calcutta Review*. Later, he was to succeed J. S. Mill as the secretary of the Political and Secret Department of the India Office. His most influential work was to be his history of the sepoy Mutiny, which we shall look at briefly later. If this biographical information indicates Kaye's deep imbrication in the colonial power structure, his 1846 novel *Long Engagements* carries deep awareness of the problematic nature of the narratives that sought to privilege that structure. The novel begins with a staunch 'reformist' reading of the then

[100] Hockley, *Memoirs*, 25.   [101] Ibid. 134.
[102] Ibid. iii. 75.   [103] Ibid. 154

most humiliating defeat suffered by the British Indian army—in the first Afghan war. Kaye attributes this debacle to a failure of surveillant gaze: 'The political eye appears to have lost all keenness of vision, as it wilfully closed against the truth.'[104] It is this failure of the British vision that leads to a grave misunderstanding of the essential lawlessness of the Afghans: 'Do what we may, we shall never make the Afghans an orderly people, according to our English notion of order. We think a vast deal of an ordinary insurrection; they think nothing of it.'[105] The mistake, it is said, is to treat the 'savage' mountain tribes of Afghanistan like the 'effeminate' Bengali of the plains. The Afghans demand a rougher form of policing than the average Indian. This failure of colonial surveillance is also seen in the superiority of the network of native intelligence gathering: 'the native rumours always are the precursors of more certain news—and . . . these reports appear to be credited by the native bankers—and they are not bad judges of the authenticity of news.'[106] This particular representation of the war, then, is also a prescription of stronger surveillance of essentially lawless subjects, and thus firmly aligned to principles of new policing. But under the cover of this narrative, the novel soon slips in another story that neutralizes the colonialist thrust.

For example, the Afghan experience also firmly dispels the myth of the necessary triumph of the 'just' British arms over criminal Asians/Indians: 'Where was our boasted British valour this morning? . . . we have tried our strength fairly against the enemy, and the result has been most disastrous . . . the enemy have taken compassion on our weakness and the chiefs issued orders to their men not to harm the runaways.'[107] Carrington, the 'Christian knight' of the novel, exemplifies the fatal limitation of the monolithic view of Indians and other 'orientals' that the language of criminality promoted. Unable to see the Afghan as anything but a 'criminal dog', he disagrees with his senior officer when the latter suggests a more nuanced approach: 'I do not think the Affghan quite so black as it is the fashion to paint them. They are the only people in the East who know what love is . . . it is too much in our way to kick a man, and then to complain that he is not grateful. This is the way we treat the Hindoos . . . this is the way we treat

---

[104] J. W. Kaye, *Long Engagements* (London: Chapman & Hall, 1846), 19.
[105] Ibid. 38.   [106] Ibid. 98.   [107] Ibid. 119.

the Affghans.'[108] It is this 'blindness', produced as a result of the criminalization of the colonial subject, that the novel now exposes as the source of British moral weakness. Conditioned to see the Afghan only as murderous, Carrington kills a faithful servant in the act of saving his friend's life

> What had he done? What dreadful deed had he committed? . . . A weight of horror had descended upon him . . . he had murdered a devoted Affghan whilst in the act of staunching the blood which streamed from a wound . . . what so intolerable as the knowledge of the dreadful fact that he had murdered the man who had saved his life?[109]

With considerable insight, Kaye shows that the moral rhetoric of the colonialist regime essentially cleared the way for a murderous rulership. Like Carrington, British colonialism would murder countless subjects in the name of progress, after having formulated them as essentially criminal. In the novel, 'justice' takes the form of Carrington's death at the hands of an Afghan. There is no room left for the reformation of the colonial ruler, despite the promptings of his conscience.

The years from 1829 to mid-century were decades of the domination of discipline and new policing both in Britain and India. However, this domination can only be charted against the massive disruptions and contests that seem to have been the very condition of the formation of these discourses. We have taken the case of two kinds of crime fiction of this period, one with British and the other with Indian criminals, to show that the novel, despite its collaborative aspects with new policing, could also emerge as a sophisticated record of these oppositions. In novelistic fiction, one may trace the deep-seated fractures that permeated the discourses of both criminalization and colonization. Perhaps more significantly, in this fiction may emerge parallels in the construction of criminality at 'home' and 'abroad' and thus glimpses of the common investments of the ruling elites in these constructs. In doing so, these novels released, as we shall see in the next chapter, the possibility of using a figure of the 'criminal Indian' to interrogate both domestic and colonial authorities.

---

[108] Kaye, *Long Engagements*, 123–5.   [109] Ibid. 304–5.

6

Representing the Mutiny:
'Criminal' India after 1857

The rise of the 'new police' in Britain, then, had a palpable effect on the administration of India. If, at home, the improved network of surveillance resulted in the 'discovery' of a tide of criminality, the same technique was applied to represent the colony where allegedly rampant criminality could then serve to justify British presence there in the name of progress and reform. But there was no smooth transference of the technologies of rulership from Britain to India. Resistance to colonial 'new policing' arose from two sources. There was material resistance from the Indians themselves with their complex socio-political organization, and this constantly belied the ideological justifications for colonialism. But the deep contradictions within the rhetoric of crime itself proved to be a rich source of interrogating colonialism. The figure of the 'criminal Indian' arose from this confluence of a variety of contradictions and was now being increasingly used to contest both colonialist and domestic British authority.

In this chapter, we will see how the Mutiny of 1857 produced a version of Indian criminality that further problematized the myth of the British rule of law. This may seem odd, because the event is traditionally (and with good reason) seen as a fertile source in the construction of a version of 'criminal India' where all the natives were represented as variations of the stereotypical Thugs and rebels. However, once placed within the context of the shifts in ideas about crime and punishment emerging in Britain during the period, the colonial 'just retribution' (which was in reality large-scale war crimes) paradoxically threw up disturbing questions about the claims to a rule of law.

By mid-century, the success of the penal reformers seemed complete in Britain. The last relics of the Georgian criminal system were being swept away by an increasingly refined and rigorous system of 'productive punishment'.[1] Capital punishment and even corporal punishment were now seen as counter-productive, and the criminal increasingly as a victim of forces like heredity and insanity which could not be 'cured' by a blindly punitive intervention. Placed in this context, the mass hanging, shooting, and blowing up from cannons of rebels and innocent Indians alike was always likely to disturb an authority that was derived from the rhetoric of crime. The punishment meted out to Indians often raised the spectre of the 'bloody assize' that reformers claimed to have erased from Britain. As a result, the 'criminal' Indian could often be used, instead of justifying the colonialist rule, to criticize its relapse into barbarity. From there, to use the same figure to interrogate the domestic condition of Britain was a small but significant step. The retributions inflicted by military commanders like Neill on Indians would come back to haunt Britain in unforeseen ways.

Recent historiography has reread the Mutiny to expose certain fictions about 'criminal India'. Rudrangshu Mukherjee has revised the representation of the events of 1857, showing how the intricate planning of the rebels suggested the existence of a well co-ordinated decision-making body.[2] Similarly, Rajat Ray has seen the event as the major contributor to the development of the political theory of the Indian struggle for independence.[3] Describing the Mutiny as a war of religion that had political dominion at stake, Ray observes: 'the idea was not simply communal harmony, but . . . a confederation of two separate peoples tied into one political unity by the social prescription of Hindustan as one land.'[4] And while the rebels' role in the formation of a germane nationalism is not in doubt, it is perhaps also useful to remember that there were not one, but several mutinies with conflicting aims and interests.

[1] See Weiner, *Reconstructing the Criminal*, 100.
[2] Rudrangshu Mukherjee, 'The Sepoy Mutinies Revisited', in M. Hasan and N. Gupta (eds.), *India's Colonial Encounters* (New Delhi: Manohar, 1993), 123.
[3] Rajat Kanta Ray, 'Race, Religion and Realm: The Political Theory of the "Reigning Indian Crusade", 1857', ibid.
[4] Ibid. 134. Ray shows how the Islamic word for faith, 'deen', was adopted as the battle cry for rebels both Hindu and Muslim, and 'what the Congress leaders later called the "Indian nation", the rebel leaders already spoke distinctly as the Hindus and Mussalmans of Hindustan'. See 139.

Ranajit Guha's study of peasant insurgency in colonial India shows how 1857 also unleashed popular rebellions against the elite triad of the 'Sarkar (government), Sahukar (native money-lender) and Zamindar (native land owner)'.[5] Moreover, if, as Gatrell reminds us, the history of crime is of 'how elites used selected law-breakers to sanction their own authority', then one of the central problems of colonialist attempts to legitimize the British actions after the Mutiny also becomes clear.[6] The year 1857 produced not only the 'rebel hordes', but also a vast majority of loyal and elite Indians whose strong identification with colonial interests made it difficult to represent them as criminals deserving the retributions of Neill and Havelock. Some 'liberal' British accounts, while refusing to question the basis of colonialism, tried to oppose the hard-line calls (like that of Charles Dickens) to exterminate the whole 'criminal' population of India, and did so from this awareness of 'loyal' India. The Mutiny's paradoxical foregrounding of both 'criminal' and 'loyal' India was one of the important factors that led to the fracturing of the rhetoric of colonialism and criminalization after 1857.

Another important consequence of Guha's work has been to expose the basic economic paradox of colonialism and the implications for its cultural life. Noticing the weakness of capitalist development in Indian agriculture before 1900, Guha explains that the extraction of the peasant's surplus was determined less by the free play of the market than by the extra-economic forces of a semi-feudal social structure maintained by the British. For Guha, this was the central paradox of the Raj: 'to assign to the most advanced capitalist power in the world the task of fusing feudal landlordism and usury in India so well as to impede the development of capitalism both in agriculture and in industry.'[7] In a colony as overwhelmingly agricultural as nineteenth-century India, this economic paradox was one factor that contributed to the 'fracturing' of the ideology of colonialism. Rising out of, and geared to function in a relatively advanced capitalist economy, the technology of criminalization stumbled in India where the colonialist regime relied more on feudal structures no longer politically relevant in Britain. The

---

[5] Ranajit Guha, *Elementary Aspects of Peasant Insurgency in Colonial India* (New Delhi: Oxford University Press, 1983), 27.

[6] V. A. C. Gatrell, 'Crime, Authority and the Policeman State', in F .M. L. Thompson (ed.), *The Cambridge Social History of Britain* (Cambridge: Cambridge University Press, 1990), iii. 245.   [7] Guha, *Elementary Aspects*, 8.

whole thrust of the police reformation in Britain had been on the *replacement* of a system that served agrarian interests. But in India, this technique was given the task of producing authority for a regime whose political organization, paradoxically, was fundamentally opposed to the tactics of reform. Hence, British officials frequently complained that the 'orientals' only understood the feudal display of power, not its subtle bureaucratic forms. On the other hand, their representation of India was relentlessly bound to the language of reform, punishment, and progress. The representation of 'criminal India' was caught between this split generated by the very nature of the colonial contact. Frequently, Indians would be seen simultaneously as 'natural criminals' who only merited capital punishment *and* as candidates for reform through the enlightened policing of the colonial regime. In a time of an acute crisis of legitimacy like 1857, this fracture in the vital instrument of rulership could become the site of the radical questioning of authority both at 'home' and the colony. A little later, we will look at the contemporary debates about criminality that provided the context for these contradictions within the colony. Here, we will look at the other major source that rendered the figure of the 'criminal Indian' problematic from mid-century onwards—the British responses to the trauma of the Mutiny.

One obvious response to the Mutiny, and one often stereotyped as the only kind of response, was the hysterical call for revenge. In the 'revenge' narratives, all rebels were murderous criminals meriting the death penalty, and all Indians were, to varying degrees, rebels or criminals. Thus, the massacres conducted by Generals Neill, Renaud, and Havelock could be represented as 'terrible, but just retribution'. The Church often took a lead in the making of this figure of the murderous Indian. In sermons strongly flavoured with the titillation of violence and violation, Victorian churchmen sought to invest British atrocities in India with legal and moral authority:

These tender, gentle, unoffending mothers, tortured with a torment worse a thousand times than death!—these little bright children, torn to fragments, the flesh forced into the mother's and father's mouths ... these little feet with little socks and shoes, cut off by the ankle with a tulwar!— that English gentleman nailed to the ground by his hands, feet and knees— the barbarians one day cutting off ears, nose and feet, and the next day other pieces. ... India was one of the dark places of the earth and the cruelest of cruel habitations. The head was indeed educated, but there was no power to elevate the heart.[8]

Still, in a culture increasingly averse to public executions, the Church often struggled to accommodate the mass murders inflicted on Indians within the language of 'justice'. Thus, the Reverend Francis Gordon admitted that far from being interested in teaching any moral lessons to the Indians, it was sheer vindictiveness that fired the zeal for punishing the rebels.[9] Because they came up against accepted notions of punishment that favoured the 'productive' and discrete punishment over 'spectacular' death penalties, the attempts to construct a legal and moral defence of British massacres in India could not be unproblematic. Even in the Church propaganda, opposing voices like that of James Charles could trace the source of the Mutiny to the essence of the colonial rule in India: 'One case may be found in the crimes and aggressions, the deeds of spoliation, butchery, lust . . . the unscrupulous and unblushing violation of law . . . which ushered in the establishment of British rule in India . . . The wholesale injustice, the extortion, robbery, and rapine, the cruel oppression of the native.'[10] There were even debates about the extent to which the Indians themselves were the victims of a 'criminal' British tyranny.

Like the church sermons, the historical accounts of the Mutiny demonstrated the paradox inherent in colonialist representations. Some eyewitness accounts contributed to the building of official British propaganda about the Mutiny. Henry Metcalf proudly recorded how he beat up a 'very consequential sort of native' who protested at his defacing of a Hindu temple—'I let him have a straight one from the shoulder . . . I repeated the dose several times,

[8] Revd John Baillie, 'God's Avenger,' in *Fast Day Sermons* (London: Joseph Masters, 1857), 7. These sermons can be used as an index to the paranoia of the British ruling classes. Edward Bickerstem preached that the Mutiny was divine punishment for the lack of piety of the 'masses of labourers and mechanics' in Britain. In making the British working classes responsible for the Mutiny, the preacher intuitively evoked the technique of criminalization that linked the domestic subalterns to their colonial counterparts as being dangerously opposed to 'progress'. See Edward Bickerstem, 'A Sermon', ibid. 16.

[9] Admitting that he spoke against the 'current phraseology', Gordon argued that 'all punishment . . . no matter what ulterior good consequences may be looked forward to by the inflictor, is in its primary ground and essential nature vindictive': Revd Francis Gordon, 'Vengeance Right and Holy', ibid. 19.

[10] James Charles, 'The Lord's Voice to Britain from the Far East', ibid. 10.

we left Mr. Native not in a very enviable position.'[11] It is not so much the soldier's gloating over the beating up of an Indian civilian that catches the eye, but the verdict that his was a just action by the 'impartial' military court that tried him.[12] Once British propaganda had succeeded in locating the source of the Mutiny in the treacherous heart of 'every native', all Indians were fair game in the pursuit of 'just' vengeance. Fred Roberts recorded how he took part in an expeditionary force with orders 'to slay every man unless the ringleaders were given up'.[13] In a series of letters, Roberts described British looting and massacres in Lucknow as a 'very necessary punishment', adding that the sight of old women and little children leaving their burnt houses made him melancholic. But above all, he insisted on punishing Indians whom he thought had been spoilt by soft British administrators and enthused at the prospect of taking charge of a 'bad district' to 'break them in'.[14]

Not only was capital punishment prescribed for the mutineers, but the colonial lawgivers also seemed to prefer the kind of violent, public, and spectacular executions that had been the very target of reforms in Britain. F. C. Maude's account of a typical execution of a rebel exemplified the reason for the liberal opposition to such punishments—that it generated a counter-productive sympathy for those being punished. In Maude's detailed description, the hitherto dehumanized rebel is converted into a brave human being:

> The young sepoy looked undaunted at us during the whole process of pinioning; indeed, he never flinched for a moment . . . we saw two legs lying in front of the gun; but no other sign of what had been a human being and a brave man . . . I became aware that I was covered, from head to foot, with minute blackened particles of man's flesh.[15]

As soon as this rhetorical transformation occurs, the possibility of securing legitimacy for a regime that meted out this kind of punishment becomes problematic.

---

[11] Henry Metcalf, *The Chronicle of Private Henry Metcalf* (1858; repr. London: Cassell, 1953), 20.

[12] Indeed, in Metcalf's account of the Lucknow campaign, the criminals can hardly be called human: 'you would have thought, with Shakespeare, that hell had become uninhabited and that all the demons were transferred to Lucknow.' Ibid. 31.

[13] Fred Roberts, *Letters Written during the Indian Mutiny* (London: Macmillan, 1924), 12. [14] Ibid. 75.

[15] F. C. Maude, *Memoirs of the Mutiny* (London: Remington, 1894), i. 276-7.

Maude realized as much when he admitted that during the course of the retributions 'a good many innocent natives may have been put to death by us'. His account of the events questioned each crucial component of the colonialist propaganda about the Mutiny. The mutineers emerge not as a cowardly and criminal rabble, but as often skilful, always brave and determined men fighting against superior firepower and resources.[16] General Neill, so often written into colonialist history as the Christian hero, is exposed as a ruthless and murderous commander who derived pleasure from mass executions.[17] Even the guilt of that most demonized of all the rebels, Nana Sahib of Kanpur, dubbed the beast of Bithoor, was questioned by Maude: 'one must doubt whether the Nana Sahib was as guilty of complicity in the murders of our women and children as he is generally believed to have been.'[18] Fittingly then, Maude's account of the Mutiny does not climax with the tale of Indian criminality brought to justice, but with an anecdote that implies the reverse. Recalling the murder of a Major Neill in England by an Indian soldier called Mazhar Ali decades after the Mutiny, Maud explains:

Major Neill was a son of General Neill, and that Sowar Mazhar Ali, who shot him, was a son of Suffar Ali, who was unjustly accused of having murdered General Wheeler . . . and was hanged after having been flogged by sweepers and made to lick up a spot of the blood-stained floor of the slaughter house of Cawnpore.[19]

This transformation of the figure of 'criminal' Indian into that of a victim and, eventually, of the avenger was one of the most dramatic results of the employment of the language of crime in the context of empire.

Several other British histories of the Mutiny produced in the latter decades of the nineteenth century displayed profound unease about the punishment of 'criminal India'.[20] The most influential of

---

[16] Ibid. 63.

[17] Tales of his heroic military performances, like the famously rapid forced marches, were now demythified in accounts that revealed how he yoked Indian farmers to transport carriages to achieve such logistical miracles. See ibid. 81.

[18] Ibid. 108.   [19] Ibid. 70.

[20] Maude's history was written decades after the Mutiny. Other military memoirs closer to the event could, of course, be more unquestioning in their employment of the rhetoric of crime. Captain M. Thomson, for example, laid the whole blame of the Kanpur massacre on the 'subtle, intriguing . . . unscrupulous and blood-thirsty'

these 'liberal' accounts of the Mutiny attempted to preserve the myths of progress by acknowledging the excesses committed by the rulers. By balancing the descriptions of the plight of the Indian people under the 'tyranny of sepoys' with those of the gross failings of the British, what these histories hoped to do was to reinscribe colonial presence in post-Mutiny India as an enlightened authority willing to acknowledge its past excesses in order to proceed with the task of civilization. But as this narrative strategy hinged on at least a revision of the figure of the 'criminal' Indian and criticism of colonial punishment, the extent of its interrogation of the legitimacy of colonial authority could also be significant.

G. O. Trevelyan's retelling of the story of the alleged massacre of British civilians at Kanpur is a good example of this. Although he described the events there as a crime greater than 'Sicilian vespers, or September massacres', he attributed the tragedy to the brutalization of the Indians under colonial administration rather than proposing any theories of 'natural' Indian depravity.[21] Trevelyan concluded that one of the chief causes of the Mutiny was the callous racism of the rulers who delighted in stigmatizing the natives of India as hypocrites and infidels.[22] He dismissed the atrocity rumours as propaganda which served to justify British war crimes. In this kind of historical narrative, it was the colonialist retribution that emerged as crimes and the Indians as the victims:

Our proverbial tendency to give a dog a bad name and hang him was most barbarously and literally exemplified in the case of the unfortunate Muslim. After the capture of Delhi, every member of a class of religious enthusiasts were hung . . . more than one individual whose guilt consisted in looking as if he belonged to a sect which was hostile to our religion. It would have been equally humane and logical if the ministers of Queen Elizabeth had burned as a Jesuit every one who was bald on the crown of his head.[23]

Azimoolah Khan, Nana Sahib's chief adviser. Special hostility was reserved for this figure because he was a highly accomplished diplomat who pleaded Nana's case in London and had been very popular in the fashionable circles there. But even in this hostile account, Thomson's attempt to reduce Indians to the 'type' of Azimoolah was hardly complete, as he was forced to admit 'noble' actions of the sepoys, such as their frequent escorting of their officers to safety after the declaration of rebellion, which provided a strong contrast to the British conduct towards their prisoners of war. See M. Thomson, *The Story of Cawnpore* (London: Bentley, 1859), esp. 57–9.

[21] G. O. Trevelyan, *Cawnpore* (London: Macmillan, 1865), 47–8.
[22] Ibid. 29.   [23] Ibid. 57.

For Trevelyan, the Mutiny had brought to the surface a character-
istic feature of the rulers that, for him, had hitherto lurked unsus-
pected. What Joseph Conrad was to immortalize as the 'heart of
darkness' later on in the century was already foreshadowed in this
history of the Mutiny—the regression of the white ruler into a
savagery and atavism normally ascribed to the subject races.
Trevelyan's indictment of British conduct was an example of how
the rhetoric of crime could be used, although without challenging
the racist basis of colonialism, to turn the tables on those who
armed themselves with the power to commit murder in the name of
law: 'After the first outbreak of joy and welcome, the inhabitants
of Cawnpore began to be aware that the English were no longer the
same men, indeed, if they were men at all . . . of what took place
the less said is the better . . . for a parallel to such an episode we
must explore far back into the depths of time.'[24]

The opposition to colonialist justice outlined in these histories
written after the Mutiny was no doubt influenced by the contemporary debates about crime and punishment.[25] But there were also
other accounts written during the heated atmosphere of 1857–8 that
rigorously exposed the British legal and moral claims as spurious.

---

[24] Ibid. 355–7. Another good example of this oppositional historiography was
Kaye's account of the events. Like Trevelyan, he found the seeds of the Mutiny in
the racist excesses committed by paragons of British manhood like Lord Dalhousie,
whose greed, cruelty, and bigotry he saw as indivisible from his nobler attributes.
Kaye illustrated this with accounts of colonial tyranny like the injustice suffered by
the Rani of Jhansi, and a ringing indictment of British punishments: 'Our military
officers were hunting down criminals of all kinds, and hanging them with as little
compunction as though they had been pariah dogs . . . young boys, who perhaps in
mere sport had flaunted rebel colours and gone about beating tom-toms were tried
and sentenced to death . . . volunteer hanging parties went out into the districts, and
amateur executioners were not wanting for the occasion.' See J. W. Kaye, *A History
of the Sepoy War* (London: Chapman & Hall, 1876), ii. 236. Among his most effective revisions of the official narratives of the retributions was the description of
Captain Hodson's murder of the Mughal princes as a 'game of royal hunting', thus
laying to rest the myth about the officer's bravery and sense of justice. See ibid. iii.
652.

[25] The entanglement of the debates about crime and accounts of the Mutiny
could frequently be seen in journals such as *Fraser's Magazine*. If Kaye and
Trevelyan incorporated the arguments against capital punishment in their histories,
an article on capital punishment in 1864 could contradict this by drawing on the
Mutiny to enlist support for it: 'Ought capital punishment to be inflicted for any
crime whatever . . . we think it ought . . . the mutineers no doubt, thought themselves in the right; yet the tremendous vigour with which they were punished effec-
tually put them down. By executing every man taken in arms, a lesson was read to
them which as long as India is India will never be forgotten.' See 69 (1864), 754.

Some of these, like the diary of the *Times* correspondent W. H. Russell who went to India specifically to investigate the atrocity rumours, were categorically opposed to the colonial regime. Russell set Kanpur in context by saying that the only unique thing about the massacre was that it was committed by a subject race.[26] He exposed how the anecdotes of the atrocities (like the supposed scrawlings of the victims on the walls of the slaughter house) were fabricated. He faithfully recorded General Neill's hangings and the massacre committed by British troops, giving them a startling immediacy in anecdotes like this: 'A Kashmir boy came towards the post, leading a blind and aged man, and throwing himself at the feet of an officer, asked for protection. That officer . . . drew his revolver and snapped at the wretched suppliant's head . . . The boy's lifeblood flooded at his feet, amid indignation and outcries of his men.'[27] Russell correctly pointed out that it was the despotic nature of colonialism that enabled the British to get away with tortures like sewing Muslims in pig skins before burning them and forcing Hindus to defile themselves before execution, as 'legal' punishments. He concluded that not only the suppression of the Mutiny, but the very basis of British rule in India had nothing to do with morality and legality. He was able to see that law was merely an instrument of the brutal and exploitative nature of the occupation:

That force is the base of our rule I have no doubt; for I have seen nothing else but force employed in our relations with the governed . . . as the great instructor of the people, the exponent of our superior morality and civilisation—does it (the government) observe treaties, show itself moderate, and just and regardless of gain? Are not our courts of law condemned by ourselves? Are they not admitted to be a curse and blight upon the country? In effect, the grave, unhappy doubt which settles on my mind is, whether India is the better for our rule.[28]

[26] W. H. Russell, *My Indian Mutiny Diary* (1858–9; repr. London: Cassell, 1957), 29.   [27] Ibid. 110.
[28] Ibid. 7. Russell's was not an eccentric voice on the conduct of the supposed lawgivers in the colony. Memoirs of eminent people like Sir George Campbell bore out his investigations about Neill's massacres: 'Neill . . . seems to have affected a religious call to blood . . . If these people had been really guilty of massacre, it would have been disgusting enough, but Neill himself does not say that they were found guilty of the murders . . . when we know how these things were done, we may well doubt if there was any proof of that.' See ibid. p. xvii.

Russell's disturbing conclusions about the nature of colonial rule found a worthy analytical companion in the writings of the Chartist Ernest Jones. His experiences of the brutalities of domestic British authority helped Jones to formulate a perceptive account of the activities of that authority abroad. In a series of articles published mainly in the *People's Paper* in 1857–8, he developed a history of the Mutiny that opposed the official stereotyping of the event in every detail. Like Trevelyan, he attributed the sepoy atrocities to their brutalization in the British colonial army.[29] His thorough reporting exposed the reality of the colonial civilising mission. He contrasted the £53,000 spent on the East India Company directors' dinner ('a greedy race of harpies') with the £3,000 spent to educate twenty-two million people in the Madras presidency where there was not a single government school in 140,000 square miles. And with admirable courage, he invited his readers to participate in what he called India's national war *against* Britain:

There ought to be but one opinion throughout Europe on the revolt of Hindostan. It is one of the most just, noble and necessary ever attempted in the history of the world . . . the Pole, the Hungarian, the Italian still own their own soil. The Hindoo does not . . . Naples and France, Lombardy and Poland, Hungary and Rome, present no tyranny so hideous as that erected by the miscreants of the Leadenhall Street in Hindostan.[30]

But one did not have to be a former Chartist to arrive at similar conclusions about the nature of colonialism. Four years before the Mutiny, John Cupper had already analysed the myth of the 'just' rule thus:

and to compare their life as infinitely more tranquil and free from the calamities of war, than during the rule of Mahommedan dynasties! As well might they boast of the safety and security of the poor captives pining away their existence in the dungeons of the inquisition . . . Take away the power of resistance, paralyse his energies, sweep beyond his reach everything that can make life worthy of a man and though he be told he enjoys the privilege of being the subject of the most honoured and powerful sovereign in the world, I fear he cannot be made to appreciate the wonderful change.[31]

---

[29] Ernest Jones, 'England's Rule in India and the Cry for Vengeance', in *Ernest Jones: Chartist*, ed. John Saville (London: Lawrence & Wishart, 1952), 221.
[30] Ernest Jones, 'The Indian Struggle', ibid. 219.
[31] Quoted in Russell *Diary*, p. xxiii.

British non-fictional accounts of the Mutiny, then, could often turn the project of criminalizing Indians on its head by discovering atrocities committed by the colonial rulers on a scale which disturbed the fiction of progress and justice. As the 1860s progressed, the fictional accounts of the Mutiny recast this questioning of British authority found in the non-fictional accounts in a more popular form.

MEADOWS TAYLOR AND OTHER NOVELISTS OF THE MUTINY

Like their non-fictional counterparts, novels presented a wide range in their response to the Mutiny. Some, like the anonymously written *Childhood in India*, were aligned to historical narratives like Metcalf's, apparently promoting the same colonialist myths with a different narrative tool. There were others like George Lawrence's *Maurice Dering*, and Meadows Taylor's *Seeta*, that questioned that version of 'criminal India' and struggled to restore the idea of enlightened colonialist rule and its future in India. And finally, there were those like Meadows Taylor's *Ralph Darnell* and Wilkie Collins's *The Moonstone* that dealt with a particular product of the Mutiny—the 'criminal Indian'—and not the event itself, in order to constitute searching questions about the British domestic and colonial authorities.

Even those novels that were apparently engaged in constructing a simple tale of British 'just victory' over the rebels usually managed to distance themselves from the puerile rhetoric of 'divine' justice that dressed up the murderous assaults of Neill and Hodson. *Childhood in India*, for instance, was about the adventures and survival of two British children caught up in the 'devil's wind' of 1857. The India that the children see as they grow up is in equal measures bestial and criminal. There is little to distinguish the actual human beings from the large monkeys that throng the town. When the children are not learning about the threat of bestial India, they are amused with the tales of Major and Mrs Gordon who wake up one morning to find everything in their house, including the clothes they were wearing, stolen by thieves.[32]

---

[32] See 'The Wife of an Officer', in *Childhood in India* (London: Jackson, Walford & Hodder, 1865), 22, 52.

But the Mutiny upsets this bestial/criminal schematization of the colony. Engaged in the task of reviving the myth of progress and reform under the queen's authority, the novel now tells the story of loyal Indians and their bond with the masters that had been all but severed in the aftermath of the retributions. When the children's father rescues Ghulab, the son of his native servant, from drowning, he is rewarded with the eternal native gratitude and servility that was the stuff of colonialist fantasy. This loyalty is shown to course through native veins and when the mutineers attack the town little Ghulab's only thought is of the children: 'He remembered that his little master and mistress were going to the Tamarind Tope . . . he must meet them and prevent their return to the station, thus only could he save their lives.'[33]

The novel's distance from the retributive frenzy may be measured by its advocacy of the paternalist bonding, indeed almost fusion, between the British and Indians. This was very different from the popular British racism during the Mutiny as recorded by Kaye: 'the very sight of a dark man stimulated our national enthusiasm to the point of frenzy. We tolerated those who wore our uniforms, but all else were the enemies and persecutors of our race.'[34] Indeed, not only do the children discover that Indians out of uniform can be good, but in order to survive, they must temporarily go native in the most complete way possible and disguise themselves as Indians living in a village with their nurse. Not only racial but gender identities are temporarily blurred as Robert is dressed up as a little native girl, hiding from the rebels under the purdah (veil). The unmanning of the British male that was so often a part of colonialist fears of going native is here treated as a ritual vital to the reconstruction of the myth of harmony between the races.

Ranged against the loyal natives and their masters are the sepoys, and religious fanatics like the Fakeer. The novel reaches its climax when the mutineers appear in the nurse's village and demand the surrender of the children. At this juncture, the story departs from yet another stereotypical Mutiny formula—the rescue of the innocents by the gallant British forces. Instead, the demonic rebels themselves are suddenly transformed into loyal human beings who can no longer see the British as enemies of their race.

33 Ibid. 65–70.   34 Kaye, *History*, iii. 636.

This magical transformation is ushered in by the loving and forgiving words of Robert: 'All that was hard and cruel in the man's heart melted away at the resting words of the innocent child. He ... would have been a ruthless savage who had harmed the fair, sick child who trusted him.'[35] In its contention that the 'criminal' Indian could be reformed, not by the gun, but by the loving trust of the masters, the novel distanced itself from the jingoism of 1857, and cast doubts on the entire validity of punishing the 'rebel' Indians.

By contrast, H. P. Malet's *Lost Links of the Indian Mutiny* cannot be said to have been concerned with producing the comforting vision of loyal Indians. At the same time, however, it attempted to explore the extent of the Indian grievances by giving prominence to the rebel leader Hoosain, whose contrasting of Britain's anti-slavery zeal with its oppression of India challenged the notion of 'just' white rule. The novel begins with the stereotypical tracing of the origins of the Mutiny among the Thugs and other Indian criminals. Chapters with titles like 'How the Natives of India eat up one another' seemingly attempt to show the full range of the secret rapacity of Indian society.[36] Against this grim backdrop, the British administrators stand out for their commitment to justice and courage. Ideal colonial administrators like the anonymous 'young Englishman' are shown single-handedly to transform 'criminals' like the Bheel tribe into a loyal body by hunting with them and showing: 'There could be no use in opposing one who would as soon face the tiger as the hare—whose horse could catch the buffalo ... who could do everything. ... Where anarchy and crime had been, he found the people contented ... the chaos, which had existed only a few short years before had gone.'[37] Malet implies that any rebellion against this noble rule must be both futile and criminal.

But against this grain of the narrative lie Hoosain's experiences as a 'coolie', press-ganged as a slave labourer in overseas colonies like Jamaica and East Africa. It is in Jamaica that Hoosain is introduced to the idea of rebelling against colonial masters. His teacher in the 'dark art of Mutiny' is a 'diabolic African' ex-slave, seemingly

[35] *Childhood in India*, 127.
[36] H. P. Malet, *Lost Links of the Indian Mutiny* (London: T. Cauley & Newby, 1867), 19–21.   [37] Ibid. 50.

well suited to exploit Hoosain's already corrupt nature. By bringing these two figures together, the Indian Mutiny is 'linked' to both
the 1831 slave rebellion in Jamaica, as well as the 1864/5 rebellion
made infamous by the massacres carried out by the British governor, Eyre. Hoosain's African teacher becomes the cipher of all
other 'criminal natives' who rebelled against British authority: 'his
favourite theme was the destruction of property upon which he had
been employed as a child, where he had nothing to complain of but
too much love and kindness.'[38] But juxtaposed to this relentless
criminalization of colonies is a counter-narrative that calls into
question the validity of designating rebel Indians as criminals. This
is achieved mainly by allotting a nationalist consciousness to
Hoosain, as seen, for instance, in his vivid description of the
destructive effects of colonialism:

> The venom spreads over the system, like the poison of the cobra . . . till the
> whole body becomes dormant, insensitive to its sufferings . . . so shall we
> die, my friends; burden after burden is placed upon us, we are covered
> with ignominy; the caste of the Hindoos are laughed at, the religion of the
> Mahomedan is scorned; our women are defiled and all of us called
> niggers.[39]

Hoosain's African teacher shows him how freedom could be won
through a violent struggle that had now brought 'ease, indolence
and plenty' to all who were slaves before.[40] Although his revolutionary aspirations apparently stand condemned by their origins in
the 'criminal' slave rebellion of Jamaica and his own past, the
novel's admiration for Hoosain's nationalist sentiment and the
exposure of the British hypocrisy about the slave trade challenge its
own cover story of colonial crime and justice.

Malet suggests that all colonialist acts, even apparently progressive ones like the British abolitionist movement, arise from self-
interest.[41] Thus, even as it condemned the African slave trade,
Britain summarily displaced and enslaved thousands of its Asian
colonial subjects and transported them as labourers to other parts
of the empire. The novel deliberately evokes memories of the infamous Atlantic 'middle passage' in its description of the voyage of
Hoosain and other Indian 'coolies' to Jamaica. The so-called liber-
ators of African slaves are shown to practise a system of surrogate

---

[38] Ibid. 109.   [39] Ibid. 184–5.   [40] Ibid. 270.
[41] Ibid. 98–100.

slavery. This considerably reduces the British empire's claims of being a force of morality and rule of law. As a result, despite its criminal lineage, the Mutiny can now be portrayed as a genuine, if misguided, attempt of the Indians to redress the wrongs suffered by them. The novel ends with the rebellious sepoys breaking open the jails and letting hardened criminals loose, from whom they soon become indistinguishable. There is a tinge of heroic defeat about Hoosain, who has laboured throughout to turn the rebels into a respectable and disciplined body: 'His worst fears were realised; zeal and order were confounded, like the confused waves of a troubled sea . . . wickedness overthrew order . . . His arguments were all lost; his title did not impose on the furious Hydra.'[42] Although the novel appears to propose that the lost link of the Indian Mutiny could be found in similar mutinies in the Caribbean, it also hints that what was 'lost' may well have been a genuine attempt to protest against the sham morality and legality of British colonialism.

One of the chief aims of the atrocity rumours of the Mutiny was to empower the colonialist masculine subjectivity that was always threatened with being unmanned.[43] In the colony, this could work on various levels. The industrial progress of nineteenth-century Britain brought with it the challenge of a proto-feminist consciousness, often figured as the spectre of the unnatural, strong (later, 'new') woman. British 'manhood' often had to turn to the solace of a colony like India to reaffirm its own dominant status. India, with its paradoxical mixture of underdeveloped capitalism and semi-feudal agrarian economy, did not allow the mobilization of the British women as a viable economic or political group. There, the women could still be defined within the domesticated boundaries of wives and mothers. On the other hand, the colony's social complexities could often pose their own special threat to this masculinist identity. The British hero could easily be unmanned by his encounters with the exotic threat of the 'oriental' sexual codes, as the captivity narratives we saw in the last chapter show. Also, the relatively porous social boundaries could enable a subversive assertion of the 'Memsahib's' sexuality. An event like the Mutiny

---

[42] H. P. Malet, *Lost Links of the Indian Mutiny*, 304–5.
[43] See Nancy Paxton, 'Mobilizing Chivalry: Rape in the British Novels about the Indian Uprising of 1857', *Victorian Studies*, 36 (1992), 5–30.

could then provide an opportunity to contain these various threats to British masculinity by deploying strategies of male chivalry and gallantry. The lurid rumours of rape, carefully fabricated and exaggerated to satisfy the masculine desire to see 'their' women violently possessed and subjugated, contained a moral against any alliance between the domestic and colonial subalterns. At the same time, these provided the perfect opportunity to restate the macho credentials of the British man abroad, always ready to sacrifice himself to save the embattled women from the demonic colonial masses. The tale of rescue and revenge could be conflated to empower the political and sexual prowess of the master gender/race.

George Lawrence's novel *Maurice Dering* (1864) implemented this strategy of empowering British masculinist nationalism, but, at the same time, raised questions about its legal and moral investments. From the very beginning, the hero is presented as the essence of the Anglo-Saxon male. His bright eyes and firm hand-clasp are meant to convey that he is a 'thoroughly genuine and real man'.[44] Paradoxically, it is precisely his masculinity that jeopardizes the harmony of 'domestic' Britain by raising forbidden desires in the fiancée of his best friend, Phillip Gascoigne. Dering's moral fibre has already been deemed sufficiently worthy in episodes such as the whipping of insolent servants: 'Chastisement proper, or juridical, not erring on the side of mercy, nor yet degenerating into brutality; where every blow descends with the deliberate emphasis of scientific strength.'[45] Armed with this proper physical and moral prowess, Dering meets this temptation with a noble rejection and a departure for India.

But it is in India that more unease about Dering's manliness emerges. Like many other novels about the taming of colonial spaces in India and Africa, hunting operates in the novel as a metaphor of the white male's supremacy over the bestiality of the benighted spaces of the world. Indeed, Maurice is shown to practise the slaughter of 'native animals' to instil perfect discipline on his 'inner self'.[46] However, his unease in the pursuit of this noble aim is suggested by his succumbing to a 'feminine' emotional outburst after one such hunting expedition where he kills a bear

[44] George Lawrence, *Maurice Dering*, 3 vols. (London: Timely Brothers, 1864), i. 22.   [45] Ibid. 134.   [46] Ibid. ii. 13.

cub and watches its mother mourn over it.[47] In the excessively sentimental description of these victims of Dering's disciplining effort, the novel creates an ambiguity about the manly morals it has seemingly been privileging. It hints at an iconic linking of all Dering's victims in the novel, his servants, rival in love, and, ultimately, the unarmed Indians he massacres later, to undermine the moral authority built on the basis of these acts.

The victim of Dering's next bout of punishment is Gerald Annesleigh, whom he finds, during his brief return to England, on the verge of seducing the very woman he had rejected in the name of honour. With such a subversion of the domestic order looming, Dering decides he has to temper 'written law' with the 'light of nature' and punish the seducer with death. He accordingly fabricates an insult, challenges Annesleigh to an illegal duel, and kills him. But this apparently 'honourable' punishment is shown to be little more than murder, as Dering himself confesses: 'to keep her innocent, I have taken your blood on my head . . . it cruelly looks like murder now.'[48] Instead of condoning these attempts to save the domestic stability and suppress 'deviant' female sexuality, the novel covertly conflates masculinist authority and honour with crime.

This subversive presentation of the violent authority of the Anglo-Saxon male climaxes in the questioning of the British retribution during the Mutiny. Like the rest of his punishments, Dering's massacre of the Indians is shown to be murderous and devoid of any legitimacy. His response to the rumour of the death of his wife in fact serves to undermine the official narratives of 'just revenge'. On hearing that his wife has been killed in the uprising, Dering expresses relief for the fact that she has died before being 'sullied' by the natives. The novel then vividly describes his systematic murder of surrendering unarmed rebels. The language of one particular passage deliberately evokes the comparison with the massacres at Kanpur:

This carnage was worse a thousand-fold; for it was wrought in a close, darkened slaughterhouse. Every now and then one of the executioners came staggering out into the open air—drunk and feint [*sic*] with the scent of blood. And Dering stood by—with that dark pitiless look on his face whereof we have before spoken.[49]

---

[47] George Lawrence, *Maurice Dering*, 17–19.
[48] Ibid. 135–6.   [49] Ibid. 242.

Although the novel apparently ascribes the moral failure in the British hero to the pressure of protecting the women—from seducers, from native violators, and, most importantly, from themselves—the confessions of Dering about the 'criminality' of his acts question the official interpretation of 1857.[50] Colonialist propaganda derived the moral and legal claims for its civilizing mission by showing how 'real' Anglo-Saxon men protected society by their firm control of both domestic and colonial subalterns. But by covertly exposing the very real violence with which this control was maintained, George Lawrence succeeded in further questioning the related stereotyping of the criminal colonial which was central to the maintaining of colonialist authority.

As we saw in the previous chapter, Philip Meadows Taylor's personal and professional lives gave him ample opportunity to come in close contact with Indians, and this experience proved to be a constant lens through which any colonialist stereotyping he was tempted to adopt had to pass. Unlike most of his contemporaries he did make the most of that opportunity, and one result of

---

[50] 'Atrocity rumours' could be used in a far less sophisticated way by novelists to strengthen the official propaganda about the Mutiny. James Grant's novel *First Love and Last Love* (London: Routledge, 1868) is a good example of relatively unproblematic criminalization of Indians. The rebels are shown to protest against the benign civilizing mission of the masters: 'our widows are forbidden to perform the sacred rite of Suttee . . . our thugs are hung as murderers for following the profession taught to them by our fathers' (i. 274–5). There are detailed descriptions of public rapes and murders of British women and children to bring out the essence of India: 'Like all heathens, they regard women merely as animals . . . many of the Hindoo women bitterly mocked the dying misery of ours, and of their children; but what could be the maternal love of the females, who at times set their infants afloat in a basket, and quietly watch them borne away by the current, and feel a glow of fraternal joy?' (ii. 77). The heroine, Kate, is repeatedly molested by her rebel captors, and Grant gloats in the description of her naked and violated body. Indians could thus be used to shore up colonialist/masculinist authority by 'punishing' dangerously independent British women in the colonies. In this way, strong women like Kate learnt the value of submitting themselves to the protection of British valour. Unsurprisingly, British heroes of the novel learn to recognize 'criminal Indians' as sexual threats. When young Dickey sees Mughal princes courting his cousins his comment is typical: 'I'm blowed . . . if I don't think some of these niggers are spooney upon my cousins! When they come upon the course like a couple of Ali Babas, with all their forty thieves after them, there is no getting near uncle's carriage' (i. 61). This finally justifies the mass executions of the Indians by the avenging British troops and Hodson's shooting of the unarmed Mughal princes. Indeed, the novel's last image captures the 'justness' of the retributions, in its juxtaposition of the murdered body of a British girl 'nailed by her hand and feet against the masonry' with the naked and hanging figures of the 'three last descendants of the Great Mogul'.

this was that the rhetoric of crime was rarely deployed unproblematically in his novels. In the decade after the Mutiny, during which the question of 'criminal India' and the legitimacy of British colonialism had been dramatically foregrounded, Taylor's attempts to 'illustrate events in Indian history by works of fiction' stressed the reformative, rather than the punitive possibilities of British rule.[51] Of course, this liberal colonialist view always sought to legitimize the occupation of India. But since this process involved reclaiming imperial credentials by questioning the propaganda about the 'criminal Indian', it also hinted at the possibility of using this figure in the interrogation of British authority.

Taylor's tracing of the 'lost links' of the Mutiny begins with his account of the rise of the Hindu Maratha power and the gradual decline of the ruling Muslim dynasties in India. His trilogy of the 1860s and 1870s offered a narrative naturalization of British colonialism as a force that filled the vacuum left by the fall of the Mughal power in India. At the same time, the lines of continuity he drew between the earlier Indian kingdoms and the British regime neutralized the progressive claims of the latter by hinting at a cyclical historical model. As we shall see, this seriously questioned the propaganda of Indian criminality and refuted the British monopolizing of morality, legality, and authority. *Tara* (1863) begins with Taylor's patterning of Indian history:

It was very strange . . . to observe the remarkable interval of exactly one hundred years, between the attack of Sivaji on the Bejapore Mahomedans in 1657 and the victory of Lord Clive over those of Bengal at Plassey in 1757. Both results led directly to the establishment of powers widely differing in their aims and characters . . . But this curious accordance of the dates becomes still more interesting when we observe that, on the anniversary of the third century, June 1857, the heads of Mahomedan and Mahratta power were leagued against that which had subdued both; and know that their combined efforts however desperate, and their intrigues however virulent, proved alike futile.[52]

This historical scheme did, of course, operate as an attempt to represent British occupation of India as an inevitable sequence in the chain of history. But his very attempts to write a fictional history of India before the political ascendance of the colonialist

[51] Philip Meadows Taylor, *Tara* (London: William Blackwood, 1863), i. p. vii.
[52] Ibid. p. xii.

power resulted in the removal of the privileged and controlling viewpoint of the anglophone reader, who was suddenly faced with the description of a culture that was bewilderingly different from the version produced by dominant colonialist narratives. Taylor disturbed the racist formulae of colonialism by underlining the essential equality of the rulers and the colonized: 'same passions and affections exist among them as among ourselves.' It was this disempowerment of the colonialist eye that disturbed Taylor's British readers and the most common complaint was a feeling of 'estrangement'. Geraldine Jewsbury predicted that the public would not be interested in a story that turned on 'native Indian intrigues', and William Blackwood, Taylor's publisher, told him: 'We fear that your Indian novel without any European element will be almost too strange.'[53] One critic advised Taylor on the flaw of his technique, pointing out that the great masters of the historical novel always carefully chose themes with 'home interest'.[54] This 'estrangement' was caused precisely by Taylor's 'unfamiliar' depiction of India, where not all people had criminal inclinations and successfully managed their affairs without any help from the British.

Taylor's Indian heroine, a beautiful and scholarly Brahmin widow, is an effective refutation of James Grant's assertion that all Indians treated women like chattel animals, and that it was only under European rule that they could achieve a measure of equality with men.[55] Although Tara and her father are shown to be exceptional in their refusal to submit to the prescribed harsh rituals of Hindu widowhood, the fact that they can do so without suffering some horribly twisted Indian vengeance refuted the 'official' propaganda about India. Of course, Tara is the object of the lustful intrigues of the villain Moro Trimmul, but Moro's actions are not endorsed by Indian society in general. In fact, Moro's lack of moral fibre is shown to be exceptional amongst the Indians. Even Sivaji, the Maratha leader whose early career seems to be a sign of stereotypical Maratha criminality, is shown to have sufficient control and moral insight, seen, for instance, in his refused to succumb to the temptation of taking a mistress: 'it would be a burden, a disgrace

---

[53] See Finkelstein, *Philip Meadows Taylor*, 11–12.
[54] See ibid. 13.
[55] See Grant, *First Love*, ii. 77.

which he dared not encounter . . . it was a hard struggle, but the young prince, whose firm will and self-control finally won him a kingdom, successfully resisted the opportunities deliberately offered.'[56] In this, Taylor's Sivaji stood at the opposite end to those representations of Indian political leaders that invariably marked them with exaggerated 'oriental' depravity.

Equally, the emancipated Tara is by no means an exception to the general condition of Indian women. Jeeja Bye, Sivaji's mother, is a typical representative of Indian women, who are shown to be the 'motors behind all the great deeds and fortunes of the family'.[57] Even a woman like Ganga, who as a temple dancer would usually be the signifier of a depraved oriental religion, is shown as the embodiment of a Victorian version of monogamous, selfless, and chaste love. When threatened with murder by her wayward lover Moro, she declares: 'I was not afraid of you when that dagger's point was at my heart. For myself I am not afraid of your threats, or your words . . . say it Sir, and I follow you through Dekhan, through Hind, till I die by your hand.'[58] In matters of gender and sexuality, Taylor's Indians are hardly marked by any signs of 'naturally criminal depravity'.

Taylor's problematic relationship with the rhetoric of crime is strengthened by his representation of the novel's 'outlaw', Pahar Singh. At one level, Pahar Singh is created with all the materials used in the propaganda about 'criminal' India. He is a robber baron who establishes a fiefdom through extortion, blackmail, and violence. Like other Indian deviants, he is often disguised as a religious mendicant and meets his gang in ruined temples. He is also well versed in the Thug lore, and thus combines in him the dreaded triumvirate of the rebel, the mendicant, and the dacoit.

Yet, his relationship with authority, in this case that of the Muslim rulers of Beejapore, is bound by codes of honour and morality. Taylor plays with the stereotype of criminalized Indian politics to endorse native statecraft as both progressive and pragmatic. His outlawed status enables Pahar to act as the unofficial arm of the state, and to thwart the conspiracy concocted by the Prime Minister and the magistrate. The treason of these officers is perhaps shown to be typical of the 'oriental' government, but Taylor indicates that the same political system also had means to

[56] Taylor, *Tara*, i. 81–2.   [57] Ibid. iii. 83.   [58] Ibid. ii. 234.

check its own weaknesses. If contemporary British law advocated the reformation of outlaws like Pahar Singh through 'useful' punishment, Taylor shows that these tactics were anticipated by native political systems long before they were brought to India by the colonizers. Pahar Singh is made useful to the state through the personal intervention of the ruler, and the bond between them is not one of material reward like that between Thug approvers and the British police, but one reminiscent of the feudal value of noble honour: 'Remember . . . these words cannot be revoked. Whatever happens, I do but thy bidding . . . Let us not speak of reward; there is nothing between us but true faith . . . and that faith was never yet given for gold.'[59]

Taylor hints that this ability of Indian princes to transform robbers into legitimate subjects actually served as the model for later British administrators. The history of Pahar Singh's service to the state is a version of the relationship between Ameer Ali and the recording magistrate in *Confessions*. Taylor drives this point home by comparing the treatment of outlaws in the respective eras. Describing the 'lawless' Beejapore frontier, Taylor points out that things were still the same under the British administration and thus puts to rest the colonialist claim of improving law and order. He then constructs the 'family history' of Pahar Singh to show how his descendants replicated his fate of being transformed from outlaws to law-keepers: 'In 1828–29, the family were found to be largely connected with Dacoity and thuggee, and the leading members of it were tried, convicted of both crimes, and sentenced to various terms of imprisonment . . . One member only of the family survived free, and, as late as 1860, was a private in the police of the—district.'[60] Taylor decriminalizes Indian politics by showing its lines of continuity with the colonial administration, and also revises the myth of 'criminal India'. His Maratha society certainly has its criminal elements, but it resembles other contemporary European societies in its largely law-abiding subjects and politically able administrators. Likewise, his Muslims bear no resemblance to their 'bloodthirsty murderous brethren' of Delhi during the Mutiny. The massacre committed in Tooljapoor is used as an example of the hysterical cruelty fomented by the Islamic propaganda of *Jihad* or the 'holy war'. At the same time, Taylor refuses to see this as

[59] Ibid. 85–7.   [60] Ibid. iii. 327–8.

constituting the essence of the religion or the country. Fazil Khan, the novel's Muslim hero, is clearly more enlightened than any of his British counterparts on the issue of religious tolerance: 'Fazil Khan by no means shared the grim detestation of Hindus as infidels, in which his fathers gloried; and he had been no willing listener to the denunciations poured out against them by the Peer.'[61] His popularity among the Hindu soldiers is not only a mark of his own enlightened view of religion, but also acknowledges a nationalist vision of India based on the unity of its two major communities that colonialist histories often took considerable pains to deny.

The novel's most striking example of this vision of unified India is provided in the romance between Fazil and Tara. Fazil's rescue of Tara from the attack on Tooljapoor and her life in a Muslim aristocratic household demonstrate the possibility of the harmonious existence of the two communities and an exorcism of their common evils through mutual respect for each other's cultural norms.[62] Similarly, Taylor's account of Sivaji is focused more on his political acumen than his supposedly dissolute Hindu nature. Even his treacherous murder of Afzool Khan is admired as an instance of realpolitik:

Treacherously as it had been gained, the Rajah Sivaji did not slumber on his victory . . . He was everywhere active and persevering . . . he became virtually independent equally of Delhi and Beejapoor . . . died in 1680, after a life which was a romance from first to last, but not before the power he had aroused and created had become invincible from Delhi to Rameshwar.[63]

In his ambition, empire-building, and ruthlessness, Sivaji closely resembled the historical figure that would dominate the next phase of Taylor's history of India—Colonel Clive.

As outlined in Taylor's 'pattern', the next link to the Mutiny was provided by his account of Clive's victory over the ruler of Bengal in 1757. *Ralph Darnell* (1865) also continued Taylor's interrogation of dominant colonialist representations of India. From the opening scene set in an English public house where Ralph's drunken carousal, volley of profane oaths, and gambling recall scenes of 'oriental' debauchery, Taylor's novel represents the establishment of British power in India as the triumph not of superior

---

[61] Taylor, *Tara*, ii. 317.   [62] Ibid. iii. 50.   [63] Ibid. 323-5.

morality and justice, but of violence, of the clash of 'stratagem against stratagem, deceit against deceit'.[64] The conquest of India is motivated not by the moral duty of a civilizing mission, but by a lust for possession stirred equally by the 'soft Hindoo girls' and the country's fabled wealth. Trade is an enterprise hardly distinguishable from thieving:

The local official pay of Mr Henry Wharton was not much above twenty pounds sterling per year, and how it was that he contrived to send to England some fifty thousand pounds' worth of goods every year, seems incomprehensible to us, though it was not in the least so either to Mr Roger Darnell or John Sanders . . . a very pretty trade resulted.[65]

Clive, the leader of this scramble for India, does not pretend that his mission is anything other than one of rapacious aggression. In his inspirational speech to the hero, Clive also demonstrates the basic techniques of legitimizing aggression by reiterating the fiction of Indians yearning to be 'ruled strongly':

For . . . among Gentoos and Moors—who look more to the effects of physical than moral power than you are accustomed to do in a free country like England—tis only by showing ourselves prepared to resist and overcome any attempts at oppression, that we can insure that weight and respect, which are the foundations of all commercial transactions . . . power can alone insure us respect, and the faithful observance of all our treaties and agreements with it.[66]

In fact, the novel proceeds to expose the spurious morality of Clive's rhetoric. The pursuit of 'respect and commercial transactions' is shown to be the naked lust for power. Clive berates the traders for their obsession with silk and sugar, and urges them to take advantage of the decline of Mughal authority in India to set up a despotic power.[67] In juxtaposing Clive's vision of the British juggernaut forcing Indian states to submission, his commercial rapacity, and his claim that this mission had divine sanction, the novel delineates the process of the manufacturing of legitimacy for brutal expansionism.

Clive's thin claim of civilizing India is also shown up in the novel's description of a Britain that is at least as permeated with

---

[64] Philip Meadows Taylor, *Ralph Darnell* (Edinburgh: William Blackwood, 1865), iii. 170.   [65] Ibid. i. 72–3.   [66] Ibid. 90–5.
[67] Ibid. 101–2.

criminality as India. Clive himself is shown to be the product of a time when desperate men often took the law into their own hands. Scenes like London's Temple Bar, adorned with the heads of executed traitors, 'that ghastly row of pale faces, blistering and rotting in the sun', subvert Britain's claim to be the arbitrator of civilization. In fact, Taylor's Marathas and Muslim rulers in *Tara* operated in a more sophisticated and humane political environment than the Britain of *Ralph Darnell*. A typical British street scene is captured in the riot that nearly kills the hero: 'Hard at the heels of the watchmen, followed a confused rabble of men; some carrying torches, and waving them in the air, some brandishing naked rapiers . . . all shouting damnation to Hanovarian rats and Tories in one of the obscene Mohock "war cries".'[68] No less than in India, the British political climate is charged with factionalism, espionage, and corruption. Ralph's friend Foster is a spy, and Taylor emphatically refuses to allocate any superior political morality to Europe over Asia: 'Do we not see such parties even in present existence about ourselves? Fenians and Nationalists in Ireland; Orleanists, Bourbons and Red-Republicans in France; Mazzinists in Italy.'[69]

The novel's questioning of colonial legitimacy operated in both the national and the personal context. *Ralph Darnell* could well be Taylor's most structurally accomplished work, as the micro-history of the hero is intricately woven into the larger history of the rise of British power in India. If Clive's story is a morally spurious attempt to legitimize aggression in India, Ralph's story is also one of a struggle in order to prove himself a legitimate son and heir to the family estates. The novel's refusal to accord superior moral and legal stature to Britain is replicated in its problematic closure to Ralph's quest for legitimacy. Ralph is revealed to have sprung from the 'criminal seed' of his father Henry, an aristocratic smuggler who eloped with the local village beauty. Marked by the dual signs of smuggling and bastardy, Ralph's chief concern is to find any evidence of his parents' marriage that will end his marginalized status in society. Driven by the taunts of his uncle Geoffrey, Ralph attempts to rob and murder him. This crime is hushed up when the family arranges for his secret transportation to India: 'the sudden transmission of an obnoxious relative to His Majesty's plantations

---

[68] Philip Meadows Taylor, *Ralph Darnell*, 212.   [69] Ibid. 248.

in Virginia, or to a friend in Calcutta, Madras, or Bombay, was by no means uncommon and attracted no particular attentions if known.'[70] Far from being the subject of a civilizsing mission, the novel showed the colony for what it often was, a receptacle of British 'refuse'.

During Clive's campaign at Plassey, a dying soldier provides Ralph with a vital clue about his parents' marriage, and Ralph's legitimacy is confirmed by the person responsible for the spurious legitimization of British power in India—Robert Clive: 'And you are the heir of Melcepeth, Ralph, and so God bless you . . . of course it is true . . . this must be certified, and we must not delay about that. Who knows who might not say that thou hadst invented it?'[71] But even as British colonialist morality is shown to be a fiction invented by Clive, Ralph's legitimacy remains tantalizingly 'fictional', always at one remove from reality. He returns to England only to find the original papers of his parents' marriage irrecoverably lost. He can never become the rightful heir and Britain only serves to remind him of lost opportunities and his criminal past. His friend Foster is finally arrested on charges of highway robbery and murder, and his faithful and devoted lover Sybil is dead: 'what could he do in England? In India there was future service for his country; a noble leader, and a crowd of struggling princes and people, among whom he might have his portion of usefulness.'[72] He returns to the colony, jettisons the aristocratic Darnell for the more plebeian 'Smithson', marries an ex-wife of Bengal's Nawab, and dedicates his life to building a government with Robert Clive, finishing his career as a general. This ending of the Ralph Darnell story could indeed be used to reinscribe colonialist authority by showing that although without any legitimacy to begin with, Britain invented its own moral and legal rights to occupy India through the laudable work of building a stable government. But such comfortable possibilities are avoided as Clive and Ralph's civilizing work is shown to lead paradoxically to a tyrannical chaos. Ralph's career ends not in the fulfilment of his grand design, but in a return to India where:

To the natives an almost reign of terror had begun, which made them fly to the protection of one of their oldest and ablest advocates with a confidence which General Smithson could not refuse. Remonstrances, private

---

[70] Ibid. ii. 87.   [71] Ibid. iii. 136.   [72] Ibid. 287.

or public, produced no effect, and were perhaps ill-received . . . So, sick at
heart, he perceived plainly that he had lived out of his time.[73]

Clive's prediction about hundreds of years of enlightened British
rule proves to be just as fictitious as the rest of his inventions, and
colonialist legitimacy, like Ralph's own, proves just as tantalizingly
unreachable.

The novel's deconstruction of colonial authority is accompanied
by a parallel questioning of dominant representations of Indian
criminality. Not only do the descriptions of British criminality relativize the crimes of the Bengali Nawab, Siraj-ud-Daulah, but
crucial colonialist myths like the 'Black Hole' of Calcutta are dealt
with in a manner that shifts the burden of guilt away from the
Indians. All the stereotypical signs of the depraved oriental prince
are attached to Siraj, yet he is not denied astute insights into the
aggressive nature of European colonialism: 'First there was a ship
and a few merchants, and one nation; now there are three nations,
and the ships come in fleets, like the flocks of birds at harvest
times.' He is innocent of the alleged massacre in the infamous
'Black Hole' incident, where the deaths of the British prisoners are
instead attributed to the confusion of battle and drunken panic.
Taylor's Indian guards try to help the prisoners by providing plen-
tiful water, and the description of the 'hole' shows more the savage
and cannibalistic survival instinct of the Europeans than Indian
cruelty:

all that could be seen was a dim surging mass of naked men—English,
Dutch, Portuguese, and natives—rising, falling, climbing on each other's
slippery shoulders. . . . Again and again he had fiercely and desperately
struck down the poor wretches who thus assailed him. There was little pity
between man and man that night.[74]

Siraj himself is shown to be unaware of the incident, and refuses to
give in to the more bigoted demands of European blood from his
priests.

Subsequently, the punishment of Siraj by the British forces is
shown to be driven not by the historical force of the civilizing
mission, but by a destiny that was not subject to any mortal
schemes: 'Listen! That coward prince's good destiny was but for a
year . . . Now men begin to say that the destiny of your people will

---

[73] Philip Meadows Taylor, *Ralph Darnell*, 334.   [74] Ibid. ii. 248–53.

follow his without a check, and of all Hind ye will be kings.'[75] As we have seen before, if this formulation produces colonialism as inevitable, it also undercuts the claims of reform and progress by taking the control of future events and the power to judge and punish away from the rulers. Siraj, like Tippoo before him, stands already judged and condemned by a mysterious force that merely uses the British presence as a judicial instrument. It is by the decree of this same force that the administrative efforts of Ralph and Clive degenerate into the reign of terror with which the novel concludes.

Meadows Taylor's insistence on linking the Mutiny to the 200 years of past Indian history and his analysis of the colonialism which developed during that period is also a sufficient indication of his unwillingness to interpret the events of 1857 as a random burst of Indian criminality. By placing his 'Mutiny' novel as the last in his trilogy, and by refusing to deal with the more sensational episodes of the event, Taylor steered well clear of the contemporary jingoistic hysterics. Indeed, his preface described the Mutiny as a political and nationalist event, not as an expression of the chaotic nature of the Indians: 'The new power ... deprived both the Mahrattas and Mussulmans of independent political existence and influence; it had introduced new and powerful elements of western civilisation, and the struggle of 1857 was a combination to regain what had been lost.'[76] For Taylor, the event's culmination in India passing from the East India Company to the direct authority of the British crown was also the fulfilment of the Indian prediction that the Company would only rule for 100 years till 1857. In *Seeta*, Taylor's concern was the reinventing of the post-Mutiny imperialist British authority by forging a paternalist bond between the rulers and the subjects. This tactic demanded a strong focus on the loyal and not the 'criminal' side of India.

The novel tells of the struggle between the British 'just' administrator, Cyril Brandon, and the rebel/dacoit Azrael Pande, over the body and soul of the embodiment of 'loyal' India—Seeta. Typical of Taylor was the acknowledgement that opposition to 'progressive' British efforts came not only from 'criminal' India, but also from within the ranks of the racist colonizers themselves. The sneering British civil servants, the haughty aristocratic family, and

[75] Ibid. iii. 87–8.
[76] Philip Meadows Taylor, *Seeta* (London: Henry King, 1872), i. p. vii.

even the sympathetic but disagreeing friend of Cyril are all linked to Indian criminals like Azrael Pande and Raja Harpal Singh in their opposition to the Brandon–Seeta union. They share the racist assumptions that, according to Taylor, lay at the bottom of the catastrophe of the Mutiny.

Meadows Taylor introduces Azrael Pande with the traditional signs of Indian criminality. He is the leader of a dacoit gang who, disguised as a priest, uses Hindu temples for rendezvous. From the nefarious activities of the gang as illustrated in their raid on Seeta's house and the murder of her husband, conclusions are drawn about the pitiless nature of these criminals: 'Was there no misgiving, no remorse, no pity? None . . . only a feverish desire for consummation. A hideous and devilish plot . . . such as one as many Indian judge has had to unravel . . . shuddering over the mental depravity which they described.'[77] When it is revealed in court that Azrael Pande was also an insurrectionist who had incited the sepoys to various minor mutinies, the link between crime and the Mutiny is seemingly clinched.

But as the preface and, later, the portrayal of the Rani of Jhansi shows, one of the novel's contentions was that not all the aspects of the Mutiny and not all the mutineers could be reduced to simple 'criminality'. The old order of Indian politics is criminalized and both the Muslim and the Hindu princes, neighbours of Brandon's 'realm', are shown to have strong links with dacoits. The Nawab Dil Khan actually shelters Azrael, and Raja Harpal Singh reveals his true colours once the Mutiny inspired by Azrael spreads to his territory:

The Rajah and his courtiers . . . amused themselves for several days with their own peculiar methods of ingenious extortions, that is, by laying out people in the sun with their hands and feet tied to the tent pegs . . . all the modes of torture which, as the people could not help thinking, did not exist in the days of the English . . . the anarchy and disorganisation of the rural districts was as complete as if there never had been any English.[78]

However, Azrael Pande himself does not operate entirely on the basis of the narrow criminal covetousness that, for instance, marked the behaviour of British merchants in *Tara*. His enterprising and tireless commitment to the rebel cause elicits admiration.

---

[77] Philip Meadows Taylor, *Seeta*, 33.   [78] Ibid. iii. 152–3.

His propaganda for the Mutiny is the closest the novel comes to admitting the dissenting voice of a subject people and creating an alternative history of colonization. It momentarily lifts him from the category of a 'mere robber' and provides a glimpse of how political dissent was criminalized by colonial authority in order to defend its own oppression:

I have been tried and sentenced to die . . . I have travelled throughout the length and breadth of the country . . . I have heard but one cry—a cry that came from the very souls of the people—deliverance from the English . . . where do those great ships yonder take the cotton, and the indigo which the poor ryots have produced, but to England?[79]

Azrael's analysis of the cause of the Mutiny is affirmed by the heroic Rani of Jhansi. The queen is so strict an interpreter of codes of honour and justice that she does not hesitate to berate her own allies like Dil Khan for their ingratitude towards the British. She herself is driven to mutiny solely by the need to resist oppression:

We loved the English; we hoisted their flag over our own; and it would have been there now, had their old justice been continued to us . . . The English, with all the empire of Delhi belonging to them, refused to continue what they themselves had once granted to us freely and generously . . . They are a mean, covetous race, farming our country . . . seizing every scrap of land, every rupee of revenue they can.[80]

The novel's presentation of the queen not merely as the ablest of the rebel leaders, but also as a noble and just human being, results in the generation of considerable sympathy for the 'native' view of the Mutiny. The fact that her views on colonial oppression coincide with those of the 'criminal' Azrael Pande's is significant. Under cover of representing the admittedly skilful instigators of the Mutiny as dacoits and Thugs, the novel suggests that there was ample truth in their accusations against the illegal and immoral British expansionism. The Mutiny could now be shown as a reaction to the reign of terror unleashed on India by the British regime that had left Taylor's other hero Darnell heartbroken and forced his return to England.

Cyril Brandon continues the task of Ralph Darnell in his commitment to the reformation of India. If one of his tasks is to discipline and exorcize the savage and criminal aspects of the country, his

[79] Ibid. ii. 31–2.   [80] Ibid. iii. 253.

other is to bring its humane side to prominence. His story articulates Taylor's refutation of the fabrication of the Mutiny atrocities and his criticism of the 'race war' unleashed upon Indians. In writing the romance of Brandon's civilizing mission, Taylor may have aimed to camouflage the fundamentally oppressive nature of colonialism that the Mutiny had made difficult to disguise. It was a damage limitation exercise and an effort to rearticulate British legal and moral authority after Neill and Havelock's mass murders. But as Taylor realized, this could only be performed by rhetorically limiting Indian criminality to the margins of society and admitting that the civilized majority had suffered at the hands of the British 'avengers'.

Taylor's aim, then, was the idealizing of the relationship between the 'good' ruler and the masses. Accordingly, Brandon's sympathetic mingling with 'his people' is shown to elevate him to the rank of a local deity. Women repeat his name in their prayers and worship him in the 'simple shrines of their faith'. He is incorporated into the oral culture of ballads and legends composed by village poets. The farewell message of the villagers sums up the essence of this fantasy of paternalistic colonialism: 'what can we say? You were like a parent to the people; a kind and merciful parent; for in the troubled season of sumbut 1914, you came to us . . . and purged this district of rebels, dacoits, and gang robbers, and not a trace of them remains.'[81] This passage sums up the aims and achievements of Taylor's narrative strategy—the colonial administrator is converted from the alien tyrant of the rebel propaganda to a 'father of the people', and the Indians themselves have internalized the colonialist logic of producing the rebels as criminals. Brandon outlines the profits of adopting the paternalist instead of the purely punitive strategy: 'Be just, be patient, be firm and true; be always accessible and courteous, never forgetting your position, and they will always love you. They are almost like children . . . easily led, when once they have given their faith.'[82]

As we have seen, this strategy required the separation of 'criminal' from civilized India and Brandon is geared to deal with each on their own merits. In his avatar of the magistrate he is the very image of colonial justice:

---

[81] Philip Meadows Taylor, *Seeta*, 291.   [82] Ibid. 295.

he had put down crime with a strong unswerving hand, as far as he could trace it; and he was equally stern in the suppression of all petty exaction, oppression and peculation ... and while his official duties necessarily brought out the strongest points of deceit and crime, *he would turn, with never-failing appreciation, to the higher qualities by which he was surrounded.* (my emphasis)[83]

It is this capacity of separating liminal India from its 'reformable' core that makes Brandon the ideal colonial administrator. When required he is able to adopt disguises and kill the likes of Azrael Pande and other rebels. And yet, on the other hand, he is also able to detect the almost animal loyalty of Indians like Seeta and forge an unbreakable link with the country. His first encounter with Seeta is a set piece that captures the erotics of the construction of colonial legitimacy. Brandon is presiding over a court dealing with Azrael Pande, and Seeta the supplicant is demanding the justice that only the colonizers are capable of giving to Indians. It is appropriate that Brandon should fall in love with Seeta in a law court while he is doling out justice because it neatly captures the particular masculine fantasy of just colonialism that Taylor was promoting. The civilized essence of India, here seen also as its feminine side, is being saved from its 'criminal' side—the male rebel/dacoits like Azrael—by the colonial lawgiver. It is also entirely appropriate that Brandon's desire to possess Seeta is sanctified by the judicial atmosphere of the court, since it both legitimizes his desire and represents India as actually supplicating to be saved, in a way, from itself: 'as she took the place assigned to her, the light from without fell full upon her, and the young magistrate thought he had never seen any woman more lovely ... her eyes were large and soft, of that clear dark brown which, like a dog's, is always so loving and true.'[84]

Brandon's marriage with Seeta becomes the legal possession of the 'soul' of the country, and Seeta in her turn performs the task of representing Britain as the enlightened saviour of herself and India: 'How little do we know of you English ... how little of your faith, or your books; teeming with glorious thoughts and the fresh stores of knowledge ... While for us—no one writes now; no one thinks; we are as the dead, with those whose very language is dead too.'[85] The resuscitation of this dead India is shown to be

---

[83] Ibid. i. 145–6.   [84] Ibid. 126–7.   [85] Ibid. iii. 61.

the responsibility of colonialism and may be seen in the awakening of Seeta's spiritual life under Brandon's tutelage. By the time of her death, Seeta's soul is claimed equally by the colonizer's language and religion, and she dies while chanting the Hindu invocation of the sun and the vision of the Christian 'father-God' calling for her from heaven. Her death is converted by the novel into a propaganda for a 'new' kind of paternalism

> Seeta is only a type of thousands and thousands of her own countrymen and women, who feel the truth, and who, until some unforeseen crisis in their lives arises, dare not make the final plunge . . . Too many among us blame the hardness of the heathen, and call this belief in their own faith by very ugly names; but I think the utmost bound of charity needs to be extended to them when we think on . . . the force of the reality of the struggle.[86]

Yet, despite this revision of the strategy of criminalization and the staking out of the grounds for a restoration of the myth of enlightened and reformist colonialism, Meadows Taylor's novel ends by expressing significant doubts about its own project. The romance of the union of India and Britain, of master and subject, of justice and reformative possibilities, is not shown to be sustainable. If 'criminal' India in the form of Azrael Pande could be pushed to the liminal margins and hunted down by colonial law, it could also snatch loyal India—Seeta—with it to underline the implausibility of such a union between the ruler and the ruled. This is dramatized in Seeta's death as she tries to save Brandon during the last desperate attempts by Azrael to kill him. This dramatic episode clears the way for a legitimate and more comfortable remarriage of Brandon with the British heroine Grace Mostyn, a union that had been the cherished project of the entire Anglo-Indian community. By killing off Seeta and thereby annulling her transgressive marriage with Brandon, Meadows Taylor may have been bowing to the dominant ideas of racial miscegenation and degeneration theories that had gained strength during this decade. But it also was a symptom of his lack of conviction in the strategy of legitimizing colonialism that he employed in the novel. If India was to be shown as containing both a criminal and a reformable essence, there could be no guarantee that one could be separated from the other. The rebel

---

[86] Philip Meadows Taylor, *Seeta*, 207.

could be demonized as the dacoit/thug Azrael Pande, but he could also irredeemably spoil the marriage of loyal India to its colonial masters.

Written mostly during the aftermath of the Mutiny, the novels we have looked at display a complex response to the non-fictional colonialist discourses. On the one hand, they generally refuted the universal criminalization of Indians as mutineers, Thugs, and dacoits and opposed the atrocity rumours. On the other hand, they often sought to produce their own version of legitimizing colonialism by splitting India into liminal/criminal and loyal/legal halves, and focusing on the latter as a site for the operation of the humane reformism of British power. But in this process, the figure of the 'criminal Indian', be it the rebel or the outlaw, often emerged with justifications if not excuses for his opposition to the colonial regime. While this figure could be used to call for suppression of all dissent as illegal and hence punishable by law, the suspicion that their 'criminality' may actually be a legitimate critique of British oppression could never quite be removed. And this was precisely the unsettling use to which it was put by another kind of novel that was emerging during this period, one that dealt with sensational crimes committed in the circles of the respectable bourgeoisie from which British colonial and domestic power emanated.

↳ Sensation
novel

7

Shifting Images of the Criminal

THE CRIMINAL AS VICTIM

Like the 1820s, the 1860s was a period of complex and crucial changes in British responses to deviance and punishment. In this context, the post-Mutiny revision of the 'criminal Indian' figure may be seen as an example of negotiation between colonialist narratives and the 'new' strategies of criminalization emerging during this time.

The twin Victorian strategies of a carefully regulated penal system and an ever-extending network of 'new policing' were now seen as a success. But, paradoxically, fears about the product of this success—the 'overdisciplined individual'—now replaced the earlier bogey figure of the uncontrollable individual. The prison, once seen as essential to the reformation of character, was now increasingly seen as a vast and oppressive machine that dehumanized its inmates. In the debates over the important Prison Bill of 1877, Dr Keneally painted a dark picture: 'In nearly all our prisons a vast amount of moral and physical torture is inflicted on prisoners that was never contemplated by law ... Most tyrannical proceedings were permitted, which, if generally known, would excite great public indignation.'[1] In this environment where manacling a prisoner's legs was being seen as torture, blowing up Indian mutineers with cannons, despite the racist assumptions of colonialism, was bound to arouse significant levels of discomfort.

In the analysis of the Mutiny novels, especially Meadows Taylor's Indian trilogy, we saw how the prominence given to the

---

[1] 'February 9, House of Commons Debate', *Hansard*, 232 (1877), 135, 415.

idea of destiny subverted the concept of individual culpability (in the case of Indian 'criminals') and even merit (in case of pioneers like Robert Clive), and thus questioned the validity of the self-proclaimed burden of the civilizing process that colonialism declared as its rationale. This curious acceptance of what had earlier been frequently described as 'oriental' superstition was actually born out of the cultural environment of the 1860s which saw significant changes in ideas about individuality. Martin Weiner points out: 'As novel technology and the expanding market extended the effective reach of actions . . . the dominant paradigms reinforced a sense of determined system of mechanical causation in which there might be room for chance, but not for conscious will, a system of large force in which the individual counted for little.'[2] One of the first consequences of this was the sympathetic representation of the criminal as a victim of larger forces like destiny. One of the most popular scientific writers of the period, Henry Maudsley, argued that vast numbers of criminals did not voluntarily choose to do wrong, but were predestined to do so. As the 'stepchildren of nature', they were said to suffer from the tyranny of 'bad organisation'.[3] One popular example of 'bad organisation' was the hereditary mental diseases that were thought to fuel criminal activities. William Guy conducted a massive statistical survey and concluded that 'the disproportion between the ratio of the insane to sane convicts and the ratio of lunatics to the population is so great as to justify the assertion that the criminal population is much more liable to insanity than the community at large'.[4] In Europe, Théodule Ribot challenged the very idea of the individual's free will by proposing that it was embedded in the physical organization of the body and hence subject to the 'fatalistic and immutable laws' of heredity.[5] Of course, this location of deviance in hereditary madness or 'destiny' legitimized the intervention of hospitals and asylums, in addition to that of the prisons, into the lives of individual subjects. At the same time, if the criminals were themselves seen as victims and were held not to be responsible for their crimes, then the vocabulary of blame and punishment, even in

---

[2] Weiner, *Reconstructing the Criminal*, 160.

[3] Henry Maudsley, *Body and Mind* (London: Macmillan, 1870), 43.

[4] William A. Guy, 'On Insanity and Crime', *Journal of the Statistical Society*, 32 (1869), 167–8.

[5] T. Ribot, *Heredity* (London: Henry King, 1875), 340–4.

the case of the colonized, had to be adjusted. This opened up fresh debates on everything from capital punishment to prison reforms and the insanity plea. The 'criminal' once again became the terrain over which the battle to discover a new kind of legitimacy of the state was conducted.

Inevitably, there was opposition to this new image of the criminal as a victim. *Fraser's Magazine* cited examples of the Indian and Irish rebellions and the 'reign of terror' in France to support capital punishment as 'equally effectual and cheap' punishment.[6] In a throwback to the language and temper of the cries for vengeance during the Mutiny, the article sneered at the reluctance to award the death penalty to criminals as a sign of moral degeneration and a collective loss of confidence in personal and national ability:

To the present writer it appears manifest, that in our age especially, it is desirable that the stern and harsh view of the case should be fully recognised, and the tender view should be discouraged. We are too soft and pitiful . . . an increase of comfort makes men look with indulgence on matters that ought to stir up the warmest indignation.[7]

But this opposition was increasingly outweighed by the support for the theory of 'weak' criminals and calls for them to be treated humanely. In a witty essay that captured the flavour of the contemporary debates, Leslie Stephen deplored the degeneration of the energetic criminals: 'the style of our murderous artists has woefully degenerated . . . the act which is only practised by inferior hands has lost a good deal of its former refinement.'[8] Despite the playful tone that, *pace* de Quincey, seemed to construct an aesthetics of murder, Stephen's article touched on several important points of the contemporary debate on crime and individuality. The spectre of 'dull' criminals captured the gloomy flavour of the theories of degeneration of the individual in the face of forces like heredity and environment.

The image of the weak criminal was also incompatible with the idea of corporal punishment. Weiner points out that the very idea of inflicting pain was becoming culturally unacceptable throughout the 1860s and the 1870s. The legal expert Fitzjames Stephens saw that 'we shrink not from the notion that a fellow creature is

---

[6] J. F. Stephen, 'Capital Punishment', *Fraser's Magazine*, 69 (1864), 753–4.
[7] Ibid.
[8] Arthur Leslie Stephen, 'The Decay of Murder', *Cornhill Magazine*, 20 (1869), 725.

unhappy, but from the idea of cutting, tearing, or bruising flesh and limbs like our own'.[9] As the controversy over Frederic Farrar's interpretation of the biblical image of hell shows, even the idea of a punitive divinity and divine punishment of the body was under attack.[10] Given the extent of this debate, it is small wonder that the narratives of Mutiny displayed a distinct ambiguity both about the kind of punishment they advocated and the extent to which they held the Indians responsible for their 'crimes'. As if taking their cue from the assertions of Maudsley that 'we may, without much difficulty, trace savagery in civilisation, as we can trace animalism in savagery', the fictions of Indian crime blurred the boundaries between the masters and their subjects, Indians and Europeans, lawgivers and criminals, legitimacy and illegitimacy, all the binaries that structured British colonialist discourse.

This shift in the image of the criminal meant that simple deterrent or punitive strategies could no longer be acceptable as sufficient for criminals who were at once victims and too weak to bear harsh punishments.[11] As a result, the three central elements of the Victorian discourse of crime—prisons, capital punishment, and hereditary criminality—were opened up to new debate. We will now briefly consider each of these cases to give some idea of the extent to which the 'official' British position on criminality, and, indeed, the concept of the criminal, continued to be fractured, contested, and uncertain.[12]

[9] Quoted in Weiner, *Reconstructing the Criminal*, 178.

[10] Farrar sparked off controversy by challenging the 'official' account of the punishment of hell: 'I have shown reasons to repudiate and condemn—i; the physical torments, the material agonies . . . ii; the supposition of its necessarily endless duration for all who incur it . . . iii; the opinion that it is incurred by the vast mass of mankind, and iv; that it is a doom passed irreversibly at the moment of death'. See Frederic W. Farrar, *Eternal Hope* (London: Macmillan, 1878), p. xxiv.

[11] Martin Weiner observes: 'Deterrence was thus to play a steadily smaller part in social policy, and its place was to be filled by more direct methods of State intervention, regulation and assistance.' Weiner, *Reconstructing the Criminal*, 185.

[12] A typical example of this new uncertainty about the technique of incarceration and supervision of criminals may be found in the parliamentary debates about discharged prisoners. Refomers like Adderly and Lord Houghton opposed the extensive powers given to the police to rearrest the 'ticket-of-leave men', while proponents of the system argued that such supervision was necessary to guard each criminal 'against himself'. The debate originated precisely in the ambivalence about the status of the criminal—seen both as a weak-minded individual who must be constantly watched, and as someone whose privacy and individuality must be respected after release. See *Hansard*, 174 (1864), 1263.

The clash of opinions about the suddenly threatening spectre of the prison and the concern for the welfare of criminals often surfaced in 'official' documents like the Prison Bill of 1865. The Bill proposed to set up an extensive network of prisons 'at the expense of every county, riding, division, hundred, liberty, franchise, borough, town, or other place'. But it also attempted to temper this proliferation of carceral institutions with welfare measures such as the placing of thermometers in every cell to maintain a comfortable level of temperature and allowing prisoners to 'take such exercise in the open air as the surgeon may deem necessary for their health'.[13] These uneasy attempts to balance extensive incarceration with the welfare of the criminals would mark British penal policy right up to the landmark Prison Bill of 1877 when 'all powers and jurisdiction at common law or by Act of Parliament or by charter vested in or exercisable by prison authorities' would be transferred to the Secretary of State.[14]

Again, what was most evident in the parliamentary debates over the latter Bill was precisely the spectre of the prison as a punishing machine that both 'diminished' the individual and attacked what were considered to be the traditional foundations of British society. One parliamentarian, Whaley, warned that the 'gigantic and almost unparalleled centralisation' was 'not called for by the voice of the country' and another, Mr Newdegate, thought that 'by invading the province of the local authorities in the counties and boroughs, they might be sapping the foundation of the constitutional system which had grown up in this country'.[15] The most trenchant criticism of the punitive machinery came from Dr Keneally, who firmly declared, 'I say that no man, no matter what crime he may have committed, ought in this England of ours, which affects to be so free, and professes to be so civilised . . . to be shown to any of the outside world in dungeons of this description.'[16]

[13] 'Prison Bill', *Parliamentary Papers*, 3 (1865), 624–51.
[14] 'A Bill to Amend the Law Relating to Prisons in England', *Parliamentary Papers*, 5 (1877), 61–2.
[15] *Hansard*, 232 (1877), 133–5.
[16] Ibid. 138. In fact, historians like Weiner have concurred with these 19th-century critics of the Bill: 'they were rapidly creating a network of officialism throughout the country . . . it was this policy of centralisation and officialism that supplied the reason why the Bill found such favour on the treasury bench'. Weiner, *Reconstructing the Criminal*, 395.

What these debates of the 1860s and 1870s show above all is that, caught at the point of transition where the image of the criminal was shifting from the culpable offender to a helpless victim, the prison was often seen as the embodiment of one of those vast systems that diminished and oppressed individuals. It was one of the cultural moments when there was significant investment of sympathy towards the criminal, and this in turn could strengthen 'unofficial' fictional narrative's attempts to question the construction of criminality and legitimacy, be they domestic or colonial.

The dominant views of capital punishment of this period were also changing along with attitudes towards the prison. As we saw, the reluctance to punish people with death was evident well before mid-century and, by the 1860s, more than 90 per cent of those convicted of indictable offences were receiving prison and not death sentences.[17] Now, even as the prison was being seen as an oppressive force, calls to refine and minimize the death sentence grew even louder. Admittedly, the accusation that found most favour with the authorities had little to do with the allegedly inhuman nature of the punishment. Rather, it pointed to the notoriously inflexible nature of the death sentence that resulted in providing the criminals with more chances of acquittal than any other punishments.[18] But often this legal and authoritarian point was articulated as a plea to 'civilize' Britain: 'Will it be said that there are nations more refined than ours, and that the English are too barbarous to dispense with executions?'[19]

It is difficult to square this debate over 'barbaric' capital punishment with the calls for the wholesale slaughter of the Indians that had rung loud only a few years earlier. But what this debate shows is the cultural environment in which the novels about the Mutiny and other Indian 'crimes' were written in the 1860s and 1870s. When the laws on capital punishment did change after 1866, the death penalty for most crimes (including treason, which was among the chief accusations against Indian mutineers) was abolished and a distinction was made between first and second degree murders, a clause that would make almost all the executions

---

[17] See Weiner, *Reconstructing the Criminal*, 308.

[18] In 1864, a Select Committee found that while 'in all other crimes the chances of escape were but 22 per cent, for the crime of murder for which there was only the death sentence, the chances of escape were 50 per cent'. *Hansard*, 174 (1864), 2056.   [19] Ibid. 2063.

carried out by the British 'army of vengeance' during the Mutiny illegal.[20] It was precisely this questioning of the morality and legality of capital punishment that the novels drew on while revising the accounts of the 'just execution' of the mutineers. This in turn contributed to their interrogation of the colonialist 'civilizing mission' in India.

A third crucial result of the change in the concept of the individual was the revision in the concept of the 'habitual criminal'. This debate was exercised to limit the subversive potential of the idea of the biological root of deviance. If criminality arose from the same 'germ' that produced individuality, then everybody, irrespective of class or social position, was liable to succumb to it. Thus, the 'hereditary' theories of crime also had to invent a particular group of people who were more likely to be carriers of the 'germ' than the others. Maudsley attempted a definition of these deviants: 'there is among criminals a distinct and incurable criminal class, marked by peculiar low physical and mental characteristics . . . Crime is hereditary in the families of the criminals belonging to this class; and . . . this hereditary crime is a disorder of mind.'[21] In the parliamentary debates over the Habitual Criminals Bill, the effectiveness of this ideological construction could be seen in the manner in which this formula was used to raise the old spectre of war against crime.[22] The Earl of Kimberley labelled the habitual criminals a 'great army making war on society' and called for their perpetual imprisonment: 'Nobody honours more than I do the good old maxim of English law that a man shall be presumed innocent until he shall have been proved guilty; but . . . men who by repeated crimes have shown that they set the laws of society at defiance should be placed under a different code . . . under a disability.'[23] Again, there was no consensus on this issue and calls for such extreme measures were frequently opposed by those urging for a reform of the penal techniques. Ultimately, the formula of 'habitual criminal' itself was shot through with an uncomfortable

---

[20] 'Report from Commissioners on Capital Punishment', *Parliamentary Papers*, 21 (1866), 48–9.

[21] Maudsley, *Body and Mind*, 66.

[22] Gatrell observes, 'after the 1869 Habitual Criminals Act and the 1871 Prevention of Crime Act . . . they [professional criminals] became an especially well-defined target of law-enforcement . . . police supervision, different penal treatment . . . served to segregate them from the universe of respectable working class'. Gatrell 'Crime, Authority', 302.   [23] *Hansard*, 191 (1869), 340.

awareness of its arbitrariness and the impossibility of any consistent application.

It is interesting to note how short the interval was between the passing of the Bill in Britain and its consequences for the colonial administration of India. Within two years of the parliamentary Act in Britain, the 'Criminal Tribes Act' was passed to 'provide for the registration, surveillance and control of certain tribes'.[24] These tribes were marked with the brand of 'habitual' criminality, and the despotic nature of the British colonial rule in India made it possible to realize the Earl of Kimberley's dream of order to near perfection. Once notified as a criminal tribe, they had no legal recourse to remove the stigma, and were laid open to completely arbitrary intervention by the British colonial police who did not make any efforts to separate the guilty from the innocent. As Yang points out: 'extended to India, the equation of a separate criminal class with the dangerous classes turned up the caste system . . . since the caste was a "thing" . . . which was concrete and measurable; above all it had definable characteristics . . . the ramifications for prevailing theories of crime causation were inescapable.'[25] Far from attempting to reform the existing caste divides, British colonialism used them to mark out the marginalized groups for 'special surveillance'. And once these groups had been targeted, the rest of India could be represented as a population of the higher order that could learn the enlightened European principles. Of course, as we have seen in the previous chapters, the peculiar despotic and racist nature of the colonial rule meant that time and again, especially during periods of significant challenges to the British hegemony, this technique could be used to criminalize all Indians. However, equally often, efforts were made to produce the Indians as divided between a reformable population and the non-curable criminal sections. Significantly, the lines between these two images of India and those between them and the 'lawgivers' were never stable and often created opportunities of questioning the moral validity of a state that imposed them.

An important strand in English writing during the decades after the Mutiny was dedicated to rescuing this vision of the reformable 'normal' subjects after the criminalizing hysteria of 1857. This also served to reinscribe the humane and benign face of colonialism

---

[24] See Yang (ed.), *Crime and Criminality*, 109.   [25] Ibid. 112.

after the mass executions. The novels, we have seen, often participated in this strategy by attaching signs of habitual or incurable criminality to rebels and separating them from the rest of 'loyal India'. But significantly, the very efforts to recreate the benign face of colonialist authority were often subverted by their questioning of its absolutist and despotic assumptions and the attempts to dress up its brutal excesses with the force of law. So far in this chapter, we have contextualized this fictional impulse by looking at the cultural environment the words were written in, where shifts in ideas of individuality and culpability triggered off debates and ambiguous responses towards criminalization and techniques of punishment. Using a sensibility that was aware of the possibilities of blurring the distances between legitimacy/deviancy, authority/ subject, Europeans/orientals, domestic/colonial, the novels often linked the question of Indian criminality to that of the legitimacy of the British presence in India. They were to use Indian criminals not merely to question Britain's colonial role, but also to expose the systematic oppression that lay at the heart of the empire, in 'domestic' Britain itself. The prime example of this was to be found in the remarkable fiction of Wilkie Collins.

THE MOONSTONE AND SPECTRES OF PROXIMATE CRIME

If the 1860s saw a decline in the national crime rate, it also saw the flourishing of a genre that was concerned with the prevalence of crime in the nooks and crannies of bourgeois and upper-class Britain.[26] If Collins borrowed the figure of the 'criminal' Indian from Mutiny fiction to critique 'domestic' Britain, he also made use of the insights into criminality found in the genre of sensation fiction. Both *The Moonstone* and sensation fiction have received extensive critical attention. Our purpose here will be to examine the manner in which sensation fiction interrogated the dominant strategies of criminalization. By fusing this sensibility of sensation fiction with the problematic figure of the 'criminal Indian', we will see how Collins charted the route on which British fiction of crime would travel for much of the century.

The questioning of law and morality in sensation fiction was

[26] See Weiner, *Reconstructing the Criminal*, 247.

conducted mainly by targeting two crucial elements of British authority—the categories of the 'domestic', and that of masculinity. Critics of the genre agree that its overriding feature was 'its introduction into fiction of those most mysterious of mysteries, the mysteries which are at our own door'.[27] Proximity, as the critic in *Quarterly Review* observed, was the great element of sensation fiction. Crime was brought uncomfortably close to respectability to introduce chaos at the very heart of social order. Anxieties inherent in the prevalent theories of madness, heredity, and crime were magnified to disturbing proportions, thus effectively attacking the legitimacy of the structures of authority. These anxieties were often illustrated by the critical outrage against the novels of Mary Braddon. The *North British Review* complained:

According to Miss Braddon, crime is not an accident, but it is the business of life. She would lead us to conclude that the chief end of man is to commit a murder, and his highest merit to escape punishment . . . if she teaches us anything new, it is that we should sympathise with murderers and reverence detectives. Her principles appear to us to resemble very strikingly those by which the *Thugs* used to regulate their lives. (my emphasis)[28]

The critic's anxiety is well expressed in the telling use of the word 'Thugs'. The subversive potential of the genre lay precisely in annulling the empowering distance between the self and the Others. In this fiction, there could be no distinction between the civilized metropolis and the colonial subjects, and Thugs may as well have been the respected members of polite Belgravia. *Blackwood's* critic Margaret Oliphant attacked such dangerous assertions:

we do not believe, as some people do, that a stratum of secret vice underlies the outward seeming of society. Most of our neighbours are very good sort of people, and we believe unfeignedly that our neighbour's neighbours resemble our own . . . nasty thoughts, ugly suggestions, an imagination which prefers the unclean, is almost more appalling than the facts of actual depravity . . . it is a shame to women so to write; and it is a shame in the women who read.[29]

[27] Winifred Hughes, *The Maniac in the Cellar* (Guildford: Princeton University Press, 1980), 7.
[28] Anon., 'Sensation Novelists: Miss Braddon', *North British Review*, 43 (1865), 202.
[29] Margaret Oliphant, 'Novels', *Blackwood's Magazine*, 102 (1867), 260, 275. Indeed, Oliphant's reaction seems to substantiate Jenny Bourne Taylor's suggestion that 'sensation' was a keyword that described the particular way in which the

Along with the notion of pervasive crime, sensation fiction used the 'woman question' to subvert the ideological claims of British masculinity.[30] Collins would use this subversion of the economy of power to link domestic and colonial subalterns in his work. To hint that Indians and British women (especially, women of a certain class) were linked in their struggle against the same oppressive authority was to strike at the heart of the cherished myth of the civilized (and civilizing) metropolis. Tamar Heller has shown how it was often by disturbing the conventional stereotypes about gender that the stereotypes of class and legality were ultimately subverted. Tracing the central role played by what she calls 'buried texts'—fragments, journals, hidden letters, and clues—in the sensation novel, Heller notes that the authors of these buried texts were 'typically either feminine . . . or, like the outcast Ezra Jennings (who claims he has a "female constitution"), in a powerless and hence stereotypically feminine position'.[31] If these marginalized figures of women or 'feminine men' were allocated the crucial narrative position in the tales, it was because their buried texts both solved the crisis in the realm of authority *and* did so in a manner that exposed authoritarian shortcomings.

Heller shows how this reversal of conventional power relations closely reflected the ambiguous position of the sensation authors, which 'in this changing Victorian literary marketplace was in many ways a double one, both feminine and masculine . . . associated with the low and heavily feminine genres of the Gothic and sensation fiction, yet . . . an active participant in the process of professionalisation'.[32] Sensation fiction thus not only promoted the subversive representation of the domestic sphere as a site open to

middle classes expressed the contemporary cultural crisis as a collective nervous disorder. Even while vehemently criticizing it, Oliphant seems to be actually affected by the feelings of disgust and horror allegedly provoked by the genre. Thus, the critics' attacks on this kind of writing were also a covert submission to the effects of that writing. See J. B. Taylor, *In the Secret Theatre of Home* (London: Routledge, 1988), 2–4.

[30] Jonathan Loesberg has noticed this capacity of the genre in his comment that 'the difference between this use of the question of identity in sensation fiction and that of other works of fiction is that the sensation novel sees the problems in its class and legal aspects . . . a fear of a general loss of social identity as a result of the merging of the classes'. 'The Ideology of Narrative Form in Sensation Fiction', *Representations*, 13 (1986), 117.

[31] Tamar Heller, *Dead Secrets: Wilkie Collins and the Female Gothic* (New Haven: Yale University Press, 1992), 1.   [32] Ibid. 7.

crime and hence to policing, but also privileged strong women and transgressive 'female-men' like Ezra Jennings. Ambiguity, Heller notes, was the key feature of the 'female gothic' that she finds replicated in sensation fiction: 'a double voice of both rebellion and acquiescence to convention . . . the subversive plot is coded within the conventional one . . . it is the female gothic's ability to engage the political dimensions of gender . . . that will be of greatest significance to such Victorian gothicists as Wilkie Collins.'[33]

Along with the subversive use of the rhetoric of crime and gender, the sensation novels also blurred the borders between sane and insane. This again was incorporated in the 'Gothic' element of illegal and immoral incarcerations of women and outbursts of hysterics in the male protagonists. In the sensation novels, 'madness itself often operates as the bleached out echo as much as the transgressive underside of the dominant order; it is as likely to be the sign of ultimate powerlessness as the unrecognised wild beast in one's own heart'.[34] In this, the novels closely echoed the fears voiced, for example, in an article in *The Times* as early as 1853: 'Nothing can be more slightly defined than the demarcation between sanity and insanity. Make the definition too narrow, it becomes meaningless; make it too wide, and the whole human race becomes involved in the dragnet.'[35]

Not only would sensation fiction attribute this madness to criminals like Lady Audley to generate a subversive sympathy for her, it would also make its male heroes, like Franklin Blake, Robert Audley, and Walter Hartwright, victims of this 'morbid' disease. This made the male heroes both 'criminal' and, at the same time, closer to the 'Others' (whether female or foreign). The importance given to insanity in the novels also indicated yet another pervasive and familiar theme, the helplessness of the individual in the face of larger forces beyond their control. As we saw earlier, the contemporary theories of madness and heredity contributed to the anxieties about shrinking human capability and sapped the confidence about progress and reform. And this diminution of the individual was not merely seen in the theme of madness within the sensation plot, but had crucial structural importance. As Walter Kendrick has noted:

---

[33] Ibid. 16.   [34] Taylor, *Secret Theatre*, 17.   [35] Quoted ibid. 27.

The complaint most commonly brought against the sensation novelists was that, because they devoted all their attention to the construction of intricate plot, they ignored the painting of character. This deficiency was seen as not only an aesthetic, but also a moral flaw ... At its best, the sensation novel aspired towards the condition of a crossword puzzle, a system of language which is governed only by its own design ... it was potentially subversive to the belief that fiction is and must be mimetic.[36]

Other critics such as Patrick Brantlinger and Winifred Hughes have also seen this subordination of the character to the plot as the over-riding feature of the genre.[37] Such intense plot machination and deliberate reduction or diminution of the individual characters were perceived as threatening flaws because they tapped into the collective cultural fears of degeneration and entropy of individual energy. It was as if the plot mimicked the irresistible forces that undermined the individual character's capacity for free will and action. Each of these elements of sensation fiction—subversive use of proximate criminality, gender relations, and insanity/diminution of the individual—were to be found in Collins's seminal detective novel. It grew out of both the general cultural anxieties of the decade as well as the specific literary responses to it.

One of the most popular targets for critics of sensation fiction was Mary Braddon. The article I have already looked at in the *North British Review* sneered at her overwhelming popularity:

if the test of genius were success, we should rank Miss Braddon very high in the list of our great novelists ... By the unthinking crowd she is regarded as a woman of genius ... but there is a faction which does not think her 'sensation novels' the most admirable products of this genera-tion, and consider that, judged by a purely literary standard, they are unworthy of unqualified commendation.[38]

Braddon's own position as an 'outsider', a struggling author who began her career on the stage in order to support her aged and ailing parents, was enough to ensure the hostility of the critics. But above all, it was the encoded subversiveness of novels like *Lady Audley's Secret* that enraged the establishment. As this novel is an

---

[36] Walter M. Kendrick, 'The Sensationalism of *The Woman in White*', in Lyn Pykett (ed.), *Wilkie Collins* (Basingstoke: Macmillan, 1998), 72–3.

[37] See Hughes, *Maniac*, 137 and Patrick Brantlinger, 'What is "Sensational" about the "Sensation Novel?" ' in Pykett (ed.), *Wilkie Collins*, 39.

[38] 'Sensation Novelists' (1865), 180–1.

almost perfect example of the genre, we may briefly point out the clinical fashion in which it illustrated the central subversive features.

Braddon used the spectres of hereditary madness and proximate criminality to challenge authoritarian structures. In her novel, the male lover/detective can only incarcerate the subversive female criminal at the price of a radical questioning of the moral and legal basis of his own authority. This effect is achieved by raising a suspicion that the male authority figures are energized by the same mania and ambition that they denounce and punish as 'criminal' in the woman. A clue to this subversive flavour of the text is provided by Braddon's architectural motifs. All the buildings conventionally used to construct the vision of stable social order—the manor, the inn, the respectable home—constantly evoke the irregular, the secret, and the unfamiliar that has been formulated as the 'uncanny'.[39] This neatly echoes the contemporary fears of the capacity of the apparently 'normal' to house dark, insane depths.

Lady Audley herself closely resembles her home in the ambiguous mixture of respectability and dark depths. Her 'soft, melting blue eyes' can emit a fiendish 'strange, sinister light'.[40] Braddon's authorial intervention links this to a murderous criminality that is seen to lurk behind the commonest façades: 'what do we know of the mysteries that may hang about the houses we enter? If I were to go tomorrow into that common place . . . in which Maria Manning and her husband murdered their guests, I should have no consciousness of that bygone horror . . . I believe I may look into the smiling face of a murderer and admire its tranquil beauty.'[41]

Lady Audley claims that it is the 'diseased' faculty of madness inherited from her mother that has driven her to murder, arson, and attempted murder—all to keep her bigamous past a secret. Here, Braddon taps into the contemporary debate on the 'insanity plea' by questioning whether Lucy Audley can be held responsible for her crimes if indeed she is a victim of hereditary mental disorder. As it is, she turns out to be a nightmare of Victorian male authority—a carrier of 'latent' insanity with 'the cunning of

[39] On a useful reading of Todorov's formulation of the 'uncanny', see Taylor, *Secret Theatre*, 15.
[40] Mary Braddon, *Lady Audley's Secret* (London: Tinsley, 1862), i. 141.
[41] Ibid. 285.

madness and the prudence of intelligence'. Straddling the borders of sanity and insanity, she attempts to escape the disciplinary network of authority that incarcerated both the criminal and the lunatic. In the end order is restored when she is 'buried alive' in a Belgian asylum by the 'detective' Robert Audley and thus the madness and criminality that gave suspicious depth to all conventionality is apparently successfully contained.

It is under the cover of this comforting tale that Braddon slips in her codes of subversion. The containment of the spectre of insanity and respectable criminality in fact leads to a discomforting examination of justice, legality, and male authority. Braddon shows that the madness/criminality of Lady Audley is the same instinct of survival and self-aggrandizement that is trumpeted as a laudable quality in the male hero/detective Robert Audley. Lady Audley's secret is not so much that she was hereditarily mad or a criminal, but that she had dared to use her intelligence and duped the male authorities to achieve a social and economic security denied to her.

From the very beginning (like her namesake Limping Lucy in *The Moonstone*) Lucy Audley displays a subaltern defiance and a refusal to stay blinded by the empowering myths of male authority. When pursued by the rich Baron Audley, she makes it clear that even as her social disempowerment and vulnerability attracted him to her, she could only attach herself to him to reverse her economic position. She is too intelligent and experienced to be taken in by the Baron's protestations of love and promises of domestic bliss for she knows well that these promises too often turn out to be hollow. Further, when it is revealed that the reason for her deprivation was the desertion of her husband, George Talboys, the same man whose alleged 'murder' Robert Audley would avenge, the separation of justice from morality is initiated by the novel. Robert Audley's 'just revenge' is revealed as being on the behalf of a selfish and irresponsible husband who has deserted his family. Lucy Audley's bigamy and her desperation to conceal it can now be seen in the light of the wrongs inflicted on her by individuals like her former husband and social codes that leave him unpunished:

I looked upon this departure as a desertion . . . I resented it by hating the man who had left me with no protector but a weak, tipsy father, and with a child to support . . . I became your wife, Sir Michael, with every resolution to be as good a wife as it was in my nature to be . . . I took pleasure in acts of kindness and benevolence . . . fate would not suffer me to be good. My destiny compelled me to be a wretch.[42]

This decriminalization of Lucy Audley leads to the paradoxical criminalization of the 'detective' hero Robert Audley. Even as Lucy's insanity and criminality are shown to be invented by the penalizing codes that attempt to curb her quest for economic and sexual independence, the male detective mind that pitilessly and efficiently weaves the chain of circumstantial evidence to trap the criminal is shown to border on true madness. Social order may rest on the painstaking process of detection that takes into account 'a scrap of paper; a shred of some torn garment . . . a thousand circumstances, so slight as to be forgotten by the criminal', but this is an obsession that can much more accurately be called insane.[43] In a verdict resonant with irony, Lucy takes stock of the contemporary signs of insanity to pronounce Robert Audley a monomaniac.[44] Moreover, her conclusions are confirmed by the musings of the 'detective' himself as he wonders whether his much-vaunted chain of evidence was actually woven out of 'the nervous fancies of a hypochondrical bachelor'. Braddon deliberately inflames this subversive implication in the guise of a comforting intervention to soothe the reader: 'Do not laugh at poor Robert because he grew hypochondrical after hearing the horrible story of his friend's death. There is nothing so delicate, so fragile, as that invisible balance upon which the mind is always trembling; Mad today and sane tomorrow.'[45] This exposure of the mind of the detective leaves more disturbances in social conventions than the final incarceration of the criminal can contain.

If social order is maintained by a kind of manic policing, the motives of that policing can be shown to be a desire to dominate, and dominate brutally. Robert Audley's attempt to detect Lucy's crime is already prefigured in his fantasy about his unborn daughters:

If I ever marry, and have daughters (which remote contingency may heaven forefend!), they shall be educated in paper buildings, take their sole exercise in the Temple Gardens, and they shall never go beyond the gates till they are marriageable, when I will take them straight across Fleet Street to St. Dunstan's church, and deliver them into the hands of their husbands.[46]

[42] Ibid. iii. 90–4.   [43] Ibid. i. 244.   [44] Ibid. ii. 268.
[45] Ibid. iii. 193.   [46] Ibid. i. 236–7.

It is this 'ideal', however fanciful, of disciplining women and other
subalterns that motivates his obsessive conversion of Lucy Audley's
story into one of female, instead of male betrayal. But Braddon's
triumph also lies in showing the plight of the human agents whose
task it is to enforce social codes of patriarchal power. Robert
himself cannot fully account for his 'detective fever', and he repeatedly voices his confusion: 'why do I go on with this . . . how pitiless I am, and how relentlessly I am carried on. It is not myself, it
is the hand which is beckoning me farther and farther upon the
dark road.'[47] It is a significant confession since it clearly locates the
source of insanity and oppression *outside* the individual agents.
The ominous image of the compelling 'hand' is precisely the product of anxiety about the diminution of the individual that shaped
the social, political, and cultural temper of the period. The detective ends up as a defender of an order to which are attached images
of overpowering oppression, and the lines between the diseased
criminal and the law-maker are radically blurred. By the end, the
incarceration of Lady Audley carries signs of overwhelming
oppression instead of enlightened justice: 'From the moment in
which Lady Audley enters that house . . . her life, so far as life is
made up of actors and variety, will be finished . . . if you were to
dig a grave for her in the nearest churchyard and buried her alive
in it, you could not more safely shut her from the world.'[48] The
image of live burial undercuts Robert's moralizing about the necessity of the punishment for a safe society, and completes this sensation fiction's exposure of law and morality as effects of power.

Although it is not directly concerned with 'criminal India', we
have deliberately dwelled on Braddon's novel.[49] Each of its key

[47] Mary Braddon, *Lady Audley's Secret*, 37.   [48] Ibid. iii. 147-8.

[49] However, Lillian Nayder has persuasively argued about the covert echoes of
the Indian Mutiny that she finds in Braddon's novel. Nayder shows that Braddon
linked her criminal heroine to the rebelling Indian sepoys through the image of the
well that had already secured a firm place in imperial mythology about the Kanpur
massacre. Like the rebels, Lucy Audley's effort violently to usurp male authority is
dramatized in her attempts to murder George Talboys by pushing him down the
well. Writing in the context of the Marriage Law Reform Bill, Braddon can then be
shown to be attempting to criminalize Englishwomen agitating for their rights to
divorce and property by conflating her heroine with established images of the colonial criminals. See Lillian Nayder, 'Rebellious Sepoys and Bigamous Wives: The
Indian Mutiny and Marriage Law Reform in *Lady Audley's Secret*', in M. Tromp,
P. K. Gilbert, and A. Haynie (eds.), *Beyond Sensation: Mary Elizabeth Braddon in
Context* (Albany: State University of New York Press, 2000), 31-42.

features—the threat of the repressed, respectable and proximate criminality, and the use of the criminal to call into question the oppressive nature of authority—also features in Collins's detective novel. That is to say, although Collins would use the colony to interrogate British authority, he did so in the context of an inter-rogation already being performed in another kind of fiction of crime. This mirrored the cultural temper of the 1830s and 1840s when the Newgate novels formed a parallel and supportive rela-tionship with the works of Meadows Taylor and Hockley that focused on 'criminal' India. This is not an effort to discover the originary moments of the fiction of either domestic or colonial criminality. Rather, we have been asking why it should be that both these kinds of fiction were able to situate themselves in an essentially ambiguous relationship with authority. As we have seen, it was the very rhetoric of crime they employed, grounded firmly in the socio-historical reality of the period that enabled them to do so.

Earlier, we saw D. A. Miller's discussion of *The Moonstone* as the classic example of the detective genre, in so far as it covertly instilled the norms of 'discipline' by appearing to privilege an ideal domesticity against the rude incursion of the official police force:

> The work of detection is carried forward by the novel's entire cast of char-acters, shifted not just from professional to amateur, but from an outsider to a whole community ... the system is implied in the very 'knowledge' characters have of one another. Everyone's behaviour in this world is being constantly encoded according to shared norms of psychological and moral verisimilitude. Invariably, the points at which behaviour seems insuffi-ciently 'motivated' by these norms are points of suspicion.[50]

That is to say, in a decade when their very success had made the Victorian police overbearingly visible, the novel promoted a more diffused form of surveillance in its portrayal of a community that automatically policed themselves, each member contributing to the process of detecting any departure from the norms and thus containing the spectre of proximate criminality.

Miller's analysis is an accurate summing up of the critical posi-tion that denies or at least delimits the novel's capacity of dissent. This has been challenged by those who have refused to see the genre as a completely pliable tool in the relentless dominance of

---

[50] D. A. Miller, 'From *roman policier* to *roman police*: Wilkie Collins's *The Moonstone*', in Pykett (ed.), *Wilkie Collins*, 204–7.

panoptic power in modern capitalist society. Critics arguing in favour of the novel's subversive credentials show how it high-lighted issues of colony and class which Miller seems to ignore in his otherwise careful analysis. Lillian Nayder has focused on Gabriel Betteredge's obsession with the canonical colonialist story of Robinson Crusoe to suggest that:

> Collins subtly reworks Defoe's novel in order to challenge the authority of this text—to loosen the hold its imperial ideal had on Victorian readers in a number of ways—in various relationships between the British and the Hindus, and between members of the English upper and lower classes . . . and exposes what the ideology of imperialism obscures—the connection between racial and social oppression.[51]

For Nayder, Miller's reading of the novel as monological and authoritarian ignores the centripetal effect of eleven 'unreliable' narratives through which the story is told. She suggests that these competing narratives set up a dialogic model of the novel where the construction of authority is constantly challenged. For instance, the 'unreliable' narrator Betteredge's attempts to live by the ideology of Robinson Crusoe result in the exposure of the cultural mechanism by which the British working classes were co-opted in the task of building an empire abroad that served the interests of the bour-geoisie.[52] Indeed, the novel's refusal to endorse a single authorita-tive point of view seems to provide the opportunity for the surfacing of class resentment and hints of social rebellion at home in the voices of Limping Lucy and Rosanna Spearman.

There is much of importance in this reading, which aims to correct the Foucauldian excesses of Miller. However, for Nayder, Collins's Indians seem to exist solely to expose the social injustice in Britain. Although she notices that signs of criminality are attached to the Indians by all the narrators, and that one of the central concerns of Collins's novel is to question this labelling, Nayder does not follow up the implications of this observation. This posits a question about the 'anti-imperialist' stance of the

---

[51] Lillian Nayder, 'Robinson Crusoe and Friday in Victorian Britain: "Discipline", "Dialogue" and Collins's Critique of Empire in *The Moonstone*', *Dickens Studies Annual*, 21 (1992), 215.

[52] 'Indeed, it is one of Collins's ironies that, in identifying with Defoe's European master, Betteredge overlooks his connection to the exploited native servant . . . working-class Englishmen may be masters in India, but they remain servants at home.' Ibid. 223–5.

novel. Can the text qualify as such if its 'anti-imperialism' consists
of using stereotypical representations of the colony, to criticize not
so much British aggression abroad, but the authority's failings at
home? Does not such radicalism merely preserve the basic colonialist assumption that the colony only exists to serve (even if as a
critical index) 'domestic' interest? That is to say, does not Collins
perform the age-old trick of radicalism at home at the cost of refusing to disturb the authority in the colony?

In the Introduction, we had begun to look at Ashish Roy's
sophisticated riposte to the 'anti-imperialist' readings of *The
Moonstone*. Roy moves in precisely through the gap left by discussions such as Nayder's about the Indian plot of the novel. He also
takes up exactly the opposite position to Nayder about the role of
Robinson Crusoe in Collins's text. Instead of providing a clue to
the 'unreliability' of the narrators, Roy sees Collins using Defoe's
text to signify obsolete and now inadequate myths of the empire
that had served an earlier epoch and must now be replaced by a
new kind of imperial imagination.[53] Written in the aftermath of the
horrendous spoliation of India by British forces during the 1857
Mutiny, Collins's novel is alleged to be concerned with recuperat-
ing legitimacy for the empire now governed directly by the mother-
empress Victoria. This, according to Roy, it does by 'Bringing
together a semiotic repertoire that demonstrates the structural
cohesion the imperial imagination aimed at but could never quite
achieve when challenged on issues of morality and reason'.[54]

How is this ideological recuperation of the colonialist project
achieved by Collins? First, by distancing the novel from what Roy
calls 'antagonistic Victorianism', whose crude formulation of the
ruling 'us' and the colonial 'them' paradoxically damaged the
construction of a lawful justification of the occupation of India.
Rather, Collins is fully prepared to admit the brutal nature of colonial occupation as seen in his description of Herncastle's murders
and thefts. But this generous admission of authoritarian excesses is
also a promise of a future liberal paternalist rulership.

Secondly, Roy thinks this ideological concern of the novel is
played out through the covert narrative strategy of splitting the
'Indian' and the 'English' plots so that each can bear the burden of

[53] See Ashish Roy, 'The Fabulous Imperialist Semiotic of Wilkie Collins's *The
Moonstone*', *New Literary History*, 24 (1993), 657.   [54] Ibid.

converting the historical reality of spoliation of India into a fictional one of restating the civilizing mission of colonialism. Thus, if the missing diamond is read as usurped colonial wealth, 'the Indian plot yokes past and present to the future by the question of when the diamond's usurpation will be reversed'.[55] But this, according to Roy, turns out to be a clever sleight of hand that displaces the pressing historical question of what made this usurpation of wealth possible and how it was going to be redressed, into the machinations of the 'English' plot whose 'chief concern is not the diamond's actual recovery but the violation of an English home'.[56] What apparently started as a narrative concerned with colonialist brutality is now found to be actually about the redressal of violence within the British social fabric. The contention that only by solving domestic problems can the moral question of usurping Indian wealth be solved can be then seen as a corrective to those readings anxious to establish the novel's anti-imperialist credentials.

Thirdly, and crucially, Roy sees this plot machination producing an 'ascetic ideal' of imperialism, most strikingly figured in Murthwaite's benevolent supervision of the restoration of the Moonstone to its rightful owners. In writing the history of the Moonstone, Collins seems to contrast eight centuries of Indo-Islamic rule where Indian wealth was caught in a cycle of violent usurpation, with one century of colonialism where, despite the occasional lapse into violence, it is possible for the first time to redress the wrong suffered by Indian property-holders. The covert interaction of the 'Indian' and 'English' plots seems to produce a trope of tolerance that in turn legitimizes the present colonial occupation:

The event detaches the interaction of English and Indian plots from the pre-Victorian free-bootery and recklessness, and makes it the site of action committed to empire as an ascetic ideal. And this troping of the idea of tolerance as shift in narrative (dis) equilibrium has the backing of a historiographic thesis proposed and sealed in the novel's outwork—in the provocative account of an English army officer's crime in the Prologue, and the imperial traveller's record of its redress in the Epilogue.[57]

---

[55] Roy, *New Literary History*, 660.   [56] Ibid. 661.
[57] Ibid. 665.

For Roy, then, the novel is not interested in formulating any radical critique of imperialist ideology. Rather, it seems to be engaged in the project of reclaiming a moral legitimacy for the colonialist regime in the aftermath of 1857 when its brutal excesses damaged its paternalist pretensions.

It is clear that Roy's reading displays the same kind of hermeneutics of suspicion that is the hallmark of Miller's thesis on the novel-as-police. Far from forming any meaningful challenges to the dominant ideology, the apparently 'radical' elements of the novels are seen instead as elements that either promote it, or engage in recuperative missions. While I do think Roy has successfully challenged those readings of *The Moonstone* that too easily celebrate its 'anti-imperialism', he may have gone too far in the other direction in seeing it primarily as a covert operation to restore the myth of a liberal paternalism or what he calls an 'ascetic ideal' to imperialist ideology. One of the things we have seen about the novels, especially those engaging with representations of nineteenth-century crime, is that it was rare for them to be unambiguously related to a dominant ideology. Noting the conjunction of crime and the colony in *The Moonstone* it may be possible to say that, while Collins (unlike, say, Ernest Jones) can certainly not be labelled a rigorous 'anti-imperialist', his novel could still be critical of the foundational elements of the imperialist/colonialist ideology. Indeed, it may be possible to use the insights of critics like Nayder in the light of the genealogy of the 'criminal' in the variety of narratives, both domestic and colonial, that we have been examining so far. This could result in a reading of the novel that stands at a deliberately irresolute distance from the resolutely conclusive readings of Nayder and Roy.

Indeed, Roy himself acknowledges that the (re)construction of colonialist ideology in Collins's novel may not be as unproblematic as his reading of it makes it out to be: 'Yet there is some slippage even in this fine semiotic scheme which circulates culturally intolerable ruptures only to rediscover them as the currency of tolerance. Of this lack to be healed, this side of the epilogue, Ezra Jennings is the final authority.'[58] Attempts to see the novel as a cultural agent complicit in the establishment of authority, colonial or domestic, are usually forced to take notice of its much more

[58] Ibid. 673.

problematic nature manifested through 'slippages'. And these 'slippages', we have seen, were frequently organized around the figure of the criminal. Critics have always noticed how the restoration of order in these novels only took place at the cost of admitting 'Other' voices that questioned the premises of that 'order'. For instance, the solution to the mystery of the theft, involving the exposure of the unconscious depths of the admirably 'normal' hero, is only achieved by recognizing the oppressive structure of the metropolitan society that marginalized a figure like Ezra Jennings. A product of British gentlemanly oppression, in this case a sexual indiscretion committed in one of the colonies, Jennings is the perfect hybrid:

His complexion was of a gypsy darkness . . . His nose presented the fine shape and modelling so often found among the ancient people of the East, so seldom visible among the newer nations of the West . . . From this strange face . . . eyes dreamy and mournful, and deeply sunk in their orbits—looked out at you, and (in my case, at least) took your attention captive at their will.[59]

This physical description marks out Jennings as 'both alien and native, inside and outside', enabling him to expose an oppressive social order even as he becomes instrumental in resolving its crisis.[60] The story of the unjust professional and personal persecution he is forced to undergo merely on the ground of his racial origin, and of course his birth-history itself, links him to the Indian priests. Just as the mere race and nationality of Indians are enough for them to be labelled as criminals, Jennings has to suffer a similar slander that forces him to act like a runaway convict, seeking out the obscurest of places to try and make a living.[61]

Of course, Jennings's body does not only house the sign of the colonial 'Other', but also that of the feminine. His racial origin and the resultant persecution forces him to take up a servile, 'typically feminine position'—that of a nursing assistant rather than that of a doctor. When he defies authority to save Mr Candy's life, this 'feminine' nature bursts out: 'Then, I knew that I had saved him; and then I own I broke down . . . and burst out crying. An hysterical relief, Mr. Blake—nothing more! Physiology says, and says

---

[59] Wilkie Collins, *The Moonstone* (1868; repr. Oxford: World's Classics, 1982), 358.   [60] Roy, 'The Fabulous Imperialist Semiotic', 674.
[61] Collins, *The Moonstone*, 420–1.

truly, that some men are born with female constitutions—and I am one of them!'⁶² A combination of both the colonized and the domestic 'Other', Jennings resolves the crisis of respectability with a suitably subversive use of the cultural capital of knowledge. Taylor has noted how Collins, in the two medical authorities consulted by Jennings—Carpenter and Elliotson—brought respectable and marginal bodies of knowledge together in a highly unorthodox manner perfectly consistent with Jennings's own outside/inside status.⁶³ It is this fusion of the central and the eccentric that resolves the crisis caused by the suppression of the 'Other'. Taylor further shows how Collins's description of Blake's trance closely follows scenes prescribed in such texts of experimental medicine as 'Magnetic Evenings at Home: The Controlled Experiment of the Private Mesmeric Display'. Jennings's treatment of Blake consists of bringing out the 'wildness, difference and otherness' through a 'method of generating a sense of cognitive confusion, disrupting stable means of signification'.⁶⁴ The figure of Ezra Jennings then, raising uncomfortable issues of colonialist and domestic violence in his physical appearance and suppression and marginalization of 'other' knowledges in his practice, triggers off what Roy has conceded to be a crisis of method and an opposition to rational detection that served as cornerstones in the construction of British authority.

Of course, Ezra Jennings goes only a part of the way towards refuting the important charge that the novel ultimately acquiesces in the colonialist assumption that, even as a critical tool, the colony exists only in order to serve the metropolis. Although Jennings raises the echoes of the violation of the East by the 'newer races of the West', his place remains firmly within the 'English plot'. Despite unmasking the repression inherent in the British social structure, he seems to be detached from the chief concern of the Indian plot—the recovery of the diamond. However, to maintain a rigid separation between the 'English' and the 'Indian' plots, and to see the one as a sophisticated attempt to disguise uncomfortable questions about the colonialist regime, may be to ignore the dissenting clues left by Collins in the text. Jennings's hybrid nature could well be the most decipherable of these clues. But if one can

⁶² Ibid. 414.   ⁶³ See Taylor, *Secret Theatre*, 181–5.
⁶⁴ Ibid. 188.

read Jennings together with the issue of the 'criminal' Indians in the novel, we might recover some of the novel's radical credentials.

If Jennings's racial origins condemn him to the furtive existence of a convict on the run, this oppression is much more clearly concretized in the case of the three Indians. The mere sight of them is enough to make Betteredge suspicious of a conspiracy to steal the family plate, although he assures the readers that he was the 'last person in the world to distrust another person because he happens to be a few shades darker than myself'. Even Penelope, so remarkably aware of the inherently oppressive nature of patriarchal authority, suspects the trio on sight of mistreating the British boy they use as a clairvoyant medium 'for no better reason except he was pretty and delicate looking'. And also presumably because the sight of him in the power of three members of the colonized people (although their power over him seems to be entirely benevolent) reversed deeply entrenched stereotypes of race promoted by colonialism. This is perfectly summed up in the judgement passed on them by Murthwaite:

Those men will wait their opportunity with the patience of cats, and will use it with the ferocity of tigers . . . In the country those men came from, they care just as much about killing a man, as you care about emptying the ashes out of your pipe. If a thousand lives stood between them and the getting back of their Diamond—and if they thought they could destroy those lives without discovery—they would take them all.[65]

Suffused with the authority of the intrepid colonial traveller, these words produce the Indians as both bestial and criminal, a threat to the ideal of domestic British peace.

But a central concern of Collins's novel is precisely to show up these colonialist assumptions to be utterly unreliable and thus subvert the crucial myth of the rule of law used to justify colonialisam. In part, this sustained critique of criminalization of the colony is inaugurated in the prologue with its revision of the 'official' account of the defeat of Tippoo Sultan at Srirangapatnam. In previous chapters, we have seen the importance of the narratives about the ruler of Mysore in both the construction and critique of the colonialist ideology. That Collins chose to attach the signs of criminality to the representative of the British conquerors,

---

[65] Collins, *The Moonstone*, 80.

Herncastle, rather than the defeated Indians, already provides a significant marker of the novel's stance. One must accept the validity of Roy's argument that a condition of Collins's efforts to invent a currency of tolerance involved his projection of the strategies of pre-1857 colonial rulership as morally unsustainable. Both narrative periods of the novel—1799 and 1848–50—are pre-Mutiny and, if we are to follow Roy's thesis, work as distancing devices that served to fabricate a paternalist ideology for the post-Mutiny era. But the myth of the rule of law, as we have seen in the previous chapters, remained crucial for the crown's governance of India. Indeed, a vast portion of the creative imagination of the empire was spent, as evident in the Mutiny novels, in recirculating comforting tales of justice and impartial governance.

Given this ideological agenda of imperialism, Collins's dissection of the techniques of criminalization could not but have created 'slippages' through which a critique of the entire project of securing legitimacy for British authority could be mounted. Although in the novel the 'solution' of the Moonstone mystery occurs almost a decade before 1857, Collins's representation of the colonial 'criminal' raised strong echoes of the contemporary criticism of the techniques of domestic rulership found in narratives ranging from the parliamentary debates about policing to sensation fiction. If it was concerned with the recuperation of the imperialist imagination, it only performed this by admitting a critique of some of its central assumptions about India as well as about the 'rule of law'. The 'criminal' Indians of the novel, indeed, serve to expose the structural oppression inherent in the much-vaunted British justice:

The magistrate said there was not even a case of suspicion against them so far. But ... he would contrive, by committing them as rogues and vagabonds, to keep them at our disposal, under lock and key, for a week. They had ignorantly done something ... in the town, which barely brought them under the operation of the law. Every human institution (Justice included) will stretch a little, if you only pull it the right way ... the Indians were committed for a week, as soon as the court opened that morning.[66]

There is little sign in the novel that there had been any reforming, post-1857, of the oppressive criminalization conducted by the

[66] Ibid. 92–3.

British state before that date. Concentrating on showing how the institution of British justice could be stretched in accordance with the wishes of powerful families, the novel undercuts the very basis on which the whole myth of the civilizing process was constructed.

Consistent with this internal logic of the novel, not only do the 'criminal' Indians expose the rotten heart of British justice, but they are also morally justified for their sole act of violence—the murder of Godfrey Ablewhite. The significance of their successful escape from Britain, virtually from under the noses of the infallible Sergeant Cuff and the captain of the ship *Bewley Castle*, has been generally underplayed by the critics. That during the decade when British brutality in the Mutiny was portrayed as 'just valour', and Governor Eyre's massacres in Jamaica were admired by the humanist Dickens, Collins was able to attach moral triumph to the murder of an Englishman (however hypocritical) by three Indians is a strong enough signal of his determination to upset the dominant representations of self/Other.

The murder of Ablewhite is shown to be an act of justice on two counts. First, it is an extrajudicial but moral act of punishment, not merely for the theft committed by Ablewhite, but also for his sexual hypocrisy, his swindling of his young trustee to the tune of £20,000, and his deception of Rachel Verinder. If this were the only purpose served by the 'crime' of the Indians, it would be possible to argue that Collins's criticism of British rulership only targeted its domestic dimension. But aligned to this was the much more radical assertion that it was morally and physically justifiable for Indians to resort to violence in order to regain their stolen property from the colonizers. By refusing to ensnare the Indians in the disciplinary network set up by the entire range of British characters suffering from 'detective fever', the novel allocates a heroic stature to them. This neatly reverses the criminalization procedure, now holding a British individual and, indeed, the entire British society as culpable in the theft and possession of the Moonstone and thus meriting punishment for it.

I have not been trying to make a case for *The Moonstone* being a foundational anti-imperialist text. But to say that it worked in a covert manner exclusively to strengthen imperialist ideology after the upheavals of the Mutiny may ignore its interrogation of some of the fundamental elements of that ideology. It made the important link between the class/gender oppression within Britain and its political/racial oppression of India and examined one of the central techniques that enabled the operation of this system: namely, the production and detection of criminals. It places the Indians in a parallel and analogous situation with those marginalized within Britain—most strikingly represented by Rosanna Spearman, Limping Lucy, and Ezra Jennings. Further, instead of diverting attention from the interrogation of colonialism, I suggest that it contributes to such an interrogation by showing its roots lying within the social organization and the technique of rulership within domestic Britain.

This constant linkage of the Indians and the domestic marginalized has been noticed before. Taylor has commented: 'Just as the frame (the Indian story) is marginal in both senses of the word— defining the story even as it remains on the edge, so those other kinds of marginal texts—the Brahmin's clairvoyance, Rosanna's letter . . . become central by remaining peripheral.'[67] The clearest connection between the colonized and the domestic oppressed, however, is again to be found in the signs of criminality attached to them. The parallels between Ezra Jennings and the Indians have already been noticed. The marginalized women of the novel are also connected to them by the common theme of a 'criminal' past. Like Jennings, Rosanna's past also has its origin in the indiscretion of a British 'gentleman' who seduced and then deserted her mother. The roots of the 'murderous' Indians, 'thieving' Rosanna, and disgraced Jennings may be said to lie in the common oppressive presence of the British genteel class.

Like the Indians and Jennings, Rosanna's physical appearance marks her out as a tainted figure. But by exposing the origins of this taint, Collins calls into question the social system that forces her into a subaltern position. As a servant and a woman, Rosanna is able to link the issues of class and gender oppression.[68] Her love for Blake is transgressive on these grounds: 'But a housemaid out of a reformatory, with a plain face and a deformed shoulder, falling in love, at first sight, with a gentleman who comes on a visit to her

---

[67] Taylor, *Secret Theatre*, 180.

[68] Heller observes: 'Just as Rachel's story demonstrates the analogy between Victorian ideologies of gender and imperialism, Rosanna's narrative shows how gender and class are mutually reinforcing categories.' 'Blank Spaces: Ideological Tensions and the Detective Work of *The Moonstone*', in Pykett (ed.), *Wilkie Collins*, 249.

mistress's house, match me that, in the way of absurdity, out of any story-book in Christendom, if you can!'[69] However, it is her 'criminal' past that really cements this systematic marginalization. Once marked out as a former thief, she cannot be admitted to respectability and must submit to the norms of sexual and economic subalternity. As she herself realizes, criminalization involved a permanent 'marking' of the individual: 'the stain is taken off . . . but the place shows'.[70] But paradoxically, this enforced marginalization also enables Rosanna to develop a voice against authority. It is she who is able to see in the spectacle of the Shivering Sands a fitting metaphor of the British social condition: 'it looks like as if it had hundreds of suffocating people under it— all struggling to get to the surface, and all sinking lower and lower in the dreadful deeps.'[71] Again, it is she who is able to analyse the material basis of bourgeois aesthetics of beauty:

Suppose you put Miss Rachel into a servant's dress, and took her ornaments off? . . . who can tell what men like? And young ladies may behave in a manner which would cost a servant her place . . . But it does stir one up to hear Miss Rachel called pretty, when one knows all the time that its her dress does it, and her confidence in herself.[72]

Like the Indians and Ezra Jennings, Rosanna Spearman's criminality is used by Collins to indict the 'normal', and the respectable authority of British society. Rosanna's 'buried' confession exposes the hero Franklin Blake as being guilty of removing the Moonstone. Since Blake's 'crime' is committed in a drugged state where his unconscious holds sway over the conscious, Rosanna's exposure also raises the suspicion that the inclination towards violent appropriation of another's property is embedded in the depths of the normal patriarchal façade of Britain. The hero's unconscious stands guilty by the very system of morality invented to justify a particular kind of social oppression.

Thus, Collins's treatment of the 'criminal' in the novel provides a clue towards its radical properties. Without being exclusively anti-imperialist, it was certainly concerned with criticizing one of the main techniques of rulership employed by the British colonial/imperial regimes—that of producing criminals. After 1857, the myth of the 'rule of law' became even more important to colonizers in India,

---

[69] Collins, *The Moonstone*, 50–1.   [70] Ibid. 26.
[71] Ibid. 28.   [72] Ibid. 349–50.

as the transfer of power from the Company to the crown was said to usher in a new era of universal justice equally available to the ruling classes and their subjects. Written in the teeth of such a dominant ideological current, Collins's problematic representation of criminality created the 'slippages' in its so-called colonialist agenda.

Moreover, it is far from accidental that the landmark example of detective fiction should employ 'criminal India' in order to mount its criticism of rulership. *The Moonstone* clearly shows the influence of sensation fiction, in so far as it employs the theme of proximate criminality, where the domestic interiors of respectable Britain were found to be the hotbed of deviance and crime. Elisabeth Gruner's study of Collins's major real-life source of the novel—the Road murder case of 1860—has shown that this was very much in tune with the cultural environment of the decade.[73] Collins's genius lay in fusing this disturbing issue with a subversive representation of the 'criminal colony' that fiction had already showed itself to be adept at depicting. He crucially realized that the whole discourse of crime was a determining factor in the construction of authority both in Britain and in its major colonies like India. If one could draw on the heated debate about criminality and policing that was continuously present in the 1860s, it would be possible to problematize the ideological fabric of that authority. This is precisely what *The Moonstone* displayed—an understanding of criminalization as an oppressive process of marginalization, an interrogation of the normal and the respectable in the light of this understanding, and the resultant critique of authority both at home and in the colony. One could venture to say that this was quite a price to pay for any 'recuperative concerns' the novel may have displayed about the imperialist ideology.

[73] The Verinder household's resistance to the intrusion of professional police and detectives mirrored the rejection and disgrace of the actual Inspector Whicher who attempted to prove the guilt of Constance Kent, the sister of the murdered child in the Road murder case. When, five years later, Constance confessed to the murder but refused to divulge her motive for it, the cherished image of the Victorian family was violently disturbed. See Elisabeth R. Gruner, 'Family Secrets and the Mysteries of the Moonstone', in Pykett (ed.), *Wilkie Collins*.

Conclusion

The Moonstone was not merely a significant milestone in the problematic use of the figure of the 'criminal' Indian in British imperial narratives. It also served as a model for British fiction of crime for the rest of the imperial era. Indeed, after Collins, it became more and more possible for fiction to interrogate, not only colonialist/imperialist ideology, but also its metropolitan context. Increasingly, the novels would situate the threatening figures of the colonial natives *within* Britain in order to expose the inconsistencies of the norms of the so-called superior civilization. The rhetoric of crime would continue to be used to disturb, as well as to shore up the ideological claims of British rulership.

Often, the most popular of the fictions of crime would employ this strategy. The very first novel in which perhaps the most famous fictional character of the period, Sherlock Holmes, was introduced placed the demonized colonial 'Other' within the heart of London to question subtly the solid middle-class respectability represented by figures like Dr Watson.[1] Conan Doyle would again use this figure of the 'criminal' Indian, in stories like 'The Speckled Band' and novels like the *Mystery of Cloomber*, to disturb the seemingly comforting conclusions reached by his sleuth about the durability of the dominant ideology.[2] Similarly, a highly successful novelist such as Grant Allen would use the spectre of a 'criminal' Indian doctor to expose the dark secrets of London's respectable society. In India, in the meanwhile, a detective like Rudyard Kipling's Strickland would call into question all the myths of rational and enlightened imperial policing and progress. Strickland's problematic solving of such cases as 'The Mark of the Beast' and 'The Return of Imray' would conjure up the image of a colony that never has been, and cannot be successfully yoked to the chariot of discipline.

---

[1] See Arthur Conan Doyle, *The Sign of Four* (London: John Murray, 1968).
[2] The latter novel closely shadowed the plot of *The Moonstone*, complete with the 'guilty' British army officer, avenging Indian priests, and occult Hindu practices. It is difficult not to read it almost as a parody of the successful Collins formula.

Of course, these elements of the fiction of crime of the latter half of the century did not only originate in the intuition of Wilkie Collins. At a time when post-Darwinism had given fears of atavistic degeneration a wide currency, and when Britain's pre-eminent position as an industrial and colonial power was gradually coming under threat, the debate about crime and punishment was entering a new phase of the struggle for consensus.[3] In India, this situation was further complicated by events like the 'White Mutiny' over the Ilbert Bill, which had the whole issue of justice, crime, and power at its heart.[4] Further, the constant and varied challenges to the Raj, from the formation of the indigenous bourgeois nationalist movement under the Indian National Congress to the subaltern struggles of the Wahabi and peasant movements, constantly kept the issue of criminalizing Indian dissent and the myth of enlightened progress close to the public mind. This further contributed to the complications in the figure of the 'criminal' Indian and enhanced the possibilities of the imaginative ways in which fiction could put it to use. However, these details must be the subject of another study.

I want to end by opening up the question that has, in many ways, been the primary motivation of this study: how does our look at crime, imperial Britain, and India resonate in these early years of a new and troubled century when we are embedded in yet another 'new' imperial structure? As I indicated in the Introduction, it certainly reminds us that the rhetoric of juridical progress that has accompanied the military and financial aggression of the West, especially since 1990, has a venerable lineage stretching back to the glory days of 'old' imperial Britain. What else does this fact tell us? That the rhetoric of crime has certainly been used to demonize Asian, Australian, African, and Latin American territories and peoples to legitimize European and North American dominance. That our awareness of this does not necessarily mean rejecting all calls to bring non-Europeans (or 'other Europeans' like Milosevich) to account for their 'criminal' acts, but

---

[3] See Weiner, *Reconstructing the Criminal*, for a discussion of the shifts in the rhetoric of crime in the light of the degeneration debate. See Daniel Pick, *Faces of Degeneration* (Cambridge: Cambridge University Press, 1989), and William Greenslade, *Degeneration, Culture and the Novel: 1880–1940* (Cambridge: Cambridge University Press, 1994), for excellent discussions of the debate itself.

[4] See Edwin Hirschmann, *White Mutiny: The Ilbert Bill Crisis in India and Genesis of the Indian National Congress* (New Delhi: Heritage, 1980).

being aware of the source and genesis of these calls for justice and order, especially when emerging from Britain and the USA. This also means a rigorous historicization of the use of the rhetoric of crime and order, an analysis of this language's application on a 'case-by-case' basis, and a refusal to hum along unquestioningly to the siren-song of establishing order.

What else does it tell? That this tool of empire is necessarily a double-edged one. As long as empires rely on a rhetoric of order and crime to secure consensus they will be subject to a scrutiny that uses the same rhetoric which has a potential to annul any ethics of domination. And this will not be because of some automatic trip system built into the stories of crime and policing, but because these always carry within them the historical imprint of domestic debates about these issues. Thus, despite regular conclusions about the political disengagement of contemporary western voters, the anti-war movement that gained considerable strength, at least in Britain, during the conflict with Iraq in 2002–3 drew on the perceived moral hypocrisy and authoritarianism of the Blair government within Britain at least as much as its unprovoked aggression against a foreign nation already devastated by a UN-imposed (but British and US-designed) economic sanction.[5] The British Prime Minister Tony Blair's rhetoric of restoring world order by bringing a known criminal (the Iraqi leader, Saddam Hussein) to justice was rendered hollow, at least partially, by what people saw as his government's attack on the individual rights of Britons in measures such as the revisions of the Criminal Justice Bill and the general failure to deal with a range of criminal issues ranging from youth offences to race crimes and the 'illegal' immigrants. More than half a century after the end of the British Raj, and under a very different imperial alignment and 'world order', fictions of crime remain both enabling and disabling tools of authority. And we are constantly turning to fiction (whether written or filmed) to explore those pressure points where the frequently murderous contradictions of imperial ideology continue to become evident.

[5] At the anti-war rallies (most dramatically, at the one held on 15 February 2003 at London's Hyde Park which, numbering in excess of a million, was the biggest political rally in British history) the moral, ethical, and material failures of the Labour government in both its domestic and foreign roles were regularly commented on, and not only by the socialist party members.

Bibliography

PRIMARY SOURCES

Official Papers

'April 18, House of Commons Debate', *Hansard*, 174 (1864).

'April 15, House of Commons Debate', *Hansard*, 21 (1829).

'A Bill for Further Improving the Police in and near the Metropolis', *Parliamentary Papers*, 4 (1839).

'A Bill for Improving the Administration of Criminal Justice in India', *Parliamentary Papers*, 2 (1828).

'A Bill for Improving the Police in and near the Metropolis', *Parliamentary Papers*, 1 (1829).

'A Bill for the Better Ordering of Prisons', *Parliamentary Papers*, 4 (1839).

'A Bill for the Establishment of County and District Constables', *Parliamentary Papers*, 2 (1839).

'A Bill for the Improvement of Police in Birmingham', *Parliamentary Papers*, 4 (1839).

'A Bill to Amend the Law Relating to Prisons in England', *Parliamentary Papers*, 5 (1877).

'A Bill to Regulate the Appointment of Juries in East India', *Parliamentary Papers*, 1 (1826).

'The Committee Appointed to Examine into the State of the Nightly Watch in the Metropolis', *Parliamentary Papers*, 2 (1812).

'Copy of the Minutes of the Supreme Government of India, on the Subject of Act xi of 1836', *Parliamentary Papers*, 41 (1837–8).

'February 9, House of Commons Debate', *Hansard*, 232 (1877).

'February 26, House of Lord's Debate', *Hansard*, 191 (1869).

'First Report from His Majesty's Commissioners on Criminal Law', *Parliamentary Papers*, 26 (1834).

Grant, Charles, 'Observations on the State of Society among the Asiatic Subjects of Great Britain, Particularly with Respect to Morals and on the Ways of Improving it', *Parliamentary Papers*, 10 (1812–13).

'Inquiry and Report, with Reference to the Statement of Mr. Theobald, as to the Employment of Torture by the Police', *Parliamentary Papers*, 40 (1854–5).

'June 5, House of Lords Debate', *Hansard*, 21 (1829).

'Minutes of Evidence', *Parliamentary Papers*, 13 (1833).

'Prison Bill', *Parliamentary Papers*, 3 (1865).

'Report from Commissioners on Capital Punishment', *Parliamentary Papers*, 21 (1866).

'Report from the Select Committee', *Parliamentary Papers*, 6 (1828).

'Report from the Select Committee on Prison Discipline', *Parliamentary Papers*, 17 (1850).

Report of the Select Committee, *Parliamentary Papers*, 4 (1822).

'Report of the Select Committee on Cold Bath Fields Meeting', *Parliamentary Papers*, 13 (1833).

'Reports of the Select Committee on the Petition of Frederick Young', *Parliamentary Papers*, 13 (1833).

'Rules for Establishing Uniform System for Government', *Parliamentary Papers*, 1 (1856).

'Second Report from His Majesty's Commission on Criminal Law', *Parliamentary Papers*, 36 (1836).

'Second Report of the Inspectors of the Prisons in Great Britain', *Parliamentary Papers*, 32 (1837).

'The Select Committee Report to Inquire into the State of the Police', *Parliamentary Papers*, 16 (1834).

'Third Report from the Committee', *Parliamentary Papers*, 2 (1818).

Other Publications

Ainsworth, W. H., *Rookwood: A Romance*, 2 vols. (London: Bentley, 1834).

—— *Jack Sheppard*, 3 vols. (London: Bentley, 1839).

Alison, Archibald, 'Causes of the Increase of Crime I', *Blackwood's Magazine*, 55 (1844), 533–45.

—— 'Causes of the Increase of Crime II', *Blackwood's Magazine*, 56 (1844), 1–14.

Allen, Grant, *The African Millionaire: Episodes in the Life of the Illustrious Colonel Clay* (London: Grant Richards, 1897).

—— *The Devil's Die* (London: Chatto & Windus, 1888).

Anon., 'Cautionary Hints', *Blackwood's Magazine*, 3 (1818), 176–8.

—— 'The Epidemic of Murder', *Spectator*, 62 (1889), 44–5.

—— 'Colquhoun on the Police of the Metropolis', *Monthly Review*, 32 (1800), 349–54.

—— 'Punishment of Death', *Westminster Review*, 17 (1832), 52–62.

—— *The Newgate Calendar* (London: T. Werner Laurie, 1832).

—— 'William Ainsworth and Jack Sheppard', *Fraser's Magazine*, 21 (1840), 227–45.

—— 'Review of Tippoo Sultaun', *Athenaeum* (23 Jan. 1841).

—— *Childhood in India* (London: Jackson, Walford & Hodder, 1865).

—— 'The Criminality of the Insane', *Fortnightly Review*, 2 (1865), 319–28.

—— 'Sensation Novelists: Miss Braddon', *North British Review*, 43 (1865), 18–205.

Baillie, John, 'God's Avenger', in *Fast Day Sermons* (London: Joseph Masters, 1857).

Bickerstem, Edward, 'A Sermon', in *Fast Day Sermons* (London: Joseph Masters, 1857).

Black, Clementina, 'Thrift for the Poor', *New Review*, 7 (1892), 666–9.

Braddon, Mary, *Lady Audley's Secret*, 3 vols. (London: Tinsley, 1862).

Bristow, James, *A Narrative of the Sufferings of James Bristow* (London: J. Murray, 1793).

Brougham, Henry, 'Anti-Draco; Or Reasons for Abolishing the Punishment of Death', *Edinburgh Review*, 52 (1831), 398–410.

Bulwer-Lytton, E., *Paul Clifford*, 3 vols. (London: Colburn & Bentley, 1830).

—— *Eugene Aram*, 3 vols (London: Colburn & Bentley, 1832).

Chalmers, John, *John Chalmers: Letters from the Indian Mutiny*, ed. Richard Terrell (Norwich: Michael Russell, 1992).

Charles, James, 'The Lord's Voice to Britain from the Far East', in *Fast Day Sermons* (London: Joseph Masters, 1857).

Collins, Wilkie, *The Moonstone* (1868; repr. Oxford: World's Classics, 1982).

Colquhoun, Patrick, *A Treatise on the Police of the Metropolis* (London: W. Fry, 1796).

Dickens, Charles, 'A Detective Police Party I', *Household Words*, 18 (1850), 409–14.

—— 'A Detective Police Party II', *Household Words*, 20 (1850), 457–60.

—— 'The Modern Science of Thief-Taking', *Household Words*, 1 (1850), 368–72.

Dirom, Alexander, *A Narrative of the Campaign in India* (London: W. Bulmer, 1793).

Dow, Alexander, *The History of Hindostan*, 3 vols. (London: Becket, 1772).

Doyle, Arthur Conan, 'The Adventure of the Crooked Man', *Strand Magazine*, 6 (1893), 22–33.

—— 'The Adventure of the Speckled Band', *Strand Magazine*, 3 (1892), 142–57.

—— *The Sign of Four*, in Doyle, *Annotated Sherlock Holmes*.

—— *Annotated Sherlock Holmes*, ed. William S. Baring-Gould (London: John Murray, 1968).

Ellis, Havelock, *The Criminal* (London: Walter Scott, 1890).

Empson, William, 'The Thugs, Dacoits and the Police of India', *Edinburgh Review*, 96 (1852), 33–5.

Farrar, Frederic, *Eternal Hope* (London: Macmillan, 1878).

Fielding, Henry, *An Enquiry into the Cause of the Late Increase of Robberies* (London: A. Miller, 1751).

Fitzclarence, Lt. Col., *Journal of a Route across India* (London: John Murray, 1819).

Gordon, Francis, 'Vengeance Right and Holy', in *Fast Day Sermons* (London: Joseph Masters, 1857).

Grant, James, *First Love and Last Love*, 3 vols. (London: Routledge, 1868).

Guy, William A., 'On Insanity and Crime', *Journal of the Statistical Society*, 32 (1869), 159–91.

Hardwick, J., 'Police', *Quarterly Review*, 37 (1828), 489–504.

Hazlitt, William, 'On the Punishment of Death', *Fraser's Magazine*, 2 (1830–1), 666–72.

Heber, Revd Reginald, *Narrative of a Journey through the Upper Provinces of India*, 3 vols. (London: John Murray, 1828).

Hockley, William Brown, *The Memoirs of a Brahmin, or the Fatal Jewels* (London: Newby & Boone, 1843).

—— *Pandurang Hari*, 3 vols. (London: Whitaker, 1826).

—— *The Zenana* (London: Sanders & Otley, 1827).

Holme, Frederick, 'The Secret Societies of Asia: The Assassins and the Thugs', *Blackwood's Magazine*, 49 (1841), 229–44.

Holwell, J. Z., *A Genuine Narrative of the Deplorable Deaths of English Gentlemen* (London: A. Miller, 1758).

—— *Interesting Historical Events Relative to the Province of Bengal and the Empire of Indostan* (London: T. Becket, 1766).

Hutton, James, *A Popular Account of the Thugs and Dacoits of India* (London: W. M. Allen, 1857).

Jackson, William, *The New and Complete Newgate Calendar* (London: Alex Hogg, 1795).

—— *The New and Complete Newgate Calendar* (London: Alex Hogg, 1818).

Jones, Ernest, 'England's Rule in India and the Cry for Vengeance', in *Ernest Jones: Chartist*.

—— 'The Indian Struggle', in *Ernest Jones: Chartist*.

—— *Ernest Jones: Chartist*, ed. John Saville (London: Lawrence & Wishart, 1952).

Kaye, J. W., *Long Engagements* (London: Chapman & Hall, 1846).

—— *A History of the Sepoy War* (London: Chapman & Hall, 1876).

Knapp, A., and Baldwin, W. (eds.), *The New and Complete Newgate Calendar* (London: Robins, 1824).

Lawrence, George, *Maurice Dering*, 3 vols. (London: Timely Brothers, 1864).

Maison, Malcolm M., 'The London Police', *Macmillan's Magazine*, 46 (1882), 192–202.

Malcolm, John, *A Memoir of Central India*, 2 vols. (London: Bentley, 1823).

Malet, H. P., *Lost Links of the Indian Mutiny* (London: Cauley & Newby, 1867).

Maude, F. C., *Memoirs of the Mutiny* (London: Remington, 1894).

Maudsley, Henry, *Body and Mind* (London: Macmillan, 1870).

Metcalf, Henry, *The Chronicle of Private Henry Metcalf* (1858; repr. London: Cassell, 1953).

Mill, James, *The History of British India* (London: Baldwin, Craddock & Joy, 1817).

Moor, Edward, *A Narrative of the Operation of Captain Little's Detachment* (London: Woodfal, 1794).

Munro, I., *A Narrative of the Military Operations on the Coromondal Coast* (London: T. Bensley, 1789).

O'Brien, W., 'The Police System of London', *Edinburgh Review*, 96 (1852), 1–33.

Offer, John (ed.), *Herbert Spencer: Political Writings* (Cambridge: Cambridge University Press, 1994).

Oliphant, Margaret, 'Novels', *Blackwood's Magazine*, 102 (1867), 257–80.

Orme, Robert, *A History of the Military Transactions of the British Nation in Indostan* (London: John Nourse, 1795).

—— *Historical Fragments of the Mogul Empire and of the Morattoes and of the English Concerns in Indostan* (London: Wingrave, 1782).

O'Sullivan, Samuel, 'Thuggee in India and Ribandism in Ireland Compared', *Dublin University Magazine*, 15 (1840), 50–65.

Pike, Luke Owen, *A History of Crime in England* (London: Smith, Elder & Co., 1873).

Ponsonby, Charles F. A. C., 'Crime, Criminals and Punishment', *Macmillan's Magazine*, 29 (1873), 145–54.

Pope, Alexander, *The Rape of the Lock and Other Poems*, ed. Geoffrey Tillotson (London: Methuen, 1940).

Reynolds, G. W. M., *The Mysteries of London*, vol. i (London: Vickers, 1846).

Ribot, Théodule, *Heredity* (London: Henry King, 1875).

Roberts, Fred, *Letters Written during the Indian Mutiny* (London: Macmillan, 1924).

Russell, W. H., *My Indian Mutiny Diary* (1858–9; repr. London: Cassell, 1957).

196 *Bibliography*

Scott, Walter, *The Surgeon's Daughter* (1827; repr. London: Penny Pocket Library, 1893).

Scurry, James, *The Captivity, Sufferings and Escape of James Scurry* (London: Henry Fisher, 1824).

Shakespeare, John, 'Observations Regarding Badheks and Thugs', *Asiatick Researches*, 13 (1820), 282–92.

Sherwood, Dr W., 'Of the Murderers Called Phansigars', *Asiatick Researches*, 13 (1820), 250–81.

Sleeman, William, *Ramaseeana*, 2 vols. (Calcutta: H. G. Huttmann, 1836).

—— *Rambles and Recollections of an Indian Official*, 2 vols. (London: J. Hatchard, 1844).

Stephen, Arthur Leslie, 'The Decay of Murder', *Cornhill Magazine*, 20 (1869), 722–33.

Stephen, J. F., 'Capital Punishment', *Fraser's Magazine*, 69 (1864), 753–72.

Stephen, Leslie, *The Science of Ethics* (London: Smith, Elder & Co.,1882).

Symons, J. C., *Tactics for the Times as Regards the Condition and Treatment of the Dangerous Classes* (London: John Oliver, 1849).

Taylor, Philip Meadows, *The Story of my Life* (Edinburgh: W. Blackwood, 1878).

—— 'On the Thugs', *New Monthly Magazine*, 38 (1833), 277–87.

—— *Confessions of a Thug*, 3 vols. (London: Bentley, 1839).

—— *Tippoo Sultaun*, 3 vols. (London: Bentley, 1840).

—— *Tara*, 3 vols. (Edinburgh: W. Blackwood, 1863).

—— *Ralph Darnell*, 3 vols. (Edinburgh: W.Blackwood, 1865).

—— 'State of Thuggee in India', *British and Foreign Review*, 15 (1843), 246–91.

—— *Seeta*, 3 vols. (London: Henry King, 1872).

Thackeray, W. M., 'Going to See a Man Hanged', *Fraser's Magazine*, 22 (1840), 150–8.

Thomson, M., *The Story of Cawnpore* (London: Bentley, 1859).

Thornton, E., *Illustrations of the History and Practice of the Thugs* (London: W. H. Allen, 1837).

Trevelyan, G. O., *Cawnpore* (London: Macmillan, 1865).

Wall, Charles, 'The Schoolmaster's Experience in Newgate', *Fraser's Magazine*, 5 (1832), 521–33.

Walsh, Cecil, *Crime in India* (London: Ernest Beam, 1930).

Wycherley, William, *The Plays of William Wycherley*, ed. Arthur Friedman (Oxford: Clarendon Press, 1979).

SECONDARY SOURCES

Ahmed, Aijaz, *In Theory: Classes, Nations, Literatures* (London: Verso, 1992).

Althusser, Louis, *Essays on Ideology* (London: Verso, 1984).

Altick, Richard, *Deadly Encounters* (London: Murray, 1987).

Amin, Samir, *Imperialism and Unequal Development* (New York: Monthly Review Press, 1977).

—— *Eurocentrism* (New York: Monthly Review Press, 1989).

Anderson, Benedict, *Imagined Communities: Reflections on the Origin and Spread of Nationalism* (London: Verso, 1983).

Arnold, David, 'The Colonial Prison: Power, Knowledge and Penology in Nineteenth-Century India', in Guha (ed.), *A Subalten Studies Reader*.

Ashcroft, Bill, Griffiths, Gareth, and Tiffin, Helen (eds.), *The Post-colonial Studies Reader* (New York: Routledge, 1995).

—— —— —— *The Empire Writes Back: Theory and Practice in Post-colonial Literatures* (New York: Routledge, 1989).

Bailey, Victor (ed.), *Policing and Punishment in Nineteenth-Century Britain* (London: Croom Helm, 1981).

Balibar, Étienne, and Wallerstein, Immanuel, *Race, Nation, Class: Ambiguous Identities* (London: Verso, 1991).

Bender, John, *Imagining the Penitentiary: Fiction and the Architecture of Mind in Eighteenth-Century England* (Chicago: University of Chicago Press, 1987).

Bhabha, K. Homi, *The Location of Culture* (London: Routledge, 1994).

Bivona, Daniel, *Desire and Contradiction* (Manchester: Manchester University Press, 1990).

Brantlinger, Patrick, *Rule of Darkness: British Literature and Imperialism* (Ithaca, NY: Cornell University Press, 1988).

—— 'What is "Sensational" about the "Sensation Novel" ', in Pykett (ed.), *Wilkie Collins*.

Brewer, Anthony, *Marxist Theories of Imperialism* (London: Routledge, 1980).

Campa, Román de la, Kaplan, E. Ann, and Sprinker, Michael (eds.), *Late Imperial Culture* (London: Verso, 1995).

Chandravarkar, Rajnarayan, *Imperial Power and Popular Politics: Class, Resistance and the State in India 1850–1950* (Cambridge: Cambridge University Press, 1998).

Chatterjee, Amal, *Representations of India 1740–1840* (Basingstoke: Macmillan, 1998).

Chatterjee, Partha, *The Nation and its Fragments* (Princeton: Princeton University Press, 1993).

Cohn, Bernard, *Colonialism and its Forms of Knowledge* (Princeton: Princeton University Press, 1996).

—— *An Anthropologist among the Historians* (New Delhi: Oxford University Press, 1987).

Curran, Stuart (ed.), *The Cambridge Companion to British Romanticism* (Cambridge: Cambridge University Press, 1993).

David, Deirdre, *Rule Britannia: Women, Empire and Victorian Writing* (Ithaca, NY: Cornell University Press, 1995).

Davies, Lennard, *Resisting Novels: Ideology and Fiction* (New York: Methuen, 1987).

Davis, Mike, *Late Victorian Holocausts: El Niño Famines and the Making of the Third World* (London: Verso, 2001).

Dirlik, Arif, *The Postcolonial Aura* (Boulder, Col.: Westview Press, 1997).

Eagleton, Terry, *Ideology* (London: Verso, 1991).

—— and Milne, Drew (eds.), *Marxist Literary Theory* (Oxford: Blackwell, 1996).

Emsley, Clive, *The English Police: A Political and Social History* (London: Longman, 1996).

Field, John, 'Police, Power and Community in a Provincial English Town', in Bailey (ed.), *Policing and Punishment*.

Fillingham, Alex, 'The Colourless Skein of Life: Threats to the Private Sphere in Conan Doyle's *A Study in Scarlet*', *English Literary History*, 56 (1989), 667–88.

Finkelstein, David, *Philip Meadows Taylor* (St Lucia: University of Queensland Victorian Research Unit, 1990).

Fisch, Jorg, *Cheap Lives and Dear Limbs* (Wiesbaden: Franz Steiner, 1983).

Foucault, Michel, *Discipline and Punish: The Birth of the Prison* (Harmondsworth: Penguin, 1979).

—— *The History of Sexuality*, vol. i (Harmondsworth: Penguin, 1978).

—— *Power/Knowledge: Selected Interviews and Other Writings 1972–1977*, ed. Colin Gordon (Brighton: Harvester Press, 1980).

Freitag, Sandria B., 'Collective Crime and Authority in North India', in Yang (ed.), *Crime and Criminality*.

Gallagher, J., and Robinson, R., 'The Imperialism of Free-Trade', *Economic History Review*, 2nd ser. 6 (1953), 1–15.

Gatrell, V. A. C., *The Hanging Tree* (Oxford: Oxford University Press, 1996).

—— 'Crime, Authority and the Policeman State', in Thompson (ed.), *Cambridge Social History*.

Goldman, Lucien, 'Towards a Sociology of the Novel', in Eagleton and Milne (eds.), *Marxist Literary Theory*.

Gordon, Stewart, 'Bhils and the Idea of a Criminal Tribe in Nineteenth-Century India', in Yang (ed.), *Crime and Criminality*.

Gramsci, Antonio, *Selections from the Prison Notebook* (New York: International Publishers, 1971).

—— *Selections from Political Writings 1920–1926* (New York: International Publishers, 1977).

Greenslade, William, *Degeneration, Culture and the Novel: 1880–1940* (Cambridge: Cambridge University Press, 1994).

Gruner, Elisabeth, 'Family Secrets and the Mysteries of the Moonstone', in Pykett (ed.), *Wilkie Collins*.

Guha, Ranajit, *Dominance without Hegemony* (Cambridge, Mass.: Harvard University Press, 1997).

—— (ed.), *A Subaltern Studies Reader* (Minneapolis: University of Minnesota Press, 1997).

—— *Elementary Aspects of Peasant Insurgency in Colonial India* (Delhi: Oxford University Press, 1983).

Hardt, Michael, and Negri, Antonio, *Empire* (Cambridge, Mass.: Harvard University Press, 2000).

Hasan, M., and Gupta, N. (eds.), *India's Colonial Encounters* (New Delhi: Manohar, 1993).

Heller, Tamar, *Dead Secrets: Wilkie Collins and the Female Gothic* (New Haven: Yale University Press, 1992).

—— 'Blank Spaces: Ideological Tensions and the Detective Work of *The Moonstone*', in Lyn Pykett (ed.), *Wilkie Collins* (Basingstoke: Macmillan, 1998).

Hennelley, Mark, 'Detecting Collins's Diamond: From Serpentstone to Moonstone', *Nineteenth Century Literature*, 39 (1984), 25–47.

Hilfer, A. C., *The Crime Novel: A Deviant Genre* (Austin: University of Texas Press, 1990).

Hilton, Boyd, *The Age of Atonement* (Oxford: Clarendon Press, 1988).

Hirschmann, E., *White Mutiny: The Ilbert Bill Crisis in India and Genesis of the Indian National Congress* (New Delhi: Heritage, 1980).

Hobsbawm, Eric, *Bandits* (London: Weidenfeld & Nicolson, 1969).

Hollingsworth, Keith, *The Newgate Novel* (Detroit: Wayne State University Press, 1963).

Hughes, Winifred, *The Maniac in the Cellar* (Guildford: Princeton University Press, 1980).

Jameson, Fredric, *The Political Unconscious: Narrative as a Socially Symbolic Act* (Ithaca, NY: Cornell University Press, 1981).

JanMohammed, Abdul, *Manichean Aesthetics: The Politics of Literature in Colonial Africa* (Amherst: University of Massachusetts Press, 1983).

Jones, David, *Crime, Protest, Community and Police in Nineteenth-Century Britain* (London: Routledge & Kegan Paul, 1982).

Kalikoff, Beth, *Murder and Moral Decay in Victorian Popular Literature* (Ann Arbor: UMI Research Press, 1986).

Kelly, Gary, 'Romantic Fiction', in Curran (ed.), *Companion to British Remanticism*.

Kendrick, Walter, 'The Sensationalism of *The Woman in White*', in Pykett (ed.), *Wilkie Collins*.

Knoepflmacher, U. C., 'The Counterworld of Victorian Fiction and *The Woman in White*', in Pykett (ed.), *Wilkie Collins*.

Loesberg, Jonathan, 'The Ideology of Narrative Form in Sensation Fiction', *Representations*, 13 (1986), 115–38.

Loomba, Ania, 'Overworlding the Third World', in Williams and Chrisman (eds.), *Colonial Discourse*.

Mackenzie, John M., *Imperialism and Popular Culture* (Manchester: Manchester University Press, 1986).

Majeed, Javed, 'Orientalism, Utilitarianism and British India' (D.Phil. thesis, Oxford: 1988).

Mansukhani, Govind, *Philip Meadows Taylor: A Critical Study* (Bombay: New Books, 1951).

Marlin, Christine, 'The Depiction of the Criminal in Victorian Fiction' (M.Phil. thesis, Oxford: 1994).

Marx, Karl, *Grundrisse* (Harmondsworth: Penguin, 1973).

—— *Capital*, vol. ii (Harmondsworth: Penguin, 1978).

Meyer, Susan, *Imperialism at Home* (Ithaca, NY: Cornell University Press, 1996).

Miller, D. A., *The Novel and the Police* (Berkeley and Los Angeles: University of California Press, 1988).

—— 'From *roman policier* to *roman police*: Wilkie Collins's *The Moonstone*', in Pykett (ed.), *Wilkie Collins*.

Moore-Gilbert, Bart (ed.), *Writing India: 1757–1990* (Manchester: Manchester University Press, 1996).

Moretti, Franco, *Signs Taken for Wonders* (London: Verso, 1988).

Mukherjee, Rudrangshu, 'The Sepoy Mutinies Revisited', in Hasan and Gupta (eds.), *India's Colonial Encounters*.

Nayder, Lillian, 'Robinson Crusoe and Friday in Victorian Britain: "Discipline", "Dialogue" and Collins's Critique of Empire in *The Moonstone*', *Dickens Studies Annual*, 21 (1992), 213–31.

—— 'Rebellious Sepoys and Bigamous Wives: The Indian Mutiny and Marriage Law Reform in *Lady Audley's Secret*', in Tromp, Gilbert, and Haynie (eds.), *Beyond Sensation*.

Ousby, Ian, *Bloodhounds of Heaven* (Cambridge, Mass.: Harvard University Press, 1976).

Page, Norman (ed.), *Wilkie Collins: The Critical Heritage* (London: Routledge, 1974).

Paley, Ruth, 'An Imperfect, Inadequate and Wretched System? Policing in London before Peel', *Criminal Justice History*, 10 (1989), 95–130.

Parry, Benita, *Delusions and Discoveries* (London: Verso, 1998).

Paxton, Nancy, 'Mobilizing Chivalry: Rape in the British Novels about the Indian Uprising of 1857', *Victorian Studies*, 36 (1992), 5–30.

Pick, Daniel, *Faces of Degeneration: A European Disorder* (Cambridge: Cambridge University Press, 1989).

Porter, Dennis, *The Pursuit of Crime* (New Haven: Yale University Press, 1981).

Pratt, Mary Louise, *Imperial Eyes: Travel Writing and Transulturation* (London: Routledge, 1992).

Pykett, Lyn (ed.), *Wilkie Collins* (Basingstoke: Macmillan, 1998).

Radzinowicz, Leon, *A History of Criminal Law and its Administration*, vol. v (London: Stevens, 1986).

Ray, Rajat Kanta, 'Race, Religion and Realm: The Political Theory of the "Reigning Indian Crusade" 1857', in Hasan and Gupta (eds.), *India's Colonial Encounters*.

Roy, Ashish, 'The Fabulous Imperialist Semiotic of Wilkie Collins's *The Moonstone*', *New Literary History*, 24 (1993), 657–81.

San Juan, E., *Beyond Postcolonial Theory* (New York: St Martin's Press, 1998).

Shaw, A. G. L. (ed.), *Great Britain and the Colonies: 1815–1865* (London: Methuen, 1970).

Simmel, Bernard, *The Rise of Free Trade Imperialism* (Cambridge: Cambridge University Press, 1970).

Singh, S. D., *Novels of the Indian Mutiny* (New Delhi: Arnold Heinemann, 1980).

Singha, Radhika, *A Despotism of Law* (New Delhi: Oxford University Press, 1998).

Spivak, Gayatri Chakravorty, 'Can the Subaltern Speak?', in Williams and Chrisman (eds.), *Colonial Discourse*.

Spurr, David, *The Rhetoric of Empire* (Durham, NC: Duke University Press, 1993).

Stokes, Eric, *The English Utilitarians and India* (Delhi: Oxford University Press, 1982).

Stoler, Ann Laura, *Race and the Education of Desire: Foucault's History of Sexuality and the Colonial Order of Things* (Durham, NC: Duke University Press, 1995).

Storch, R. D., 'The Policeman as Domestic Missionary', *Social History*, 9 (1976), 481–509.

Suleri, Sara, *The Rhetoric of English India* (Chicago: University of Chicago Press, 1992).

Taylor, David, *The New Police in Nineteenth-Century England* (Manchester: Manchester University Press, 1997).

Taylor, J. B., *In the Secret Theatre of Home* (London: Routledge, 1988).

Teltscher, Kate, *India Inscribed: European and British Writing on India* (New Delhi: Oxford University Press, 1995).

Teltscher, Kate, 'The Fearful Name of the Black Hole: Fashioning an Imperial Myth', in Moore-Gilbert (ed.), *Writing India.*

Thompson, E. P., *The Making of the English Working Class* (Harmondsworth: Penguin, 1970).

—— *Whigs and Hunters* (Harmondsworth: Penguin, 1977).

Thompson, F. M. L. (ed.), *The Cambridge Social History of Britain* (Cambridge: Cambridge University Press, 1990).

Thompson, Jon, *Fiction, Crime and Empire* (Urbana: University of Illinois Press, 1993).

Thomson, Ronald R.,'The Fingerprint of the Foreigner', *English Literary History*, 61 (1994), 655–83.

Tomlinson, M. H., 'Penal Servitude 1846–65: A System in Evolution', in Bailey (ed.), *Policing and Punishment.*

Tromp, M., Gilbert, P. K., and Haynie, A. (eds.), *Beyond Sensation: Mary Elizabeth Braddon in Context* (Albany: State University of New York Press, 2000).

Weiner, Martin, *Reconstructing the Criminal: Culture, Law and Policy in England 1830–1914* (Cambridge: Cambridge University Press, 1990).

Williams, Patrick, and Chrisman, Laura (eds.), *Colonial Discourse and Post-colonial Theory* (New York: Harvester/Wheatsheaf, 1994).

Worpole, Ken, *Reading by Numbers* (London: Comedia, 1984).

Wright, Harrison M. (ed.), *The 'New Imperialism'* (Lexington, Mass.: Heath, 1976).

Wurgaft, Lewis D., *The Imperial Imagination* (Middletown, Conn.: Wesleyan University Press, 1983).

Yang, Anand (ed.), *Crime and Criminality in British India* (Tucson: University of Arizona Press, 1985).

Young, Robert, *White Mythologies: Writing History and the West* (London: Routledge, 1990).

—— *Colonial Desire* (London: Routledge, 1995).

—— *Postcolonialism: An Historical Introduction* (Oxford: Blackwell, 2001).

Index